D0192594

THE WORLD OF THE CONCERT PIANIST

STEINWAY & SONS

THE WORLD OF THE CONCERT PIANIST

DAVID DUBAL

LONDON
VICTOR GOLLANCZ LTD
1985

First published in the U.S.A. 1984
by Summit Books, a Division of Simon & Schuster, Inc.,
as *Reflections from the Keyboard*

First published in Great Britain 1985
by Victor Gollancz Ltd,
14 Henrietta Street, London WC2E 8QJ

British Library Cataloguing in Publication Data
Dubal, David
[Reflections from the keyboard]. The world
of the concert pianist.
1. Pianists—Interviews
I. [Reflections from the keyboard] II. Title
786.3'041 ML397

ISBN 0-575-03654-0

Portions of three interviews contained in this book
have appeared in *Keynote Magazine*

Photo page 2: Larry Shmenco

Designed by Edith Fowler

Printed in Great Britain by
St Edmundsbury Press, Bury St Edmunds, Suffolk

ACKNOWLEDGMENTS

I gratefully acknowledge my debt to WNCN-GAF Broadcasting Company, where a number of these interviews were broadcast on my radio series "For the Love of Music." For granting permission for this use, I thank Dr. Jesse Werner, former chairman of the board of GAF. My thanks also to Matthew Field, WNCN's general manager and publisher of *Keynote Magazine,* for permission to use the de Larrocha, Ashkenazy and Brendel interviews which appeared in *Keynote.* Matthew Field's continued support has been invaluable to me.

In connection with the Glenn Gould interview, I thank Stephen Posen, attorney for the Gould estate, for his kind permission to use this material. Gould and I had made an arrangement whereby I would send him questions which he would answer by hand. His untimely death came before he completed my series of questions. What we have printed here is the first draft of an unfinished epistolary interview. When these pages were found among his papers, they were sent by Gould's assistant, Ray Roberts, to Robert J. Silverman, the editor and publisher of *The Piano Quarterly.* Gould's handwriting was striking but also quite illegible to me—and it was Robert Silverman who spent the many hours necessary to decipher these pages. I am grateful to him for his painstaking work.

Others who must be thanked for their help are David Antoine, Herbert Breslin, Agnes Bruneau, Jack Caslin, Peter Clancy, Sedgwick Clark, James Colias, Julie Ellner, Deborah Fleischman, Edith Fowler, Thomas Frost, John Gruen, Kathy Hurley, Ellen Kazis, Susan Koscis, Audrey Michaels, Wendy Nicholson, Robert Nissim, Grace Patti, John Pfeiffer, Ruth Pincoe, Charles Pitts, Shirley Rhoads, Frieda Rothe, James Silberman, John Steinway, and Rick Willett.

I also wish to thank Priscilla Davis and Elizabeth Hamilton for their help in transcribing these interviews.

Lola Cantor's empathy and wisdom were of the greatest importance to me during this undertaking.

My final appreciation is to my editor, Ileene Smith. The idea for this book came from her. Without her encouragement it would not exist. She was a superb editor, and her feeling for the piano enhanced this volume immeasurably.

For Margaret Mercer
and also my parents,
who on one fine day
bought me a piano

CONTENTS

PREFACE

The wise Epictetus might well have had the pianist's career in mind when he issued the caveat "Consider what your nature is able to bear before you decide which path in life you will take." The pianist's life is an arduous one, which must begin in childhood. One cannot merely will oneself to become a pianist at age twenty-five, as is possible with so many other professions. If a child does not begin to study by the sixth or seventh year, the likelihood of a career quickly diminishes. Practicing must become a relentless preoccupation, with countless monastic hours of each day devoted to its perfection. For these hours there is no minimum wage. (In old age the French pianist Francis Planté remarked, "I represent seventy-five years of piano playing at eight hours a day!") And after mercilessly denying oneself diversion, there is no guarantee that the public will want to hear *your* Brahms F minor Sonata, let alone your version of the Ives *Concord, Mass. Sonata,* if your taste lies along more iconoclastic lines.

After hearing a recital by the pianist Harry Kaufman, historian Will Durant wrote, "I spent six years writing one book, but you must have spent forty years making it possible for your powers of nerve, muscle, memory and technique to give us last evening's feast. I feel that you gave us forty years of your life and asked nothing in return . . . for such a performance must exhaust body and soul for weeks."

From the pianist's point of view we have the words of George Antheil, who took a sporting view of a recital he was about to give. Antheil wrote, "I knew that the total energy I would expend upon that piano that evening would be at least a number of tons, equal to the energy a boxer expends upon his antagonist at a prize fight, equal to killing three large-size bulls, perhaps four—and I would be ready to drop with exhaustion."

Each player who wishes to perform publicly must come to terms with the instrument in his or her own way. For some the piano is a vehicle for self-expression, even confession; for others it becomes a monster to be vanquished. Some cope with the demands of the instrument with great equanimity, while others—tormented when they are away from their piano—practice compulsively. But for all pianists, the instrument, with its monumental literature, looms very large. While Chopin may have penned his sixteen-measure A major Prelude in a "blessed hour," Moriz Rosenthal was quite serious when he said that he had worked on this piece for sixty years. For Dinu Lipatti, two days away from the piano meant "spaghetti fingers." And as Vladimir de Pachmann said, "Look, I will play the wonderful nocturne of Chopin in G. The legato thirds seem simple! Ah, if I could only tell you of the years that are behind those thirds. The human mind is peculiar in its method of mastering the movements of the fingers, and to get a great masterpiece so that you can have supreme control over it at all times and under all conditions demands a far greater effort than the ordinary non-professional music lover can imagine."

Even if the aspiring pianist does reach the concert stage, he will find that the distance from the practice studio to the hall equals that between the earth and the stars. There are the many external enemies to contend with: the man in the audience who feels he must cough as the first hushed notes of the *Appassionata Sonata* are sounded; the late-comer who cannot find his seat; the bad piano and poor acoustics. And yet these inconveniences are inconsequential when compared with the demons within. Stage-fright and the fear of memory slips can be a never-ending scourge.

Anton Rubinstein, describing his anguish, wrote, "Something like a nervous dread often takes possession of me while I am on stage in the presence of a large audience . . . one can hardly imagine how painful this sensation may be . . . this sense of uncertainty has often inflicted upon me tortures only to be compared with those of the Inquisition, while the public listening to me imagines that I am perfectly calm." In a similar spirit William Kapell wrote, "My great sadness is the realization that the first ten minutes of every concert are lost to me, while I get accustomed all over again to being there. In these ten or fifteen minutes, I suffer agony, because even if it is a heavenly piece of music, I can't feel deeply about it, as I am still in the process of getting over my embarrassment and discomfort. When this short but oh so long time has run its miserable course, I am all right, but until then, I must submit meekly to slips of the fingers, and to a heart that beats, but not enough to obliterate me, which is what I want. . . . I am nervous and apprehensive because I may not 'have it' that particular night. Because I feel the piece is bigger than me, so big I may never be able to even touch it, let alone be the master."

Live musical performance is an exciting, fragile and unpredictable experience. It demands a blend of strength, love and determination which few possess. The great pianist Ferruccio Busoni best characterized the ideal qualities of the pianist when he wrote, "The pianist must have unusual intelligence and culture, feeling, temperament, imagination, poetry and finally that personal magnetism which sometimes enables the artist to inspire four thousand people, strangers, whom chance has brought together, with one and the same feeling. . . . If any of these qualities are missing the deficiency will be apparent in every phrase he plays."

In the tremendously competitive pianistic world of today, however, even these qualities are not enough. It has become a virtual necessity to win one or more international competitions, to please the press, to find the right manager, to get substantial financial backing, to secure a good contract with a record company. But despite the unimaginably bleak odds, conservatories throughout the world are brimming with dedicated students who dream of a concert career. Not for glamour, fame or money, but from an insatiable desire to take the piano literature into the fabric of their life. Many, then, are called to this life, many take up the challenge, but only a bare fraction achieve sustaining careers.

The musicians interviewed in this book represent a good number of the survivors of their profession. These are the rare pianists who have fulfilled their dreams, indeed, their destiny. They are modern troubadors who jet around the globe, their main occupation being the *interpretation* of the piano literature. Thankfully, their interpretations are preserved on disc. Future generations will not have to guess at the glories of Arrau's Beethoven, Gould's Bach, Horowitz's Liszt, Perahia's Mozart or de Larrocha's Granados.

In a sense, *The World of the Concert Pianist* is a history book, a document for the music-lover of the way in which late-twentieth-century pianists view their world. In addition to being full of invaluable insights into the nuance of both practice and performance, it reveals their feelings about their idols, the state of the music world and, finally, the instrument itself. While interviewing these musicians I was always aware, without exception, of their extraordinary dedication to their craft and their continuing awe of the great works they play. Their medium is completely nonverbal, yet each was passionate about describing his or her life's work; and as Goethe observed, "The deepest concerns of the mind and heart, our most important observations and reflections should be discussed only by word of mouth."

David Dubal
New York City

"The virtuoso is not a mason who, with chisel in hand, faithfully and conscientiously cuts his stone after the design of the architect. He is not a passive tool that reproduces feeling and thought without adding himself. He is called upon to let these speak, weep, sing—to render these to his own consciousness. He creates in this way like the composer himself, for he must embrace in himself those passions which he, in their complete brilliancy, has to bring to light. He breathes life into the lethargic body, infuses it with fire, and enlivens it with the pulse of gracefulness and charm. He changes the clay form into a living being . . ."

—Franz Liszt

Born February 6, 1903, in Chillán, Chile, Arrau won the Liszt prize in 1919. He made his American debut with the Boston and Chicago Symphonies in 1923 and won the International Pianists' Competition in Geneva in 1927. During the first years of World War II, Arrau settled in the United States. In 1949 he was named "Favorite Son of Mexico." In 1965 he was named by France a "Chevalier de l'ordre des arts et des lettres." He was awarded the Hans von Bülow medal in 1978 by the Berlin Philharmonic. In 1983 he received numerous honors on the occasion of his eightieth birthday.

Claudio Arrau

DUBAL: Although you were just seven when you left Chile to study in Berlin, do you remember anything of the musical life of your native land?

ARRAU: It was primitive, but there was soon a tremendous development. There evolved a very sensitive audience for music.

DUBAL: You are one of the most honored citizens of Chile, with two streets named after you in Santiago.

ARRAU: I can say that this flatters me enormously.

DUBAL: Is Spanish still the most natural language for you?

ARRAU: It is German I am best in.

DUBAL: Did you come from a musical household?

ARRAU: Yes, my mother was a very good pianist, but she never played in concerts. I heard her teaching when I was three or four years old. That was the first time I heard classical music.

DUBAL: When did you know that the piano would be your life?

ARRAU: You know, I never doubted for a minute that that was the thing I was going to do in life, and nothing else. It was what satisfied me. I never had the desire to play another instrument, to compose or to conduct. The piano quite simply was the one thing I wanted to do.

DUBAL: So in 1911 off you went to Berlin to study. That is where, after searching for the right teacher, you found your musical prophet—Martin Krause.

ARRAU: I was with him only for five years. I never had another teacher. I was very lucky—he was like a guru. He watched what I ate, how I slept and looked after my general health. He walked with me every day for about half an hour or more. He guided my reading of world literature, took me to museums. I saw all the great dancers of the time with him. By age eight, I had heard Wagner's *Parsifal*. He wanted me to have an all-around education and I am truly grateful to this day.

DUBAL: Few people have had that kind of guidance. Tell me a little about him.

ARRAU: Krause was a Liszt student who was very famous in those days. He had numerous pupils as well as six or seven daughters who were all musicians. I always practiced in his house, in a special room, and the daughters would come every few hours to see if I was practicing well, to prevent me from forming bad habits.

DUBAL: Did Krause teach you once a week?

ARRAU: Oh, no, he taught me every day, and for two to three hours. I think he was very keen on developing a real modesty in me. I must add that Krause never took a cent for his work. He was that kind of person. I was only seventeen when he died, but where could I go after him?

DUBAL: Did you learn a lot of music as a child?

ARRAU: Yes, I was never lazy; I kept studying all the time. I had a tremendous urge to get acquainted with the musical language of each composer, and I always tried to develop my own way of molding their music.

DUBAL: As a young boy studying in Berlin, did you feel burdened by the need to succeed?

ARRAU: Yes, from a very early age I felt a sense of responsibility to the piano, to the works I was playing. If something went wrong, I blamed myself for it. I was very severe with myself even though I was only a child.

DUBAL: It cannot be easy to be a child prodigy: there's so much to live up to.

ARRAU: So many child prodigies get stuck at a certain moment in their development, the moment of transition from intuitive to conscious playing. That's the dangerous time.

DUBAL: Did Krause prepare you for the rigors of a concert career?

ARRAU: Oh, very much so—I can remember him saying to me, "You must know the work so well that if you are awakened at four o'clock in the morning and told to play a concerto for a conductor, you can do it instantly and without complaint. He taught me not to be too finicky about conditions. For example, Krause would say "Everybody can play well on a *good* piano; the trick is to play well on a *bad* piano."

DUBAL: How do you make that adjustment?

ARRAU: It happens automatically: One begins to account for the piano's weaknesses, to readjust, to think of the music on that particular piano.

DUBAL: With Krause gone, how did you manage in the following years?

ARRAU: As a young man, I wasn't very sure of myself. I had doubts about all sorts of things. So I went through analysis. Just as I was fortunate in having found Krause, I found an absolutely marvelous psychiatrist, another of my gurus. Of course one has to be ready to accept help. Through analysis I began to unfold and push aside my handicaps. From this time in the early Twenties my self-doubts began to resolve and I was able to move forward with my playing and career.

DUBAL: Having played some pieces for seventy years and more, have you ever reached saturation with particular works or composers?

ARRAU: If my relationship to a particular work begins to go stale, I protect the music by not playing it until I can re-create it with a new impulse.

DUBAL: What is your sense of the role of the interpreter?

ARRAU: I have a particular conception of what an interpreter should be. Interpreters must be able to transform themselves, to feel their way into a world that might be foreign to them. A good interpreter must be able to develop the capacity to play many styles. A good actor doesn't only act parts that are compatible with him. Unless you can transform yourself you are not an interpreter, but a player of certain works that suit you.

DUBAL: Does this mean you suspend all critical judgment of the piece you're playing?

ARRAU: Yes, because you have to be in love with it as you play it; at that moment it has to be the most beautiful music you've ever played. If I want, I can criticize it later.

DUBAL: You once said that at unexpected moments during a performance a divine moment of revelation can occur.

ARRAU: Yes, it's something that can happen. You suddenly know you're playing it the way you've always wanted to play it. I would call it "a little miracle." It has to do with a sense of communion between you and the composer that springs from the unconscious. You have to be in touch with your unconscious to stay creative. Sometimes in a performance something suddenly comes forth that is completely new to you. You can't push it aside. It can scare you but it's a most marvelous thing when it happens.

DUBAL: Do you ever worry about your hands' being hurt?

ARRAU: Never, no. Some people are amazed that I lift heavy things, or when I garden they say, "Don't bang your fingers." But somehow I am not scared about my hands.

DUBAL: You don't seem to be a frightened person.

ARRAU: No, not often. I don't say that I never feel fear before a performance, but I have learned to channel it. This is important, to channel feelings of fear, of anxiety, to use them—it makes you more sensitive.

DUBAL: Watching you talk and seeing you move, you seem to use your energy very economically.

ARRAU: Oh, yes. Particularly now, when I am older, I have made a conscious effort to save my strength and concentrate it on artistic creation.

DUBAL: This must be crucial considering your grueling concert schedule.

ARRAU: I have been very lucky because good health has helped me to stay more or less in form. I feel that I should actually go on playing until, really, the last moment of my life. Of course, one should probably not say that.

DUBAL: Why?

ARRAU: Because it's a challenge to fate.

DUBAL: When Beethoven was deaf he said, "I shall seize fate by the throat!" Mr. Arrau, you are a true Faustian!

ARRAU: I think that's a marvelous thing to be. Then one never takes anything for granted.

DUBAL: Are you influenced by an audience?

ARRAU: I always try to be independent of audiences. I am pleased if they understand what I am doing, but if they don't, I cannot let this influence me at all. I just go on with what I have to do with the music. The thing to beware of in a concert situation is vanity. For instance, one must never take a faster tempo because it may impress the audience. Vanity kills the whole relationship between the music and the interpreter.

DUBAL: Where are your favorite audiences?

ARRAU: There are so many, but for me one of the greatest audiences is in Mexico City. I played my first Beethoven cycle there in the Thirties. In those days, it wasn't a particularly educated audience, but they had an incredible feeling for musical values, for real values. I also love to play in Prague, which is a very musical city.

DUBAL: Certainly Berliners love you to play for them.

ARRAU: Well, they have known me since I was a child; they think I belong to them. London is, of course, absolutely marvelous for music, and so are Edinburgh, Manchester and Glasgow.

DUBAL: You had great success in Russia even though your playing is different from theirs.

ARRAU: I am more in the Germanic line. But they are wonderful, spontaneous audiences.

DUBAL: What about Japan?

ARRAU: The audiences there are incredible. The young people appear uninterested in their own musical tradition. They have taken to Western music instead. And they are so well-mannered. If somebody has a cold, they will use a mask like a surgeon uses so as not to give the cold to a neighbor, and to lessen the sound of their coughing.

DUBAL: How are Italian audiences?

ARRAU: They are going through a tremendous period of development. They used to be very superficial—disinterested and discourteous. But today, some of the best audiences in the world are in Florence, Milan and at some of the Italian festivals. To the young Italians, music seems very important, it almost plays the part that religion used to play. It's not just entertainment. The Italians react very strongly; they come backstage; they ask questions. They even argue, saying, "I didn't think your tempo was right," and things like that. I love it when they do this. One sometimes gets ideas when somebody reacts with conviction.

DUBAL: You have made recordings all your life, but in the past thirty years or so you have been relentless in recording great segments of your enormous repertoire. What motivates you to give so much of your energy to your recording?

ARRAU: The recordings are a document of my way of interpreting certain works. Not that I think it's the only right way, but it's mine, and it may be valuable for young artists. It is also, I suppose, a way of living on.

DUBAL: When you make your recordings, do you record separate sections, or do you play the whole piece through?

ARRAU: In a sonata movement, for instance, I prefer to play the whole exposition and then, if necessary, to divide that, but only into the longest sections possible. Of course, sometimes there are spots where there are wrong notes or other problems and then you have to insert the corrections. But generally, I have found that it is not good to make the sections too small, too short; something gets lost in the flow of the music.

DUBAL: Is recording exciting for you?

ARRAU: Oh, yes, I really enjoy it. I also get ideas from listening to the playbacks. Things that work in performance are sometimes not good on records and vice versa. Recording has its own laws—that's why I am not very much for the recording of live performances. I never really liked them too much.

DUBAL: Is it important for a musician to know about the era in which each composer lived?

ARRAU: Very definitely. One should know the art of the composer's period, literature, even the political situation. One should learn to get the feel of a particular historical moment. Everything contributes to an understanding of the composer's music.

DUBAL: Your depth of knowledge of each composer's output is reflected in your programming of one-composer recitals or even cycles.

ARRAU: Yes, I started that kind of thing in the Thirties, when I did all of Bach's keyboard works in twelve recitals. At first these programs had a small audience, but then they grew and grew. People liked hearing many aspects of the work of a single composer. After the Bach I did all of Mozart's solo pieces and then the Beethoven sonatas.

DUBAL: What happened with Bach in your repertoire? You never play him anymore.

ARRAU: Yes, that's right. Just after finishing the cycle I decided Bach sounds best on his own instruments, the harpsichord and the clavichord. So I stopped playing him. I felt that the listener could feel Bach most authentically when he is played on the harpsichord. His aesthetic stems from a less secular world. Indeed, he wrote on his manuscripts "for the glory of God." Any shades of crescendo and diminuendo and other inflections which can only be achieved on a modern piano hinder Bach's meaning. These qualities of the piano's creep into Bach whether you like it to or not.

DUBAL: As you were growing up in Berlin, whose programming did you admire most?

ARRAU: I remember, when I was a child, hearing Teresa Carreño playing the Third, Fourth and Fifth Concertos of Beethoven in one evening. In Berlin, of course, there was a very serious music public which thrived on such intensity. One could also hear, as I was growing up, monumental offerings from Busoni, d'Albert and Conrad Ansorge. Busoni did nine Mozart concerti in three evenings just before he passed away. I remember the incredible rhythmic vitality of his playing; it struck you from the first note. He was tremendously creative, his imagination was awesome in whatever he did. He could shock you with his playing.

DUBAL: And what about Teresa Carreño?

ARRAU: She played in the grand way, she was incredible. I think she was the greatest woman pianist who ever lived.

DUBAL: There's a story that she and her husband, Eugene d'Albert, had so many marriages between them that one day d'Albert screamed to Carreño, "Have your children and my children stop fighting with our children!" Did you ever meet Carreño?

ARRAU: Yes, she was very nice to me. Krause always took me backstage after her concerts. She would caress me and ask me how I was doing. One day we asked her, "How do you manage with all your children? How do you do your practicing?" "Oh," she said, "nobody would dare to come or even knock at the door because I keep a loaded gun on top of the piano, ready to shoot anybody who disturbs me."

DUBAL: May we now speak about the composer who has been with you more than any other: Ludwig van Beethoven? What does Beethoven's music represent?

ARRAU: In a few words, Beethoven's music represents struggle and victory. It is something that is very positive. For Beethoven, there is always victory in sight. His music spells a spiritual rebirth. It speaks to all of us in a way that is relevant to our times. In the sense that his life was an existential struggle for survival, Beethoven is our contemporary. Beethoven exemplifies in his creative output all the spiritual and psychic battles of the hero, the hero who is given superhuman tasks to overcome and who, after untold struggles—truly bloodied, but undaunted—emerges the victor and finally attains the highest state of self-realization and illumination.

DUBAL: In the 1850s Wilhelm von Lenz wrote a book about Beethoven's three periods: early, middle and, after he became deaf, the late Beethoven. What is your feeling about these kinds of distinctions?

ARRAU: In my opinion these kinds of critical commonplaces never really work. They overlook the marvelous unfolding, the incredible development of his genius. In the end, he reached a mystical union with the godhead, as it were, and this certainly transcends any category. He composed on a higher plane than almost anyone else in the history of Western music. At the beginning of his career, who could have foretold the metaphysical language of the C minor Sonata, Op. 111, and the slow movement of the *Hammerklavier Sonata,* Op. 106, for instance?

DUBAL: When you played your first Beethoven pieces as a child, did you have any idea that his music would come to mean what it does to you?

ARRAU: I felt completely at ease in his music from the very beginning and I knew instantly that Beethoven would be a major force in my musical world.

DUBAL: What was the first Beethoven work you played in public?

ARRAU: I think it was the First Concerto. I was still a child.

DUBAL: What was the first sonata you studied?

ARRAU: Op. 2 No. 3 in C major.

DUBAL: That was a very difficult sonata to start with. When did you come to the *Sonata Pathétique,* Op. 13? Most youngsters can't wait to begin it.

ARRAU: Oh, yes, I learned that early, but it was not until I was seventeen that I understood it. I had never been satisfied with the way the last movement was played. I thought, "Something is wrong; they all play it in a sort of gay way, and it cannot be—after that tragic first movement and that prayer-like slow movement." Suddenly it occurred to me that the last movement was full of anxiety, a tremendous anxiety infuses it. From that moment, I developed my own way of playing the last movement.

DUBAL: When you are playing a Beethoven work, do you feel more responsibility than you would for another composer?

ARRAU: I would say that one should feel a sense of responsibility to any great composer. Yet, when I go out on stage to play Beethoven, I find that it's almost easier than with other composers because the meaning of his music is so clear and so definite. I always feel rather at ease when I play Beethoven.

DUBAL: You have made a superb edition of the Beethoven sonatas for Peters. Why did you feel a new Beethoven edition was in order?

ARRAU: I think the last great edition of Beethoven was Schnabel's, so I decided it was time to go through everything again and compare the early editions and the available manuscripts.

DUBAL: Do you think pianists should work from many editions?

ARRAU: Oh, yes, even old ones such as Hans von Bülow's, which is wonderful in its way. However, one must be very careful about his faulty scholarship. For example, von Bülow will decide to fill in chords and certain passages in higher octaves without warning. But as to the overall musical insight into the works, it is a marvelous edition.

DUBAL: Von Bülow was one of the great Beethoven players of the nineteenth century. What do you think of the d'Albert edition of the sonatas?

ARRAU: It's seldom used now, but it was the next most influential German edition after the von Bülow. It's not very faithful, but there are a lot of good ideas and suggestions in it.

DUBAL: What do you think of the trend of playing Beethoven on original instruments?

ARRAU: I don't think Beethoven needs that. In fact I have played Beethoven's own pianos in Vienna, as well as many other fortepianos, and they seem inadequate to his size. I think he was dreaming of the modern piano. Even Mozart, to my way of hearing, comes out best on the modern piano.

DUBAL: Your repertoire contains very little Mozart, but you are one of the few German-trained pianists who have had a continuous and important relationship with Chopin's work. Your conceptions of Chopin are quite big. No rose-colored salonist surrounded by violets for you. Your waltzes are very grand, and your nocturnes are played almost as ballades.

ARRAU: Oh, the waltzes are marvelous, a little hackneyed of course, but they are all so beautiful. And the nocturnes, contrary to many people's opinion, are very important pieces, some of the best music he wrote. The last three nocturnes are indescribable. I am just crazy about them. And the great Fantasy in F minor, the Barcarolle, the *Polonaise-Fantaisie*—these are unique creations that show Chopin's enormous talent for condensation—even within these, his largest forms. He is an important and virile composer, hardly the Victorian ladies' salon composer that he is made out to be. If you just play Chopin like he's too often played, with subdued dynamics and such, he becomes weak and loses so much of his inner drama.

DUBAL: Yet, even with many of these pale performances, the world never tires of his music.

ARRAU: You are right, they never tire of him. Yet his true worth is still not fully appreciated. There are always those who refuse to think of him as anything but a salon composer. All over the world there are so-called intellectuals who speak of him still with a little condescension. But this is less so now than fifty years ago.

DUBAL: Yes, half a century ago, some of his finest music was still virtually unknown. But I know that the notion of Chopin the sentimental stylist still lingers. I recently heard your performance of the Chopin E minor Concerto, which was monumental, by the way.

ARRAU: Oh, I love that concerto. One of my fondest memories of it was when I played it with Bruno Walter. He also loved this concerto very much, and he had played it himself a lot. Before our engagement he asked me to come even earlier than usual, to have two or three rehearsals. In fact, we had three. You should have heard this performance! All the little things in the orchestra that one usually thinks are superfluous were brought out by him and given meaning. So many conductors think the orchestra is secondary in the Chopin concertos and they lose the details.

DUBAL: So Walter gave three rehearsals to a concerto which most conductors are sorry they have to conduct.

ARRAU: Exactly, and I had somehow always dreamt of that way of performing it. For me, it was an unforgettable performance. Another great performance of the Chopin E minor, from the orchestral angle, was one I did in Cologne with Klemperer.

DUBAL: Have you ever looked at Debussy's edition of Chopin? I believe it is the one Arthur Rubinstein used.

ARRAU: Yes, it's very interesting, very original. But one must be careful and consult other editions that are more faithful to the original, such as the Paderewski edition or, better still, the Henle.

DUBAL: Let's speak of Liszt now, with whom you must have felt a kinship early on. You are fond of saying that Beethoven taught Czerny, who taught Liszt, who taught Krause, who taught you.

ARRAU: I am very much conscious of this great tradition. Krause, as did many, worshiped Liszt, and I do, too. He was an awesome individual—very enigmatic. True, he had certain weaknesses, perhaps too much vanity, but this was of no importance in light of his other qualities. He was the most generous person in the world, willing to help his students with their careers in any way, always making connections for them. He also had many young composers around him, like Draeseke, Cornelius and Raff.

DUBAL: In your Liszt performances, I think it is your intention to bring out Liszt's spiritual nature and ever-searching musicality. He could read a poem or look at a painting or sculpture and be inspired to compose.

ARRAU: What strikes me again and again are the mystical qualities he reveals in his music. For instance, the mysticism of love. In this he reaches great depths. Liszt is too often trivialized, misunderstood. I shall never forget the revelation of hearing Busoni play the Liszt Sonata—such depths of passion and meaning one cannot imagine!

DUBAL: What did Krause say about how to play Liszt?

ARRAU: He used to say that Liszt demanded more technique than one actually needed, so that the performance would look and sound as if it were without effort. There must be in the playing a total freedom, the sonority stemming from the whole body, not just the fingers.

DUBAL: You once said Liszt had the very sound of the piano in his bones.

ARRAU: Yes, he knew every nuance that he wanted. But the performer must have true creative imagination to bring him to life.

DUBAL: Another composer very dear to you is Schumann.

ARRAU: Yes, since childhood I have been involved in his world. He is totally and purely romantic; there are tremendous tensions in his music, great emotional extremes. His music reveals all of the signs of the split personality, the schizophrenia which culminated in his death in an asylum at the age of forty-six. At first his music made people afraid; they thought it was crazy. It was entirely new and original.

DUBAL: But Schumann understood the split in his personality. He said that his introspective work was composed by Eusebius, while his fiery work was composed by Florestan.

ARRAU: Yes, Schumann understood the divisions in his personality, and the wonderful thing was that he was able to harness his creativity despite the ongoing battle. He kept his sanity as long as possible, but his was a tragic life.

DUBAL: What do you find to be the most popular Schumann pieces with audiences?

ARRAU: The Concerto in A minor always travels well. Of the solo pieces, I think maybe the *Symphonic Etudes,* the Fantasy in C major, certainly the *Carnaval*. Not so much the *Davidsbündler Dances,* nor the *Kreisleriana*. They demand some knowledge of the literature of the time, of Schumann's literary heros E. T. A. Hoffmann and Jean-Paul Richter. Even the name *Kreisleriana* is mysterious to today's audiences. It comes from a story by E. T. A. Hoffmann called "Kater Murr." Kreisler is the bizarre bandmaster, and for Schumann this became a sort of self-portrait.

DUBAL: Is Schumann more popular in some countries than others?

ARRAU: Yes, at the moment Schumann is not popular in Germany; while in France, he is popular but they like his lyrical side, they don't care for or, in my opinion, understand his Florestan side.

DUBAL: And yet Schumann seems to be the nineteenth-century German composer most loved by French composers.

ARRAU: Yes, that's true; his influence is wide, from Fauré to Chabrier.

DUBAL: What is your opinion of Clara Schumann's editions of her husband's works?

ARRAU: In Madame Schumann's editions the tempi are either too slow or too fast. My theory is that she was a very well-balanced bourgeois woman, and her husband's music, with its demons, made her a little afraid. So she tried through her tempo marks to make his music more acceptable.

DUBAL: As a musical conservative she often tried to tame his wildness by telling him to compose in the Classical mold. . . . May we now speak of Schubert, whose music Schumann was the first to discover after Schubert's early death?

ARRAU: And it was Schumann's fine critical writings on Schubert which helped bring Schubert to the public light. You know, for me, interpretively, Schubert is the most difficult of the great composers of the piano literature.

DUBAL: Why is that?

ARRAU: Because one must bring together a synthesis of elements. It has been said that his music is an eternal song, an infinite song. But for the interpreter, the problem is to keep the tension alive in those long melodies, and within those long movements. Schubert can present an idea, a subject, from so many different angles. For that you need a particular kind of sensitivity. Schubert has so many little shadings and those sudden modulations from major to minor or vice versa. Also, remember that Beethoven was his idol, and there are many Beethovenian elements to blend into his big sonata movements, as well as the folk-like simplicity of his Viennese background. And then the transitions are so important, from one mood into another. I played Schubert a lot in my youth, but now I think I understand him more. I am finally able to bring the many elements of his music together.

DUBAL: It is sad that Schubert, like Chopin, was loved but not regarded highly enough.

ARRAU: Oh, yes. As if he were just a charming melodist for the bourgeois salons of Vienna. In some of the later works, there is the deepest human understanding. In the last of his piano sonatas, the B-flat Sonata, for instance, you feel him giving up any kind of hope; you feel the proximity of death.

DUBAL: I'd like to venture away from the Germanic masters now to mention your old disc of some of Albéniz's *Iberia*.

ARRAU: You know, I am still quite happy with that record. In Latin America as a child I heard a lot of Albéniz. It was played in all the drawing rooms, but of course, they were the simpler, less important pieces.

DUBAL: The *Iberia* Suite is quite different—a massive edifice!

ARRAU: It is an incredible structure, isn't it? I think it is some of the most difficult music written for the piano. It is an orchestra on the piano. You know, Albéniz as a young man knew Liszt and studied with him a little.

DUBAL: Albéniz also knew Debussy, a composer that so often figures in your recitals.

ARRAU: Debussy's music is different from any other. It was a leap into a new region of art. It is like the music of another planet. I think he is one of the great geniuses of all time. His opera *Pelléas et Mélisande* is one of the miracles in music. And also in some of the preludes—*Canope,* for instance—it is unimaginable that anybody could create in those few notes such depth. When we spoke of Schubert, I mentioned the proximity of death. Debussy also has this quality. In the prelude *Des pas sur la neige,* there is a melancholy atmosphere, a sadness, an intolerable dilemma.

DUBAL: I now realize that Debussy is for you much more than just an Impressionist.

ARRAU: As an interpreter, I am not just interested in the fairy-tale qualities of his music, but in its spiritual potential. The spiritual Debussy is so often neglected. He is too often played merely for the beauty of his sound, and there is far more to Debussy than that. According to my feeling, even famous Debussy players make that mistake.

DUBAL: Has your constant touring of the world left you any time to teach?

ARRAU: Yes, I have taught quite a lot. It has been a great satisfaction. Teaching is like molding a sculpture. To help and guide a young artist, to help them step forward is very important to me.

DUBAL: Do you ever worry that your students will be so much in awe of you that they will attempt to become Arrau imitations?

ARRAU: Such a thing is a very great danger, I'm afraid. The moment one notices that the student is imitating the teacher, the teacher should encourage the student to go his own way and try to find himself.

DUBAL: Do you have general technical advice for students?

ARRAU: Let me think. Offhand, I would say if you need strength in a certain passage, practice with more force than you will actually need in performance so that the listener has the feeling, "Oh, he could play that much faster or more powerfully if he wanted to." One should not only overcome a technical problem, but one must surpass it.

DUBAL: Speaking of technique, many have spoken about the musicality of your trills.

ARRAU: A trill can't be just good, it must be in the mood of the phrase it's in, and its surroundings.

DUBAL: Do you still get satisfaction from practicing?

ARRAU: I think it's beautiful to practice; I *love* to practice. On the average I do now two to three hours a day. But sometimes I am a little bit lazy. Krause used to have me stay away from the piano for at least a month in the summer, so as not to get stale, and I still do it quite often. Then when I go back to the piano it's really an event.

DUBAL: Have you fulfilled all of your musical goals?

ARRAU: I wish I had free time to prepare some performances of contemporary music. I think the performer has a certain responsibility to living composers. For instance, I would love to play the Carter Concerto.

DUBAL: I heard that once you did the gigantic Carlos Chávez Concerto.

ARRAU: Ah, a wonderful piece! I did it with Chávez himself conducting. It was not the world premiere, but the first performance in Mexico.

DUBAL: I know you also played some Schoenberg in your career.

ARRAU: I remember once playing in Berlin Schoenberg's Drei Klavierstücke, Op. 11. Can you believe that I received a number of anonymous letters complaining that they didn't expect that from me, that I was spoiling my image!

DUBAL: But I think we can safely say that your career survived this. What do you do for relaxation?

ARRAU: I love great literature. I grew up, one might say, with Goethe. In modern literature, Proust and Hesse give me nourishment, while in painting, Turner is more and more one of my favorites; and Grünewald is, for me, one of the greatest painters. I also enjoy films, theater and modern dance. People really respond to a great dancer or dance company. And I love opera—I have often been inspired by great singing. There are so many things that enlarge us; that can influence us very much in the way we play.

DUBAL: Beyond the arts, I know that you receive great joy from taking care of your trees.

ARRAU: I love trees with a passion. I plant them, and I watch over them. You will laugh, but I have a weakness for weeping trees. I have planted many weeping willows, weeping beeches, weeping birches and weeping cherry trees.

DUBAL: Do you find the world less humane than when you were growing up under the tutelage of Martin Krause?

ARRAU: No, I have the feeling that our world now is much more authentic. Every abuse in every field is uncovered, and something is done about it. Oh, I think our historical moment is marvelous. Just think of flight itself. I never cease to be amazed at a 747 that goes up in the air with such ease.

DUBAL: What would you say to a young pianist who possibly has not won a competition, and is despairing in his career?

ARRAU: There are so many different types of talents. I always say that even a small talent has a little musical message which is invaluable if there is sincerity.

Vladimir Ashkenazy

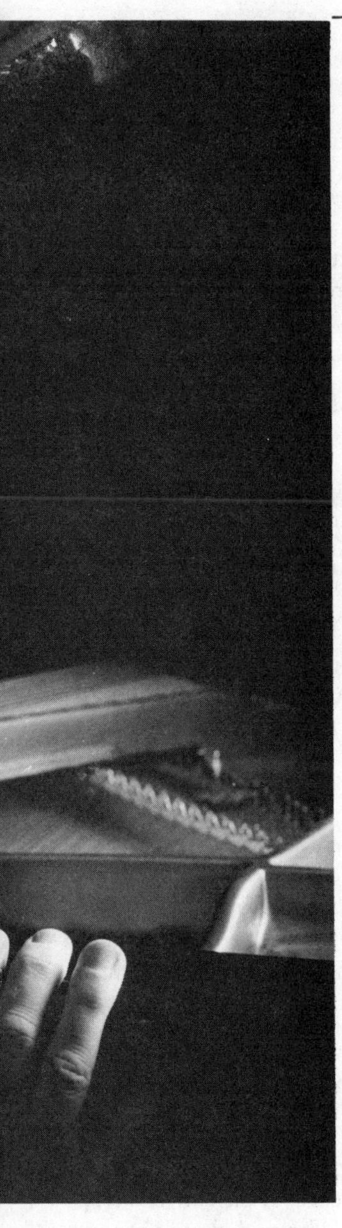

Born July 6, 1937, in Gorky, U.S.S.R., Ashkenazy began his studies at the Moscow Central Music School with Anaida Sumbatian at age eight. At eighteen he went to the Moscow Conservatory. In 1955 he came in second at the Chopin International Competition in Warsaw. The following year he won the Queen Elisabeth Competition in Brussels. In 1962 he shared first prize with John Ogdon as co-winner of the Tchaikovsky Competition in Moscow. After 1963, when he defected from Russia, his career blossomed. He vastly extended his repertoire, began to record large portions of the solo and concerto literature, and steadily toured the world. His recordings have won numerous awards. In the last several years he has conducted many major orchestras.

DUBAL: You went to the Moscow Conservatory. Was it a fiercely competitive place?

ASHKENAZY: As in any music school, there was an element of competition there, but I don't think it was harmful. Competition only becomes dangerous when it is allowed to turn into jealousy or a fight for survival. But I don't think it was like that at the conservatory, no.

DUBAL: So you were not under pressure to win big competitions?

ASHKENAZY: The pressures are imposed on you by the system, not by the conservatory. The Soviet system is such that it needs constant propaganda from every segment of life, so it constantly needs prize-winners from the musicians. The minister of culture, who is under the Politburo, prompts the conservatory to produce a constant stream of international-competition winners. And this is very hard on students.

DUBAL: Is this the reason you entered the Tchaikovsky Competition in 1962, after you were already a celebrated artist? Was there pressure from the government?

ASHKENAZY: Yes. The minister of culture called me and said that unless I participated in the Tchaikovsky Competition, I might as well forget about my career altogether, and I would not go abroad again. So I had no choice. You think that what is printed in your newspapers about the Soviet Union is just American propaganda. But having lived in the West for nearly twenty years, and having read all the Western newspapers, I must say that it is nothing of the kind. It is all truth, though only one-tenth of the truth of what is happening in the Soviet Union.

DUBAL: Would it have been possible for you to have developed fully had you stayed in the Soviet Union?

ASHKENAZY: In a society that is completely stagnated, spiritually, it is an impossibility for an individual to develop freely. You can develop to a certain degree, but it probably will be a deformed development rather than a normal, free one. You never become yourself really; you have to lie all the time. That life really destroys your soul; whatever you have inside will be destroyed. In the end, you're ruined, really. So how could I say I would develop in the same way? I am absolutely convinced, 200 percent, that I could not have become the person I am now.

DUBAL: The Shostakovich memoir, *Testimony*, gives a very bleak and tragic picture of a musician's life under the Soviet system. Of course, this was denounced as a fraud by the Soviets.

ASHKENAZY: It's a pathetic story, though I can't say with 100 percent certainty that every word in the book is definitely as Shostakovich said or thought. But as a person who lived in Russia, and who met Shostakovich a few times, and who knows the musical and social climate in Russia, I think it's a very truthful book. It sounds very much in character with Shostakovich, though I was never close to him. What a hard life he had. His son Maxim once said he remembered seeing his father cry only twice: once, at the death of his mother, and the second time, when he had to join the Communist Party. For me that says everything.

DUBAL: Bleak as Soviet life was, you did have excellent training at the Moscow Conservatory. Did you have any contact with the great teacher Heinrich Neuhaus?

ASHKENAZY: I myself studied with Lev Oborin but I did go to Neuhaus's classes a couple of times, and I enjoyed them very much. He was absolutely wonderful, a real artist and poet—a great personality.

DUBAL: In the late twentieth century, is there still a Russian school of piano playing?

ASHKENAZY: By now I don't know if there is still such a thing as a specifically Russian school. Today communication is so fast that you can have any recording or any advice from any part of the world at hand. The music world has become very international.

DUBAL: And more strenuous than ever.

ASHKENAZY: Yes, I often wonder if the lay audience realizes what an international career involves. They think you have a fantastic life, that you just come out on stage and play for your pleasure and become very rich. People aren't aware of what kind of slavery it is, except for me it is sweet slavery.

DUBAL: As a performer, what do you hope for from an audience?

ASHKENAZY: I need a lot of concentration and silence while I play, but what I expect is a different story. In different countries you expect different kinds of concentration. In some Latin countries, you don't expect very much concentration—there can be a lot of noise, though the last few times I visited Italy, I was pleasantly surprised. I found a lot of young people in the audience, which was not the case ten, fifteen years ago, and they were very quiet. I remember I couldn't stand playing in Italy because the audiences were absolutely unruly—you could not get silence. Once or twice I had to stand up before playing and say, "Unless you will be silent, I won't begin the concert!" But, as I say, in the last few years it has been absolutely marvelous. In general, I think there is developing a deeper commitment to serious music. Young people don't go to concerts because they are social occasions, but because they really want to listen to the music.

DUBAL: Your discography is one of the largest in recorded history. What do you do with your records? Do you put them on the shelf or do you study them closely?

ASHKENAZY: So much time is spent on recording a work, listening to the many playbacks, that I become numb to it. Once I approve of the recording it no longer interests me. Only if I decide to re-record it do I listen back to the original version. Then it is instructive and interesting—to listen to what you did with a piece some years back.

DUBAL: Do you listen to records of other musicians?

ASHKENAZY: Yes, all the time. I am very interested in what others do with music.

DUBAL: In what way has interpretation changed most since the 1920s and 1930s?

ASHKENAZY: I think we distort music much less now. To put it simply, that older generation distorted much more. I believe that interpretation should be like a transparent glass, a window for the composer's music. One should not be willful. I don't believe in interpretation with a capital letter. I believe in bringing the music to life from within—without artificial effects.

DUBAL: Are there composers who had more allure for you as a child than they do now?

ASHKENAZY: When I was a child I had crushes on, say, Tchaikovsky, Rachmaninoff or Scriabin. They were crazes really. Now their qualities are more in perspective, but I never lost my first love for any of them.

DUBAL: Lately you have been playing and recording a great deal of Scriabin. What can you tell us about this composer, who remains an enigma to so many?

ASHKENAZY: It's not easy to explain Scriabin—he lived in his own world.

He thought of himself as a philosopher. Through his music he believed that he would transform the world. He was in touch with the theosophists of his time and was interested in the occult.

DUBAL: Do you think it's necessary to know Scriabin's philosophy in order to play his work well?

ASHKENAZY: I think knowing about it can facilitate interpretation and appreciation of his music. He tries to capture different states of mind and spirit, and ultimately they merge in the universal spirit. This is not easy to talk about, yet the music that describes these states is very organic. It is not simplistically programmatic or superficial. The music is very impressive in musical terms and is very idiomatic for the piano, though his states of mind are certainly not easy to translate to the physical—especially when he is in flight, so to speak. He tends to use the entire keyboard and jump from place to place. So, if one wants to fly, one has to jump, and that's rather difficult pianistically. The left-hand writing is particularly difficult. But, if you can get the right sound, the right feeling, somehow you can manage him. Scriabin is maliciously, decadently insane.

DUBAL: Is he widely performed in Russia?

ASHKENAZY: He is very much a part of the Russian musical heritage—any musician will know a good deal of Scriabin. But you can't say Scriabin is a household word in Russia, like Tchaikovsky, Mussorgsky or Rachmaninoff. This is because his music is not quickly accessible.

DUBAL: Do you know the Scriabin playing of Vladimir Sofronitsky?

ASHKENAZY: Yes, I heard him a few times and I have quite a few recordings of his Scriabin. I think he was a wonderful interpreter—really marvelous. He wasn't really a great instrumentalist, though—it was hard for him physically to play the instrument. But somehow he managed technically and, in fact, he absolutely communicated his music.

DUBAL: Horowitz is also a great interpreter of Scriabin. As a youngster in Russia, was he one of your pianistic idols?

ASHKENAZY: He was for a while when I was a teenager; I was interested in the sheer piano playing. I think there was even a month or two when I tried to imitate him—but I couldn't, because my equipment was entirely different, and I suppose my inner requirements were of a different nature, too. At that stage in my life, though, Horowitz was unbelievably exciting, a demonic pianist.

Dubal: Aside from being one of the busiest pianists you are increasingly known for your conducting. How did you come to conducting?

Ashkenazy: I have been in love with the symphony orchestra ever since I can remember. My first great musical experiences were when my mother took me to see an opera, ballet or an orchestral concert at the Bolshoi Theater. I remember that I wasn't at all interested in what was happening on stage. Instead, I was mesmerized by what was happening in the pit. When I became a teenager I literally spent all my free time and all my pocket money on orchestral concerts. I was constantly buying scores and learning how to read them. I learned an unbelievable amount of orchestral repertoire that way. But I never imagined that I would be a conductor. It never crossed my mind because the sheer joy of listening to good performances was so overwhelming. I never thought of asking for more. But when I moved to the West and began my western career, I played more and more concerts with great orchestras and wonderful conductors. During this time I was growing as a person and a musician, and I was becoming more and more discriminating about what I heard, which led me to the wish to conduct. It was a slow but inevitable process. As a conductor it brings me unbelievable joy to make and shape music the way I want it.

Dubal: In your concerto playing, I have always sensed a wonderful rapport between you and the orchestra.

Ashkenazy: I'm pleased that you are aware of the rapport. In a concerto I feel very much a part of the orchestra in every way—as a person, as a musician.

Dubal: Are you ever frustrated by the quality of some orchestras?

Ashkenazy: I'm very lucky because now I conduct only very good orchestras. In the beginning I conducted some third- and fourth-rate orchestras, but then I didn't conduct very well myself. At that time it was difficult for me to decide if what was coming out was my fault or the orchestra's fault. If something was not right I tended to blame myself. But in conducting first-class orchestras I have no frustration at all. I'm absolutely sure that if something is not right it can only be my fault.

Dubal: What are the chief differences between learning orchestral and solo music?

Ashkenazy: I think the differences are only practical; there are no essential differences. If I am learning a Beethoven piano sonata, it has to become part of my motoric system, so to speak, so that I don't need to think about where my finger goes. It needs to become an organic part of me and this takes a very long time. As a conductor learning a symphony the process is much faster since you're not dealing with the actual production of sound.

DUBAL: Is it more stressful to conduct an orchestra or to play a solo recital?

ASHKENAZY: I feel much more exposed when I play the piano. Conducting an orchestra is still a shared responsibility, and if I make an error, a good orchestra will help me find my way. Psychologically, conducting is much more comfortable for me. When playing the piano nobody can help you. If something goes wrong, *nobody* can help you.

DUBAL: Is it advantageous for a conductor to be a pianist?

ASHKENAZY: Absolutely. Since the piano is a complete instrument with a wide range of color, it stands on its own. So, when you begin to conduct an orchestra you simply transport yourself to the orchestral medium. Basically, it is a continuation of what you had before. A disadvantage, though, is that the heart of the orchestra is the string section, and pianists generally have no special knowledge of bowing, sound production and so on. But one learns by experience, and I now know more than I did when I began to conduct. Friends in the string section have helped me very much.

DUBAL: Though you have a tremendous repertoire, as a pianist and conductor you have paid little attention to recent music.

ASHKENAZY: I think at this moment music is coming to a kind of dead end. Recently I spoke to an active composer whose piece was performed in the same program in which I played a concerto. It was an interesting piece. After the performance I said to the composer, "Did you like the performance of your piece?" He replied, "Yes, it was very well performed, but it's such an ugly piece of music." I said, "But you're the composer!" "Yes, I know I'm the composer but all I see and hear around me is ugliness, so that's what I put down on the paper. It's all ugly, and it should be ugly—but I hate this music." It's very interesting, his reaction to his own music. And you hear this kind of music all the time today—this is what people compose. Maybe that's what they want to compose: hateful music. I must admit I hate it too. And I don't want to be part of it.

DUBAL: What do you expect from music?

ASHKENAZY: I like all kinds of music, as long as there is some message for me.

DUBAL: What about rock music?

ASHKENAZY: I think rock has almost no message, with very few exceptions. It's basically a lot of rubbish, a lot of noise. All it does is make people restless and agitated for no reason. Music should have a spiritual dimension. One cannot put into words how music becomes a tool for our perception of the world, but the fact remains that the great composer, through his music, does perceive so much. Through music more than any other means, I have learned about humanity and all that surrounds me.

DUBAL: Which brings to mind Beethoven and his hard-fought creative development. Do you know the little book called *Beethoven: His Spiritual Development,* by J. W. N. Sullivan?

ASHKENAZY: It's my favorite book on Beethoven and perhaps on music itself. It's such a marvelous little volume.

DUBAL: Sullivan felt that music on the level of Beethoven's communicates great depths of consciousness that contain invaluable lessons for humanity.

ASHKENAZY: How much he understood of Beethoven, one of the great geniuses. That we have a Beethoven in our midst is a great solace and a never-ending experience.

DUBAL: Isn't it interesting that some of the most grossly insensitive people yearn to be artists? To think that Hitler's ambition was to be a painter. . . .

ASHKENAZY: Yes, he was a watercolorist—and at the same time, a deformed and deranged monster. The mind is a strange world. Even within the killer there can be an area of refined feeling, though this is of course hard to accept.

DUBAL: Do you believe the twentieth century is a dark age?

ASHKENAZY: I think the Dark Ages have never ceased.

DUBAL: Does this depress you?

ASHKENAZY: Yes, I often feel depression and self-doubt—there is a constant recapitulation of these feelings every few weeks or every few months. It's unavoidable, I suppose. But in the end such feelings don't help you, they cut down on your energy: One must get going again.

DUBAL: Do you ever think of your place in the world of music?

ASHKENAZY: No, I am absolutely disinterested in such things.

Born June 8, 1949, in Lvov, Poland, Ax studied with his father from the age of six, while the family was living in Warsaw. In 1959 they left Poland, settling in Winnipeg, Canada, before coming to New York, where Ax entered the pre-college division of the Juilliard School. He later attended Juilliard as a student of Mieczyslaw Münz. By 1970 he had made a tour of Latin America and began entering international competitions. In 1973 he became the first winner of the Arthur Rubinstein International Competition in Tel-Aviv. In 1974 he was the recipient of the Michaels Award of Young Concert Artists. He made his New York debut in 1975. Ever since, he has been engaged at the major festivals and in recital and orchestral appearances throughout the United States, Europe, Israel and Japan.

Emanuel Ax

CHRISTIAN STEINER

DUBAL: Who are the contemporary pianists that have moved you most?

AX: Serkin, Richter, Rubinstein, Horowitz. These are all artists with complete visions of music. They create a world of their own. For me, a great performing artist must bring you into his world, into his vision. Just listen to Rudolf Serkin play the *Hammerklavier Sonata* or Schubert's *Wanderer Fantasy*. As you listen, it seems this is the only way to play that music. I feel the same way about the cellist Yo-Yo Ma. In the case of Richter, when he's in top form, nobody alive plays the piano better. Richter's control of the instrument is unsurpassed. And if he is inspired, he explodes into the most amazing flights of fantasy. I will never forget a London performance of the Scriabin Fifth, Seventh and Ninth Sonatas —if you can imagine all of that in one sitting. The manipulation of sonorities was unimaginable.

DUBAL: And Rubinstein?

AX: He was the artist whose concerts I most looked forward to. Rubinstein was more than a pianist, he was an idea. He was like a king—his bearing, his approach to the instrument, his whole approach to the music was one of great aristocracy.

DUBAL: Clifton Fadiman called him "the last civilized man."

AX: Very well said. And I think he was much more honest and sincere and direct in his approach to most composers than a lot of people that are thought of as intellectual pianists.

DUBAL: How do you feel about his recordings compared with the live performances, where his presence counted for so much?

AX: They're wonderful recordings, and in their own right they are a great body of work. But for me, compared with the live Rubinstein, they were always somehow disappointing; and I suspect it had more to do with the playing than with the fact that you couldn't see him. He played differently on stage. He was less careful. He did not have that Damocles sword of cleanliness and accuracy hanging over him in the concert hall, and I think that was all to the good. I'm disappointed that more concert performances were not recorded. I came and saw him several times after the Rubinstein Competition and played for him.

DUBAL: Did he ever discuss your playing with you?

AX: Yes, he was a very generous man, and he spoke very honestly about my playing. On the occasions that I played for him he talked very seriously, precisely and in great detail. It wasn't like everyone said: "Rubinstein, he just plays. It all just pours out of him." Believe me, it didn't all pour out of him. He knew exactly what he was doing with every note. Of course Rubinstein had the greatest physical coordination, and I think many things came easier to him than to most pianists. He did a lot of his work mentally, and then he was able to implement his ideas on the keyboard without much practice.

DUBAL: In that way he was much like Glenn Gould.

AX: Ah, there's another musician who takes you into his world. He was an absolutely stunning pianist in every way. What creativity! And the precision of his playing is overwhelming. There's a case of someone who had no problems at all with the instrument. Oh, what a tragedy, such an early death.

DUBAL: Yes, he had no problems with the instrument and, like Rubinstein, much of it was done in the head. He didn't have to spend every minute at the instrument.

AX: That's what I gather, which absolutely astounds me, because the precision of his playing is so overwhelming.

DUBAL: You have only studied with one important teacher, Mieczyslaw Münz.

AX: He was my only teacher for fourteen years. He was a great stickler for good piano playing. I loved his approach to the piano and he made me work very hard and very carefully. I think our personalities were very well suited. I had a lot of curiosity musically, and he was permissive in that way, never imposing any view of music-making on me.

DUBAL: When did you realize you no longer needed to rely on a teacher?

AX: This is an important moment in every artist's life. In my case it was very much a matter of circumstance. After winning the Rubinstein Competition I started to go away a great deal. And around that time, Münz went off to Japan to teach for a year. So we gradually drifted apart. Soon I realized that I had to work things out on my own. I now find it very valuable to play for people other than pianists. Working with Yo-Yo Ma has been fabulous for me because he has great ears. And since he doesn't play the same instrument it is very liberating. It's all musical.

DUBAL: Do you ever feel captive to the piano?

AX: No, but that's probably because I don't work hard enough.

DUBAL: What's enough?

AX: There's enough in the piano repertory to keep you busy eighteen hours a day for eternity. But I like to balance things. I don't like to feel that I have to practice every minute. There are plenty of times when I don't want to practice, but never periods when I don't want to hear music or go to concerts or talk about it. The basic form of my life is music.

DUBAL: What is your definition of talent?

AX: Perhaps on the simplest level it's having a brain that absorbs a certain kind of pattern easily, whether it be mathematics, music or chess. A gifted chess player has a sense of the board. And a musical child will find musical patterns easy to absorb. That is talent, and many have it but many do not have the love or desire to make music. Desire is not in the genes. And finally there's a lot less perseverance than desire. A Heifetz and Horowitz have all of these qualities. But it's a very rare combination.

DUBAL: But surely there are more than three ingredients that make up talent. Where, for example, does taste fit in?

AX: By my definition taste is a sixth sense about what is harmonious and what is not. Also, a person with good musical taste is someone who has a superior sense of proportion. Everything clicks the right way. Then again, good taste is often an overrated commodity. Of course there's great value in having good taste, but it's not the only thing that makes an artist, by any means. I would rather hear an emotional, over-indulgent performance than a restrained, tasteful one anytime. Maybe this is because I've always tended to be a little constrained. I do try to put things together in a tasteful way, and sometimes that means not testing the outer limits of a work. And I'm trying more to test the outer limits. So for me, testing these limits has become very important to me. I try to stretch as far as I can.

DUBAL: I recently heard you play the Haydn Sonata in C major in a delightfully humorous way, and yet the audience did not seem to perceive the humor in your playing.

AX: Humor in music is a tough act. Probably because it implies wit, which is usually expressed in a verbal way. Unlike sounds, wit is not abstract, so it is very difficult to be witty in music, with the exception of opera, of course. But getting back to Haydn, "Was there ever a greater master of humor?" Claude Frank once said to me. Haydn's so pleased with his cleverness—he's like the brightest kid in the class who's always saying, "Look how smart I am!"

DUBAL: What are the best books on music you have read?

AX: Two books that immediately come to mind are by Charles Rosen, *The Classical Style* and his little book entitled *Arnold Schoenberg*. I was overwhelmed by *The Classical Style*. I thought, Here is a man who writes about Classical music in a way that illuminates it from the inside out. I found his analysis of the *Hammerklavier* absolutely shattering. And in the Schoenberg book, he penetrates right to the core of this very disturbing composer, though one whom I love.

DUBAL: Perhaps this is because he demands so much concentration.

AX: Yes, you have to be an active participant when you're listening to Schoenberg or other complicated music. But you don't have to be an active participant to listen to Dolly Parton. You don't need to be exposed to her for years to begin to appreciate her. But you can't appreciate classical music if you don't get involved, if you don't bring yourself to it. It's the difference between reading a great book and an Agatha Christie mystery. You've got to go through thorny passages in a great book. If you're going to read Proust, you've got to concentrate more. It's that simple.

DUBAL: Why is it that Schoenberg so disturbs us?

AX: The composer Hugh Aitken once said that Schoenberg wrote music that somehow delved into areas of our psyches that we don't want to know about. And I think he was right. In many ways it is neurotic music, but I find it incredibly expressive. And yet I know he irritates a lot of people.

DUBAL: Yes, he always has, but nevertheless he is played.

AX: True. In fact, I'll be performing the Piano Concerto soon.

DUBAL: I'll be looking forward to that. It's a piece that fascinates me and repels me at the same time.

AX: Yes. That's it exactly!

MARTIN REICHENTHAL

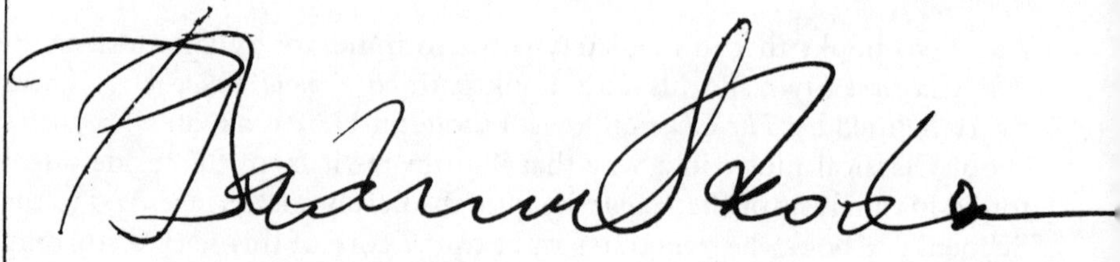

Born October 6, 1927, in Vienna, Austria, Badura-Skoda won the Austrian Music Competition in 1947 and the International Music Contest in Budapest in 1948. He graduated from the Vienna College of Music in 1948. On January 10, 1953, he made a spectacular American debut. He is one of the most-traveled concert pianists of his generation, and he has taught extensively. The Frank Martin Piano Concerto was composed for him. Badura-Skoda is also a composer. His striking Elegie for Piano *was published in 1982. In the last several years he has made many recordings on fortepianos.*

Paul Badura–Skoda

Carnegie
Hall
90

DUBAL: You've just flown in from San Francisco, and then you are off to Vienna. How do you manage to practice with all your traveling?

BADURA-SKODA: What a strain it is to be in China one day and Montreal the next. But, it seems that at long last I can do with a little less practicing; it has become a part of me. Though I always try to manage a few hours each day. Did you know that Gieseking really could do without practicing? He practiced very little.

DUBAL: Yes, he was famous for that. He studied with Karl Leimer, who taught him a visualization method, which helped his already astonishing memory. He could premiere a new concerto from memory with a week's study.

BADURA-SKODA: Gieseking was unique in many respects. And his muscular capacity was astounding. He was as precise as any pianist playing today. But today so many pianists play like robots. As a professional, I can admire their technique but they leave their audiences cold. Even if the thirds in Chopin's celebrated G-sharp minor Etude are perfectly rendered.

DUBAL: In the long run, audiences are very hard to fool. I've heard audiences wowed by press hype, or by brilliant execution. But eventually the audience realizes which artists really have something to say.

BADURA-SKODA: I definitely agree with you. In the end, the audience is captivated by a singing tone, the sheer beauty of sound as well as the personal spell. For instance, Cortot had the most beautiful piano sound I ever heard. It had a penetrating quality, and it could be accomplished even on a poor instrument.

DUBAL: I have always liked your particular sound on the piano; it is never percussive.

BADURA-SKODA: Thank you. I have always tried to measure the strength used in producing sound. The louder you play a piano, the more percussive it gets. A fine lesson in achieving a singing tone can be gotten by listening to Cortot or Horowitz, who can play an accompaniment so softly that the melody never sounds forced. Remember that the louder you play the melody the more percussive it will sound. Scriabin was said to have told his students that even a *fortissimo* should sound soft.

DUBAL: Edwin Fischer, a pianist I know you admire, also had a wonderful, non-percussive sound.

BADURA-SKODA: Yes, Fischer had all the bearings of genius. Everything he did was creative, different, touched by a different source. He found new possibilities where others thought there were none.

DUBAL: He taught only master classes, didn't he?

BADURA-SKODA: That's correct. The cream of good pianists came to him from all over the world. A student would sit down and play, and when he was finished, Fischer would say "That's very good." Then, without pretension he would sit down and open the same sonata, and you would go to pieces. Here you are, a young artist with good training and fine keyboard control, and you felt that you'd been doing child's work. All it took was three notes to know that it was Fischer at the piano.

DUBAL: Everybody felt strongly about Fischer. The other day I was talking with the British pianist Ronald Smith, who told me that one of the great musical experiences of his life was playing a Bach concerto with Fischer in London.

BADURA-SKODA: And yet his massive gifts did not always come through in public. There were moments of agony in his concerts. He was so overly sensitive that he could sabotage his own recitals. He would become upset with his own playing or with the audience for coughing in the middle of a slow movement, for instance. Suddenly he would produce bundles of wrong notes, or simply run away from himself.

DUBAL: Yes, nothing can be as precarious as public performance; one's nerves are always being tested.

BADURA-SKODA: I think every performer has to deal with this in his own peculiar way. Horowitz believes that an audience is necessary and inspirational, and yet he has undoubtedly found his audience anxiety-provoking, at times. On the other hand, Glenn Gould was at his best at the recording studio without any interference from the audience. As for myself, I have to admit that the audience can be a problem, particularly in a place I'm unfamiliar with. There are times when you feel that the public is just waiting for your slightest mistake. Concert halls are not always benevolent places. Then again, most audiences are receptive and sometimes they can inspire you. There is a give and take, a wave that increases through the recital and which pushes you beyond your ordinary limits, so that you give more than you can at home or in a recording session.

Dubal: In which part of the world have you found the most satisfying audiences?

Badura-Skoda: The warmest audiences you can imagine are in Russia, and most especially in Leningrad, with their two great halls, so rich in tradition. Liszt played in one of them and the other is the home of the Leningrad Philharmonic. It's just marvelous to play there. You feel a wonderful sense of anticipation, a special atmosphere, even before you set foot on stage. Then you begin to play and you feel people holding their breath so as not to lose the most delicate shading in the music. You see people with scores, students and teachers alike; they are there to follow everything you are doing.

Dubal: Did you play Mozart for them? I find that many Russian musicians seem uncomfortable with Mozart.

Badura-Skoda: It's interesting that you say that because many of my Russian colleagues told me that my playing of Mozart was a sort of lesson to them because it was more moderate than theirs. They tend to give too much or too little, and we have certainly had both extremes from Russian Mozart-playing. It is either too Romantic, with many exaggerations, or pedantic and ice-cold, shying away from anything which is personal. I tried to convince them that it is possible to be Romantic without going to extremes. For example, it is not necessary to undergo tempo changes within a movement.

Dubal: Is Mozart the greatest interpretive challenge for you, or is it the Beethoven sonatas?

Badura-Skoda: At one time my answer would have been Beethoven, but now I believe it's more difficult to play Mozart. Mozart is more exposed, and it is more difficult to get to the deeper meaning of the music than it is in Beethoven. The message in Beethoven is so indelible, and apart from the technical difficulties, he is clear in what he communicates. In Mozart, there's something which you cannot grasp intellectually, there is something ultimately mysterious about his music.

Dubal: It seems to me that in your Beethoven playing, you take faster tempi than most other pianists.

Badura-Skoda: I do take faster tempi than most, but they are always based on Beethoven's own indications, metronome marks, traditions and so on.

Dubal: In addition to being a pianist, you are also a scholar—a musicologist. What does it mean to be a musicologist?

BADURA-SKODA: The musical message is like a language that needs deciphering. As time goes by we lose the sense of its original meaning. Of particular importance is the cultivation and understanding of historical performance styles.

DUBAL: Is it through your work as a musicologist that you began to play and record on the wooden fortepianos?

BADURA-SKODA: Yes. I had been invited by the London Royal Association of Music to play Beethoven on both an old piano—an 1803 Broadwood—and a modern one. And I was certain that everyone, including myself, would prefer the modern piano, but I was wrong. Everybody left convinced that nothing could match the excitement of hearing Beethoven's *Appassionata* played on an early piano. The sound is quite wonderful—delicate and silvery—and there's something thrilling about the feeling that the piano might break at any moment. The stress becomes part of the performance. This is why Liszt broke so many pianos when he was conquering the musical world. It is said that he sometimes broke up to three or four pianos per recital.

DUBAL: Of course, this was before the iron frame. In recording sessions do you make special provisions for the possibility that the fortepiano might break or go out of tune frequently?

BADURA-SKODA: We always have at least one good technician standing by.

DUBAL: Lately I find that Bach is played more and more on the harpsichord; and Mozart is frequently being played on the fortepianos of the late eighteenth century. Do you think that Chopin will soon be played on old Pleyel and Erard pianos?

BADURA-SKODA: Up until recently, I would have said no because I thought that the pianos of Chopin and Schumann were more or less identical to ours. But recently I was asked to make a recording of the Chopin preludes and some mazurkas on a Chopin piano. And I was astonished by the difference. I won't say it was better or worse, but it was very, very different. I finally understood through my own hands and ears what I had read about as a musicologist. The instrument was much clearer in its textures, particularly in the lower register, and it had much less brilliance in the upper registers. It had a wonderful transparency and, particularly when I was playing the slow parts of a work, there was a wonderful feeling of poetry in the air. The vapor of Chopin's music seemed to come out more readily.

DUBAL: How did the pedals work?

Badura-Skoda: Exactly like ours. But you could easily use more pedal, which explains Chopin's original pedalings. It was reported that his right foot was always in motion. Of course the middle pedal, which was invented by Steinway, was unknown to Chopin.

Dubal: Whether on contemporary or early instruments, very few pianists have made as many records as you have. Do you like hearing your own work on discs?

Badura-Skoda: I usually listen to a recording when it comes out, to figure out if it is as good or as bad as I had originally thought. Then I put it aside. Basically, I am interested in gathering new data, in learning how other artists solve this or that problem. As for my early recordings which were made twenty or twenty-five years ago, there are times when I don't recognize my own interpretation anymore. It has happened more than once that I have asked innocently, "Who is that pianist?"

Dubal: I know you compose, because I was recently looking through your *Elegie for Piano*.

Badura-Skoda: I think everyone wants to compose, but it is more difficult to do so in our time than any time before. The artist, in earlier societies, had his function. He knew exactly what he was supposed to do, and what he was not supposed to do, what was allowed and what was forbidden. Today you have to create your own style; you are not born into it. You cannot say, "I am writing like Brahms or like Beethoven." The crucial thing is to find your own style, to make up your own limits. Because art can only exist within limits, within a framework.

Dubal: I often wonder how a composer like Haydn would have functioned in a society like ours, which is so different from the rather cushioned environment he was composing in.

Badura-Skoda: I think each of the great composers would write in a contemporary idiom; there's no question about it. Haydn today wouldn't write like Haydn of 200 years ago, and the same goes for Beethoven or Mozart. But certainly they would follow the same patterns. Haydn loved experiments, so I could see him doing a lot of electronic music, and bringing in, as he did in his time, rural music or Gypsy music. So you would perhaps find elements of jazz or rock in his symphonies. It's fun to speculate.

Dubal: Do you think it is more difficult to launch a career today than it was when you began?

Badura-Skoda: Yes, in my day you could get started by arranging a concert for yourself. Today the renting of a hall is terribly expensive. Thirty years ago it was no expense at all to send out ten thousand announcements. Today if you want to give a New York performance at Alice Tully Hall, it can cost $15,000, but can you get a good turnout? Only the very wealthy can afford this. I'm sorry to say that the likelihood of making a career is very, very dim. Few make it, and even those who win a prize in a big contest don't have any guarantee. But I don't want to be totally discouraging. I find that in Europe there is a new interest in piano recitals—particularly in Italy and France. Recently I spoke to a French music-lover who said, "At long last, France has turned into a musical country. Indeed, we have larger crowds at concerts and larger sales of classical records in France than ever before."

DUBAL: Another country with a burgeoning interest in classical music is China, where you will be playing next.

BADURA-SKODA: Yes, I will be there not only to play, but also to teach master classes. China is very eager to make up for the thirty-five years during which it was cut off from the West. Certainly during Mao's last years and the Cultural Revolution nobody dared to show any appreciation of western music.

DUBAL: Does it make you feel at all optimistic about the world situation when you are able to transcend political tensions by playing in a country like China?

BADURA-SKODA: Do you know that Beethoven firmly believed that people who listened well to his music would be better people, happier people? It's the attitude that art has moral value. Yes, I think music has a special capacity to bring harmony to all nations. Good music has a truly positive effect on people. I have seen this with my own eyes in the Soviet Union, China and many of the politically unstable countries of South America. When are we all going to live in peace? I have been everywhere, and I am always amazed at how intensely humanity can react to great art. Instead of developing nuclear weapons, when are we going to decide to live, and love, and play music, and listen to it, and survive?

JULIAN H. KREEGER

David Bar–Illan

David Bar-Illan

Born February 7, 1930, in Haifa, Israel, where he received his musical training, Bar-Illan served in the army during the Israeli War for Independence in 1948. After the war, he resumed his studies, graduating from both the Juilliard School and the Mannes College of Music. His main teachers were Dora Zaslavsky and Rosina Lhevinne. He made his New York debut in 1960, playing with Dmitri Mitropoulos and the New York Philharmonic. Later he was Pierre Boulez's first soloist with the New York Philharmonic, and he gave the first piano recital at the John F. Kennedy Center for the Performing Arts in Washington, D.C.

DUBAL: I know you do a great deal of silent practicing. This intrigues me. How did you arrive at this method?

BAR-ILLAN: I can say without exaggerating that my way of practice has changed my pianistic life. I worked, as we all do, by playing the music out loud, until one day before a concert in Buenos Aires, I was rudely interrupted by a very unpleasant woman in the apartment below. Although it was daytime, she threatened to call the police. So, necessity being the mother of invention, I tried to practice as quietly as possible. I noticed that if I depressed the keys very, very slowly, there would be no sound at all. I quickly realized that this could give me some interesting results. First of all, since some of the motions were so slow, I found this to be a marvelous way of checking on how securely I had memorized the pieces. And after that day I continued to practice in this way because it became clear that the kind of pressure used in such careful depression of the keys strengthens the fingers to such an extent that when you play at the proper tempo, it seems easy. You've seen baseball players practicing their swing with two bats in order to feel the relative lightness of one bat. This kind of practice gives you a margin of strength and security on stage, where we may be performing somewhat below our optimum level. And of course on tour this has become one of the blessings of my existence. I can practice on any bloody keyboard that is available. So many pianists say they can't practice because the piano is not good enough, and to me that's nonsense.

DUBAL: Do you use this kind of practice when you aren't on tour as well?

BAR-ILLAN: Oh, yes, in fact I even developed it to incorporate another aspect of work. As you well know, the piano is a percussive mechanism and, unlike a wind or string instrument, it is very difficult to achieve on it a legato effect, which is, of course, the connection and overlapping between the notes. I had one of my two concert grands muted in order to eliminate as much of the decay rate of the struck tone as possible. So on my piano there is almost no after-sound, which means that I am getting the minimal amount of legato. If I play on a very good, ringing piano, with long-lasting tone, I find that it becomes seductive to let the piano do the work. But then you are on one of those many concert stages where the acoustic is so dry and the decay rate is so fast that it never seems to get past the apron of the stage. So, to get a legato in a hall like this I struggle to achieve the maximum legato on the muted piano. To feel secure with the legato means that I can sing without any trouble on any instrument that you give me. Singing on the piano is one of the most important achievements of piano playing.

DUBAL: What about the pedal in this kind of practice?

BAR-ILLAN: The pedal should be for coloristic effect, not for aiding in legato. It should only be used in achieving legato as a last resort—for impractical skips, or if the hand is too small to make certain connections. But even then, one should stay on the first note as long as possible before going to the next one.

DUBAL: How do you manage to repress the natural desire to hear the music?

BAR-ILLAN: Do understand that during my soundless practicing I do hear the music in my mind. One can all too easily play music without actually listening to it. Through this kind of work I ensure that my music-making is not merely automatic. Naturally, when I feel ready, I leave my "machine" and go to the good piano, where I find out if everything I want is being achieved. If I'm not pleased with the results, I go right back to the machine. I know this sounds austere—there's no doubt that my way of work requires a great deal of persistence and attention. But for my playing I need this kind of application.

DUBAL: I know that lately you have been practicing all the Chopin etudes in order to record them.

BAR-ILLAN: Yes, and the more I work on them the more extraordinary they become. Who else could create such a world of emotion in so few moments?

DUBAL: George Sand once wrote that one little Chopin prelude contains more music than all the trumpetings of Meyerbeer's operas.

BAR-ILLAN: Yes, and I think it was Horowitz who said that one Chopin mazurka is worth all the music in a Mahler symphony. As for his economy, I don't think anyone ever managed to get more from two minutes of music. And, in the case of the etudes, also revolutionize the technique of piano playing.

DUBAL: He definitely systematized in these pieces all the technical explorations in the etudes of Clementi, Cramer, Moscheles, Czerny and Steibilt and Berger.

BAR-ILLAN: Yes, and to think he was only twenty years old. In the etudes he finally made the technical difficulties subservient to the musical purpose.

DUBAL: Yet many of those technical difficulties remain unparalleled.

BAR-ILLAN: Some are excruciatingly difficult. It's very rare that one pianist can play each of the etudes with the same kind of mastery.

DUBAL: In the 1830s, just after the etudes were published, Liszt was probably the only pianist in Europe who could play them well, besides Chopin. Do you know the letter written to the pianist Ferdinand Hiller, in which Chopin says, "I am writing without knowing what my pen is scribbling, because at this moment Liszt is playing my etudes and putting honest thoughts out of my head: I should like to rob him of the way to play my own etudes"?

BAR-ILLAN: I didn't know of that letter; how revealing it is to hear one great musician comment on the playing of another. I'm sure their approaches were totally different and yet Chopin wasn't saying "only my way is correct."

DUBAL: Great interpretation certainly is a mystery.

BAR-ILLAN: Yes, the greater the interpretation, the more impossible to figure it out. A good example is Friedman's recordings of some of the Chopin mazurkas. I don't understand what he is doing. On purpose I try to imitate them—not to play like him of course, but to understand what he does. And yet what he does with them remains an enigma. Or just listen to Cortot. What an individualist! What is it about Cortot? Even with all the wrong notes, and the variations in tempo that I simply cannot understand—yet his performances make your heart beat faster. One can talk about timing, about personality, character, tone, ability to color the music. But when you come down to the nitty-gritty, it is impossible to actually say what separates a very excellent performance by someone, and a performance by Cortot, Rubinstein, Horowitz or Gould, all of whom I can recognize in two phrases at the most. Such a thing is not definable, but whatever it is, it is essential to great music-making. Without it there will be no audience excitement, fever pitch, electricity or whatever you want to call it. This magic exists in all performing arts. There is a world of difference between the fine dancer and the star, the Nureyev, who drives the audience to rapture. They may both be doing everything correctly but they are two different species.

DUBAL: There are so many subtleties involved in making a compelling performer.

BAR-ILLAN: Yes, there are so many aspects of musicianship—technical proficiency, agility and independence of the fingers, musical feeling, musical memory, understanding of the composer, the ability to project all this and, to use a slightly inelegant term for classical music, "showmanship."

DUBAL: Showmanship was not devalued in the nineteenth century—Paganini, Liszt and Paderewski certainly had it in abundance.

BAR-ILLAN: Of course they did, but unfortunately the word has come to have a vulgar or trivial meaning. For me, showmanship means the ability to entertain, and I see nothing wrong with that. The more I perform, the more I understand that we must be entertainers above everything else. I am there to put on a show, not to educate. Otherwise there is really no justification for me to ask people to pay good money to come to a hall, sit in relatively uncomfortable seats in a not always pleasant environment, and listen to me play the piano for two hours. I don't see why they would want to be there unless they feel that they are going to be entertained. I think art should be thought of and treated in this way. Certainly Shakespeare didn't write plays to educate, but to entertain. Horowitz entertains very differently than does Liberace. They each exist on different planes. Horowitz entertains just as much as Liberace, perhaps not to the same people and not in the same manner; but all over the world people flock to Horowitz concerts because he has the great ability to transport them.

DUBAL: You mentioned Glenn Gould, who certainly understood about showmanship. It came through even in his humming.

Bar-Illan: Oh, absolutely, and on a very high level. What a stunning entertainer. To see him conducting himself, conducting the orchestra, humming, singing. He was very aware of all that. I don't think it was something he couldn't have stopped if he had wanted to. As for his performances, they were unmistakably his own. What could be more entertaining than that? Gould often said that if you can't do something differently, don't do it. If there are twenty terrific recordings of the *Waldstein,* why bother to make a twenty-first if you have nothing new to contribute?

Dubal: I know Gould was a friend of yours.

Bar-Illan: We were close friends for a long time. His death was shattering to me. He was a genius, the real article. He had a fugal mind. He could actually think on three or four levels at the same time and could listen to four conversations simultaneously. Naturally his ability to play counterpoint was unmatched. He often liked to call me and read to me his articles, which were written in literary counterpoint. To know him was an experience. He could discuss anything, from very mundane things to Greek philosophy, and it literally sounded like discussions from above. Yet he was so unpretentious and delightful. He would usually appear out of nowhere. He once called me when he was in New York and said, "David, I'm recording the *Moonlight Sonata* this afternoon. Should I play it slow or fast?" And since I thought the *Moonlight* is usually played too slowly I said, "Please play it fast." He said "Good," he hung up and then I didn't hear from him for six months. It was useless to pursue him, but then, out of the blue, again, he would phone at midnight, and our conversation would go on for hours. Though once, right after saying hello, I coughed and sneezed, and he said with worry in his voice, "What's the matter?" I told him I had a cold. He hung up. I think he actually believed he could get a cold over the wire.

Dubal: Did he show any interest in your playing?

Bar-Illan: Oh yes, I even played on his sacred piano, which he guarded with his life. He talked about his piano as if it were human. He talked of its temperaments. He was proud of it. His piano, he said, improved with age and had the ability to tune itself. Once, when the piano was dropped by movers, he was as upset as if a family member had died. I remember playing a rather virtuosic piece on it once, and as I raised my hand high, he thought I was about to come down hard on the instrument. He said, "Oh, no, no, don't, don't, wait!!!"

DUBAL: Did Gould ever play for you privately?

BAR-ILLAN: I'll never forget the time I played Mendelssohn's *Rondo Capriccioso* for him, and he said "I know that! I believe I must have played it when I was ten or eleven." He then sat down and played it perfectly in his own inimitable way, making it sound a bit Bachian of course. It was all there from beginning to end. He hadn't touched it in thirty years.

DUBAL: Did Gould ever come to any of your concerts?

BAR-ILLAN: As we all know, he hated concerts, but he actually did come to a few of mine. Of course he didn't sit in the audience. He was totally averse to it, as well as being celebrity-shy. So before the concert he would look for a place backstage and hide there. Afterward, I'd look at my scores and they'd be covered with all sorts of amusing cracks he'd made about what I did with the pieces I played.

DUBAL: Gould, of course, played Bach on the piano, but there are those who think it is a sacrilege to play Bach on anything but his original instruments. Do you think we are becoming overly concerned with the medium, perhaps at the expense of the music?

BAR-ILLAN: Did you know that Ravel, one of the masters of piano scoring, never had a grand piano in his home? He composed on an upright, which offers a fraction of the possibilities afforded by a concert grand. Should we for authenticity sake play Ravel on an upright? Wouldn't that be ludicrous?

DUBAL: Do you think there is a lack of versatility among musicians today?

BAR-ILLAN: In a way, it's inevitable, because we have technical demands made upon us that were never even dreamt of in Mozart's time. They didn't have to play a hundred concerts a year or make recordings. They didn't have to reach the technical standard we do today, so they could afford the time to be more versatile.

DUBAL: As far as I know you don't play much contemporary music, although you have played both solo pieces and concertos of Robert Starer.

BAR-ILLAN: I strongly believe in Starer's music, and I try to play as much of it as possible. I think if each of us picks one living composer that we believe in, instead of dividing our time with several out of a sense of obligation, we can really do a good selling job on that composer.

DUBAL: I know Starer lived in Israel. Is contemporary music valued there?

BAR-ILLAN: No, the Israelis are not great supporters of contemporary music; it's an excellent but conservative audience. In fact, it is the largest audience per capita in the world for classical music. The Israel Philharmonic repeats every concert sixteen times to satisfy all its subscribers. Tel Aviv is a city of about 800,000 people, and I think they have 35,000 subscribers there. That's an absolutely incredible ratio.

DUBAL: Growing up there did you receive good teaching?

BAR-ILLAN: Oh yes, in the Thirties many fine European artists, teachers, pianists, violinists, came to the country because of the Nazis. Hans Neumann, an extraordinary musician who had played many concerts in Europe, was my teacher. He came from Prague when the Nazi terror came there.

DUBAL: As a Jew, living in what is now Israel during the Nazi period, you must have wondered often how many gifted young artists had been destroyed by Hitler.

BAR-ILLAN: This was the worst tragedy in human history. We can never know what genius would have come about if Hitler had not murdered one million children. After all these were the people who produced Freud and Einstein. Just think of the kind of talent that the Jews produced in Europe from around 1850. So you can imagine what could have been in Poland, where the entire population of Jews was wiped out. These were the people that produced Rubinstein, Friedman, Godowsky, Hofmann and on and on. Not to mention what was lost in what is now the Soviet Union. Sol Hurok used to define a cultural exchange as "when the Russians send us Jews from Odessa and we send them Jews from Odessa."

DUBAL: Can you explain the great flowering of Jewish talent in the arts and sciences in the last century and a half?

BAR-ILLAN: For 1800 years, while the Jews were ghettoized, I think they must have stored up tremendous amounts of intellectual and artistic energy. When the Jew started to assimilate into European society around 1850, that emancipation brought a flood of thought and artistic achievement of which we are speaking. Before this the Jew could only pour his heart and mind into the *Talmud* and the *Torah*.

Born October 17, 1940, in Los Angeles of Yugoslav parents, Bishop-Kovacevich made his debut in San Francisco at the age of eleven. At fourteen he played the Ravel Concerto in G with that city's orchestra. Bishop-Kovacevich made his London recital debut at Wigmore Hall in 1961, and his New York debut in 1968. From 1969 to 1971 he performed all of Mozart's piano concerti at London's Queen Elizabeth Hall. For his performance of Bartók's Second Piano Concerto he received an Edison Award in 1970. His career has taken him throughout the world.

Stephen Bishop-Kovacevich

DUBAL: You are an American, yet you have played here less than in other parts of the world.

BISHOP-KOVACEVICH: That's right, I grew up in California and when I was eighteen I left Berkeley to study with Myra Hess—I thought for a few months, perhaps a year. I ended up living in London for more than two decades, which certainly was a surprise.

DUBAL: Who did you study with before Myra Hess?

BISHOP-KOVACEVICH: Lev Shorr, a Russian who came to America about fifty years ago. I studied with him for ten or eleven years in San Francisco.

DUBAL: That's a long time to stay with one teacher.

BISHOP-KOVACEVICH: That's right.

DUBAL: So he must have had something.

BISHOP-KOVACEVICH: He did indeed. He was a very fine teacher.

DUBAL: How did he take to the idea of your studying with Dame Myra Hess?

BISHOP-KOVACEVICH: I think he knew it was time, that I had to move on. Also you could not make a career by staying in San Francisco in those days. You either had to go to New York or London.

DUBAL: So off you went to London. Were you nervous the first time you were to play for Hess?

BISHOP-KOVACEVICH: I remember coming an hour early and just pacing around. But she had a way of making one feel at ease. Incidentally, I also played for Horowitz once as a young pianist and he too put me at ease.

DUBAL: How long did you study with Hess?

BISHOP-KOVACEVICH: For two very good years, just before she became ill. It was around that time that I began to get my first concerts.

DUBAL: Did your career follow the usual course—from the conservatory to the competition, that sort of thing?

BISHOP-KOVACEVICH: Not at all! After studying with Myra Hess I just started giving recitals in London. I hired the Wigmore Hall and gave five recitals there in two years. That was it. I scraped by the first couple of years and had to borrow a bit, but then the engagements started coming in.

DUBAL: Have you ever taught?

BISHOP-KOVACEVICH: I have one or two students in London but I don't teach regularly. There's just not the time and the energy, really. After I finish practicing, I want to go play snooker. I have an addiction to snooker, which is the European version of billiards. I don't want to see a student when I finish practicing, I need to relax.

DUBAL: How do you prepare for a concert on the day of the event?

BISHOP-KOVACEVICH: I wish I could tell you that I had found a formula after all these years. For me there are no rules, though it certainly doesn't do to go out and play six sets of tennis and then walk out on the stage in the evening. And I find that it's a good idea not to touch any of the pieces you're due to play, but to practice other things instead; get to know the piano, find your way into the new keyboard. And then rest.

DUBAL: Does your heart still pound before you go on stage?

BISHOP-KOVACEVICH: Oh yes, though it varies from concert to concert. But if you're very well prepared, no matter what state of mind you're in, your preparation will save the day.

DUBAL: Paderewski once said that nerves come from a bad conscience, from holes in the preparation.

BISHOP-KOVACEVICH: My preparation is always savage. Then again, there are sometimes various demons to cope with in one's head. I recently went to the hall the day before I was due to give a concert and I found myself practicing the fugue of Beethoven's Sonata Op. 101 for four hours. That's a piece that I can usually play without practicing at all. But that day, it wasn't going well and I was scared like hell.

DUBAL: Are you a good sight-reader?

BISHOP-KOVACEVICH: I'm a rotten sight-reader. It's lovely to be a good sight-reader, but I'm not one. This was perhaps because as a child my memory was so strong that I didn't have to develop the skill.

DUBAL: Do you work out your pedaling as precisely as you do your phrasing and dynamics?

BISHOP-KOVACEVICH: Pedaling is the most instinctive part of my music-making. I never even think about it. I don't want to know "how" I pedal. And yet I once got a fan letter from Stokowski about my pedaling—can you believe it? After a concert he wrote me, saying, "You do with your pedal what I tried to get with the Philadelphia Orchestra." And I was thrilled!

DUBAL: How do you keep works fresh season after season? Is it difficult?

BISHOP-KOVACEVICH: No, not in the case of very great works such as the Schubert B-flat Sonata. The deeper you go into a work such as this, the more creative you will be in performance. For instance, you might begin the first movement a little quicker one day, which will change the entire character of your performance. It will change the way you play the second movement, which will affect the way you play the third and fourth movements. But again, I must emphasize that these new insights can only come from deep knowledge of the score.

DUBAL: What is stage presence?

BISHOP-KOVACEVICH: Stage presence is a gift which defies analysis, but there is an aura that you feel when it's there. When I feel I have it, I feel closest to the audience.

DUBAL: Do you still like to perform as much as you did at the very beginning of your career?

BISHOP-KOVACEVICH: I'm less enamored of the stage than I used to be. I remember speaking with Glenn Gould about this—he tried to convince me to stop playing in public; he said it was beneath me. I argued with him at the time. But recently, I've come to see more of what he means. Let's face it, it takes only one person coughing, or turning the pages of a score to ruin a passage. This can be very discouraging.

DUBAL: Gould did not believe in the process of communal listening. He thought listening was strictly a personal thing, and that's why he loved to make records.

BISHOP-KOVACEVICH: Yes, it is a personal thing. But I believe it is possible to have a personal experience with others. But not in a hall full of people flapping their programs.

DUBAL: Do you ever experience post-concert depression?

BISHOP-KOVACEVICH: Only if I've given a bad concert. I do feel very drained of energy, however, and afterwards, a little dazed.

DUBAL: I noticed at a recent concert of yours that you didn't play any encores.

BISHOP-KOVACEVICH: At that particular concert I was very tired and cross at the audience. I thought they'd made too much noise. So that was it. But usually I love giving encores. There is a certain freedom and generosity in encore playing because you know it's a gift to the audience.

DUBAL: When do you feel best about your playing?

BISHOP-KOVACEVICH: The most satisfying thing of all can be times when you're musically "on" for yourself. Sure, moments of revelation may come at a concert, but there's something so private and uncommercial about what happens when you're on your own.

DUBAL: I was recently listening to your only Chopin recording and wondering why you don't play him in public more often.

BISHOP-KOVACEVICH: I adore Chopin, but to play him in public is extremely problematic for me because I get too excited. His music engenders such a storm in me. Actually, I have quite a large Chopin repertoire, but bringing it to the stage is complicated for me and I keep postponing it. Let me try to explain. In the Viennese Classics, even in the most convulsive pages in Beethoven, there's an incredibly strong line to hold on to. The line can be stretched nearly to the breaking point—and yet there is a certain security, because the tension builds over the whole structure. But with Chopin there are instantaneous explosions which are much more difficult to realize in the context of the piece.

DUBAL: And does the explosive element overtake your control?

BISHOP-KOVACEVICH: Yes, in Chopin, instead of letting go, I might be too careful. I seldom play him the way I want to, and for that reason I can only perform Chopin for a public I know and like. In addition, the hall has to be right. If it's dry, please don't even ask me to play Chopin. I can survive dry halls with the Classics. But to play a piece of Chopin in one . . . I just don't know how people do it. Chopin must resonate.

DUBAL: A composer you play quite often is Bartók.

BISHOP-KOVACEVICH: I came to him when I was in my mid-twenties. I heard a recording of the Bartók Second Piano Concerto, which I didn't know at that point. I was absolutely thunderstruck by this piece, which was far less well-known then than it is today. I went and bought the score, and it looked as if a printer had just thrown a million black notes on the page. I thought, "This may be a great piece, but I can never play it." It looked impossible. Soon after, I was playing a concert with Colin Davis and I mentioned my attraction to the Bartók Second and also my fear of it. The next day I got an invitation from the BBC, from him, to play the Bartók Second in nine months' time. He obviously wasn't going to let me get away with anything. So I seized the opportunity. I worked like a maniac. Frankly, I'd never played anything as technically difficult.

There are all kinds of challenges in the literature, but there is nothing more difficult than playing Bartók's Second really ferociously. I almost paralyzed my hand in the process of learning the piece. One morning I woke up and I could not hold a piece of fruit in my hand because it was so overstrained. I went to a doctor who said, "Cancel the concert. You won't be able to stand the pain." But I didn't cancel and somehow I got through the performance. I was obsessed by the music, and after that I started to play quite a lot of Bartók. I played all the concertos and some of the solo music. For five or six years I absolutely adored it. Now I love it, but not with the extraordinary passion that I once felt.

DUBAL: Do you play contemporary music besides Bartók? I know that the Richard Rodney Bennett Piano Concerto is dedicated to you.

BISHOP-KOVACEVICH: That's right, it is. But I don't play very much contemporary music. It may be brutal to say, but I think that the technical problems and the reading problems are so immense, that the rewards are not in proportion to the effort. Some of the stuff sent to me by composers hoping for a performance is just amazing. It might as well be played by a computer. I once played a work by a composer whose name I won't mention, in which I worked like a dog to learn the tone clusters correctly. When I played for him, it came out all wrong and he didn't even know the difference. I was terribly angry because of the great waste of time. I could have been learning so many other things, or even playing snooker.

DUBAL: As an exponent of the Viennese School, Schnabel must have been one of your idols.

BISHOP-KOVACEVICH: In a sense, but really Horowitz and Rachmaninoff were the pianists I was most passionate about.

DUBAL: Yet you don't play their romantic virtuoso repertoire—

BISHOP-KOVACEVICH: Yes, I know, but if you listen to the way I play Beethoven or Brahms, for example, you'll see that there's a fierceness in it, a virtuoso element, which is derived from the virtuoso school. And this is the influence of Horowitz and Rachmaninoff. Of course I never heard Rachmaninoff play but I know his recordings intimately. Some are absolutely unbelievable. In his recording of the Schubert Impromptu Op. 90 No. 4, although I think he begins rather crassly, he soon reveals a depth of passion that is really what Schubert is all about. It is not the usual Viennese chocolate-and-whipped-cream performance. It's absolutely piercing and passionate.

DUBAL: This is rather unusual, for a pianist of your age who concentrates on the Classical school to have such admiration for Rachmaninoff and

Horowitz, two Russian romantics. Don't they play with too much rubato for your taste?

BISHOP-KOVACEVICH: No. Almost everything Rachmaninoff plays has a natural motivation, and I find everything Horowitz plays to be provocative. Of course I'm not always comfortable with what he does, but what he stands for is amazing. For me he stands alone. He's like a madness, a narcotic—sometimes irrational, sometimes beautiful and poetic, sometimes violent.

DUBAL: In the Germanic school, did you admire Backhaus?

BISHOP-KOVACEVICH: Absolutely. To my mind, Backhaus was the only person who ever truly understood Beethoven's *Hammerklavier Sonata*. Listen to his recordings. It's true he may not be faithful to the text in every instance, but the wildness of what he's attempting to do is quite wonderful.

DUBAL: Do you have a "blind spot" composer, one that you are not in accord with?

BISHOP-KOVACEVICH: I think Haydn is overrated and I cannot bear the piano sonatas.

DUBAL: That's blasphemy! He's one of the giants!

BISHOP-KOVACEVICH: Yes, I know, and Beethoven liked him and all that, but when I hear Haydn, I feel like giving him a tip. He's still eating with the servants. With Beethoven, there was no more eating with the servants. You know he came in the front door.

DUBAL: Does it ever intimidate you to think there may be people in the audience who envy your gift?

BISHOP-KOVACEVICH: Unfortunately, yes, and I sometimes say to myself, "Do I dare play as well as I can?" When you play in concert, you're often doing something which most of the people in the audience can't do, and that can be an uncomfortable situation for me and for those who are envious of my talent. And the more successful and gifted you are, and the more you reveal this on stage, the bigger the problem is. But you have to be willing to take responsibility for inducing these feelings because you have to give all.

DUBAL: Do you have to be a noble person to be an artist?

BISHOP-KOVACEVICH: I would hope that the evil person would undermine his own artistic viability. But I'm not so sure. We once thought art protected us from the monster, but since the rise of Nazi Germany we have come to understand the proximity of art to bestiality.

Born November 15, 1914, in Havana, Cuba, Bolet attended the Curtis Institute in Philadelphia, where he studied piano with David Saperton as well as conducting with Fritz Reiner and later with Abram Chasins. In 1937 he won the Naumburg Award. As a lieutenant in the U.S. Army, stationed in Japan, he conducted the Japanese premiere of The Mikado. *In 1968 he joined the faculty at Indiana University. He is presently the head of the piano department at Curtis. Bolet has played a wide repertoire and has resurrected interesting Romantic scores such as the Sgambati Piano Concerto.*

Jorge Bolet

DUBAL: When did you come to music and the piano?

BOLET: I think I came to be a pianist because I was born a pianist. I say that modestly. I am sure that I heard piano playing the day I was born. I have an older sister who was really extremely talented, and played a great deal. She was my very first teacher, so music was in the air I breathed and doubtless in my genes also. My brother is a conductor.

DUBAL: You considered your home environment a wonderful thing.

BOLET: Oh, yes, I think it's a great advantage for a child who has musical talent to have music in the home constantly. I was really hearing piano playing from the day I was born until I was old enough to play the piano myself. I remember sitting beside my sister for hours on end, turning her pages—and before I could read a note of music, I knew exactly when to turn the page, all the while becoming acquainted with the repertory.

DUBAL: Is your technique also natural?

BOLET: Yes, I think mechanical aptitude is also an inborn talent. In my case, what I do at the keyboard has always been done with a certain amount of ease. That is not to say that everything is easy, of course. I find that whatever I have to do with a rather open hand position comes easily; but whenever I have to play things that require a closed hand position, that becomes more difficult.

DUBAL: There are pianists who have said that the daily grind of practicing is like going to the salt mines. Is practicing the piano odious to you or is it a joy?

BOLET: I have to be honest. I hate practicing. I've always disliked it. But it's a necessity. I have to do it because I love to play. I've always contended that I'm a performer, and that's why recording is even a horrendous experience to me, because I feel when I'm recording that I'm not performing. I'm playing to microphones and engineers in a control booth. To me, music depends on three very important factors: the composer, who wrote the music; the performer, who plays the music; and the listener, who listens to it. So if you take the listening factor away, you only have two-thirds of the music left. I have always found it very, very frustrating and really annoying not to have an audience.

DUBAL: So you need an audience for that third component. Do you think records will have revolutionized music in the long run?

BOLET: They have already revolutionized music, there's no doubt of that. But I think it has destroyed a great deal of what I consider "music-making." I use that term as opposed to just "piano playing." We have come to the point where recordings are of such mechanical perfection that any slight imperfection in a performance is not tolerated. As a result, the young generation of pianists, of which we have scores, usually have a flawless mechanical control of everything they play. Clinkers are forbidden; they never miss a passage; they never muddle up anything. They're really pianistic computers, and the records themselves now are so clean with the new digital process that everything is so clean and bright, and this for me is a little frightening.

DUBAL: This, then, is a result of the homogenization that has occurred through the technical perfection of the recording process.

BOLET: Absolutely. Recordings have been very much responsible for that. Where is the inspiration of the moment; the new idea that emerges while performing, which is something I experience all the time? I do many things in performance that I've never consciously thought of doing, and the sense of freedom is exhilarating.

DUBAL: Yes, I know from hearing you many times in live performances that you like to take chances. They don't always work out; but when they do, there is excitement in the air.

BOLET: For me, freedom and spontaneity are what make music-making really interesting.

DUBAL: Besides records, what else do you feel has taken its toll on originality and freedom in "music-making?"

BOLET: Competitions—I think they have done piano playing more harm than almost anything else. Look at it this way: A young pianist enters a big international competition. There are fifteen judges, roughly. The pianists have to get fifteen votes—or at least that is their aim. They cannot play anything that is going to antagonize any of those fifteen people in any way. They cannot do anything that could be considered controversial by any one of them; they cannot do anything that could be considered a personal idea. So, as a result, you hear one, ten, thirty young pianists and they're all alike. They all have exactly the same approach. You never hear anything that you haven't heard many times before.

DUBAL: What do you recommend to young pianists today, to capture more of what you wish?

BOLET: I wish that every young pianist would really study—I don't mean just listen, but really study the performances of Rachmaninoff, Horowitz, Moiseiwitsch, Hofmann and Friedman and really analyze what made their performances so great.

Dubal: People often talk about the tremendous technical standard of our time. Yet are there pianists around today with techniques like those of the ones you just mentioned?

Bolet: Godowsky used the term "technique" to include everything about a pianist's performance—the conception, the character, tempo—everything that concerns the whole. And by that definition, I do not think we measure up. I think not.

Dubal: What do you think is the chief difficulty that younger musicians encounter today in their efforts to build their career?

Bolet: I think it is basically the same thing I came up against when I was trying to establish my own career. The competition is extraordinary. As you know, I've had a very long career, and it hasn't always been a successful one. Anyway, I have heard literally dozens of young pianists with real talent, full of promise for an international career, and where are they now? So many of the youngsters start out brilliantly. They make some excellent recordings, they play with important orchestras and good conductors. They play all the great music festivals, but how long do most careers last? By the time they are thirty-five, a new crop has taken their place, and no one ever hears of them again.

Dubal: I think part of the problem is that the managements think they can only sell twenty-year-old competition winners.

Bolet: Yes, this has certainly gotten out of hand. To book a young pianist, he or she has to have won a major international competition. The first thing people ask about a young pianist is "What competitions has he or she won?"

Dubal: As you said, your career has had its ups and downs. But your success has been enormous, especially in the last fifteen years or so. What has sustained you through the difficult times?

Bolet: I absolutely refuse to give up. It really boils down to that. But, I must say, there have been so many times in my life when I've thought, "You know, I'm just banging my head against a stone wall. I'm getting absolutely nowhere." "Well, I'll give it one more year; and if I don't succeed, I'll just become a professional photographer." Photography has been my great hobby for many years, ever since I was very young. But then something would happen. For instance, Rodzinski heard me play in Havana and he raved about me. Another time I played for Mitropoulos and he said, "How is it I never heard of you? Where have you been?" At that point I was already a man of forty years of age and I had been everywhere. The "Where have you been?" happened again when I played for Koussevitzky—"How is it I've never heard of you?" When something like this would happen, I would tell myself: "If conductors like these will engage me, I must not quit." And of course, the music itself propelled me. I'd learn a new work, and I would just have to perform it for an audience somewhere.

DUBAL: What is the difference between audiences today and the ones Godowsky and Hofmann played for?

BOLET: Today's audiences go to the concert hall to hear Beethoven and Schubert and Brahms and so on. But back in Godowsky and Hofmann's day, we went to hear what the pianist had to say about the composer; we went to hear the pianists, and the same thing went for every other great pianist. When you went to hear Cortot play an all-Chopin recital, you went to hear what Cortot had to say about Chopin.

DUBAL: Indeed, that is a great change in music performance today—the text is sacred and so is the composer. But we're not very interested in the musician. I have often gone to all-Beethoven concerts, which have sometimes been quite dull, but the audience applauds wildly because Beethoven is a very status composer. In a sense, the audience is applauding itself for being there.

BOLET: I agree completely.

DUBAL: Let's talk about the composer you are most closely associated with in the public's mind—Franz Liszt.

BOLET: I think you have to have a special kind of mental attitude in playing Liszt. With almost any composer before Liszt, or even with his contemporaries, I think it's really quite important to study the score very precisely, to stick as closely to what the composer has written as possible. With Liszt, you have to do exactly the same thing when you first study the composition, but after you have absorbed everything that is in the score, everything that Liszt wrote the way he wrote it, you have to throw the score in the wastebasket and make the piece your own. You have to play it the way you feel it has to be played.

DUBAL: That's a very interesting trick, if it can be done, but for most students, I'm afraid it would be rather a reckless adventure.

BOLET: Yes, perhaps you have to know Liszt very well—his style, his declamation—in order for this to work.

DUBAL: Do you suppose that Liszt was really the phenomenal pianist legend tells us he was?

BOLET: Yes, I'm sure I wouldn't be disappointed, because all the testimony that we have of Liszt's contemporaries who heard him play said that he was absolutely unique. The level of his playing was something that no one had even dreamed of before.

DUBAL: Besides Liszt, you also seem to love the challenge of playing Godowsky, who was Liszt's successor from the point of view of technical acumen. How did you get involved with his transcendental technical madness?

BOLET: I studied with David Saperton at the Curtis Institute in Philadelphia for seven years. And Saperton, who was married to Godowsky's daughter, was very much involved in Godowsky's music. During the years that I studied with him, I learned quite a sizable repertoire of Godowsky. I think Saperton took a great deal of pleasure in assigning pieces to me that some of his other students just couldn't tackle. Anyway, whenever I would learn a few of these works, Saperton would have me come to New York and play them for Godowsky. So I actually studied with Godowsky himself.

I think it's really tragic that Godowsky has been so maligned. You know, a certain section of the musical public, particularly the professional pianists, simply dismiss him as the man who tampered with the Chopin etudes. Most of those people have an encyclopedic ignorance of what Godowsky is and what he did, which is understandable, since when there is prejudice, there is seldom truth. Nevertheless, Godowsky *did do* what Liszt had been able to do in his day. He managed to advance the technique, the mechanics of piano playing to a degree previously unimagined. I'm fascinated by what he was able to do because, without doubt, Godowsky symphonicized (if there is such a word) piano playing to a greater extent than any other composer who has ever lived. What Godowsky did with rhythms, polyrhythms and textures can only be termed ingenious.

DUBAL: Not long ago, you played the Josef Marx Piano Concerto with Zubin Mehta and the New York Philharmonic. What can you tell us about Marx, who is little-known today?

BOLET: Marx was an Austrian composer born in 1882, who was known mostly for his lieder. He wrote over one hundred songs which were once frequently sung but, I am sorry to say, are now neglected. The concerto was written in 1920. It has been played in Europe occasionally, but it had never been played in the United States. It's a shame because it's a wonderful work, a real post-Romantic extravaganza, with beautiful melodies and magnificent harmonies, with hundreds of thousands of notes, cavalcades of notes.

DUBAL: Is it possible that the Marx Concerto didn't receive its due as a repertory piece because, for a Romantic concerto, it was written too late? The new century was already into its third decade and there were so many new things to say musically.

BOLET: I think you are right. If it had been written in 1885 it probably wouldn't have become so obscure.

DUBAL: How did you come to revive this score?

BOLET: Well, as you know, I'm always interested in playing music that nobody else plays: I simply get tired of playing the same things all the time. Anyway, I was once given a full orchestra score of the Marx Concerto, and when I looked it over, I fell in love with it and decided that I really wanted to learn it. But, learning a piece like that from a full orchestra score is rather difficult, because the notes are terribly small; and so it's difficult to read. But then a friend of mine here in New York, knowing that I was learning the work, happened to pass by a music store on the West Side. And on a fluke, he went in, asked if they had any works of Marx, and amazingly enough they pulled out a two-piano reduction of the score.

DUBAL: I can imagine your surprise. Every time I've been in a music store lately and have asked for anything outside of the standard literature, I come out empty-handed. Fortunately there are still a few such shops as Patelson's in New York, and an excellent one in Amsterdam, the Muziekhandel.

BOLET: I know, it's getting very frustrating; good music stores are becoming very scarce.

DUBAL: Are there any recent composers of piano music that hold any interest for you?

BOLET: I think Ginastera has written some really significant music for the piano. The sonatas and the concerti are of particularly fine quality. Here in the United States, John Corigliano is writing significant music for the piano. Both composers are serious and accessible to a large public.

DUBAL: Have you played much contemporary music?

BOLET: I have played a share of it. I introduced John LaMontaine's Piano Concerto, for example, which won the Pulitzer Prize in 1958. I've played a good deal of Norman Dello Joio's music. I introduced his Third Sonata, which is an excellent piece. The Second Sonata is also a marvelous work, but no one seems to have taken it up.

DUBAL: Have you always taught the piano?

BOLET: Yes, I have always had a few students.

DUBAL: And you are now head of the piano department at the Curtis Institute. Is that fun?

Bolet: No. It's hard work. Really, I would much prefer if I didn't have to teach. I teach purely out of duty.

Dubal: But, you're not one of those teachers who kill the spirit, are you? The nineteenth-century pianist Adolf von Henselt was supposedly such a brutal teacher that his students said, "Don't go near him; Henselt kills!"

Bolet: I am a stern master, but that is because I believe that people like myself who have received so much from the great masters of the past have an obligation to pass it on to the next generation. Otherwise, the great tradition is lost and dies. I think that the real problem with piano playing today is that the great tradition of Liszt, Leschetizky, Anton Rubinstein, Godowsky and Busoni is passing away.

Dubal: In your own teaching, have you ever felt that there's a certain common fault that many students have?

Bolet: They play everything too fast. They have the misconception that speed creates excitement; and I try to get it into their head that nothing kills excitement like mere velocity. Hofmann used to say that the sensation of speed is not created by the rapidity with which one note follows another, but by the amount of space between one note and another—which is exactly right. Also, according to the acoustical phenomenon, the farther you are from the source of the music, the faster it sounds. It's sometimes difficult to persuade the student of this, however.

Dubal: Yes, that should certainly be taken into consideration, especially in large halls.

Bolet: Of course, it's something you must take into consideration constantly.

Dubal: So many pianists love to play at Carnegie Hall. What are your feelings about it?

Bolet: Carnegie Hall is one of the greatest music halls in the world. The acoustic is marvelous, it is somehow intimate and yet so grandly spacious.

Dubal: Is there any place you really dislike playing?

Bolet: The one place I dislike playing is the Royal Festival Hall in London, because the acoustic there is so dry. It doesn't matter what you do, how much pedal you use, you never feel that you are engulfed in sound, and I love that feeling of great reverberation. The music just seems to evaporate into thin air, regardless of what you do.

Dubal: Are you nervous before or during concerts?

BOLET: I'm always nervous playing in New York. I think that goes back to my young days, when a New York performance was the big test. For some reason, I'm always a little bit more nervous playing in New York than anywhere else. However, I think nerves are a wonderful thing, as long as it is the kind of nerves that increases your adrenaline, sharpens your ears, gets your mind to a really fine pitch. Such nerves sharpen all the nerve endings in your fingers. The other kind of nerves, the kind that make you go to pieces, can, of course, be the undoing of a pianist.

DUBAL: Have you heard of the new drug that some performers are now taking that is said to control adrenaline levels? I believe it is called Inderal.

BOLET: No, I haven't heard of it and I don't believe in such things. I think if you need a drug to perform, you might as well take up selling shoes or go into politics.

DUBAL: Do you feel passionately about any other art form besides music?

BOLET: Yes, I love painting. I have a houseful of paintings in California, and another one in New York. But unfortunately, my schedule is generally so tight and demanding that I have found that when I am on tour, I have to conserve every bit of my energy for actual performance, and I cannot go to museums and galleries the way I used to. For instance, when I was in London recently, there was a great Japanese exhibit at the Royal Gallery that I was desperate to see. And I did go one morning, but the crowds were so vast that I just couldn't imagine spending the amount of energy necessary to make my way through them, because I had a performance that night. I just couldn't do it. You must calculate very carefully how you spend your time before a concert.

DUBAL: When students come to you, and they want to be a Bolet, a Horowitz, a Perahia, how do you advise them?

BOLET: I tell them to study everything they can to broaden their mind, and not to limit their whole life and whole existence to piano playing. Many pianists today are overpracticing and are very limited people as a result. Anton Rubinstein and Liszt and so many of their students were very worldly and men of very great spirit. Today, this is not so often the case. But these are very difficult times for the young musicians trying to start on a career, trying to make something of themselves. I often tell my students that they have chosen the world's most insane profession: The chances of success are perhaps one in ten thousand. And I think you have to be either extraordinarily gifted or extraordinarily misguided to go into something like that with your eyes open. But sometimes one has the calling, and you go forth; and then the whole piano literature awaits you.

CLIVE BARDA

Born January 5, 1931, in Wiesenberg, Moravia. His concert career began to flourish when he received a prize in the 1949 Busoni Competition at Bolzano, Italy. In the 1950s he made a reputation through a wide range of recordings, including the first complete set of all of the solo piano music of Beethoven, for which he received a Grand Prix du Disque. He has had many other record awards, including an Edison for his recording of Schubert's Sonata in A major, D. 959, the Wiener Flotenuhr Award for his Mozart concertos, and the Japan Academy Award. In 1978 he was presented with a gold record, marking the millionth sale of his recordings on the Philips label. Brendel's book Musical Thoughts and After-Thoughts *appeared in 1976. He has played cycles of the complete Beethoven sonatas in the major capitals of the world, and in May 1983 he became the first since Schnabel to play all of them at Carnegie Hall.*

Alfred Brendel

PART ONE

DUBAL: Did you come from a musical household?

BRENDEL: Not at all. As far as I know there is not a single musician in my family—this is one of the unusual things about my career. But my parents noticed that as a child I sang a lot of songs, so they encouraged me to learn the piano.

DUBAL: Did you discover that you liked to practice once you began your piano lessons?

BRENDEL: My desire to achieve results became very clear when I was twelve years old. However, there was hardly any musical stimulation at home, nor did my parents take me to concerts, so my development was probably much slower than it would otherwise have been. But in a sense my development was all my own. I learned early on that I needed to find things out for myself.

DUBAL: So you mean you had no real teaching?

BRENDEL: I had piano teachers who didn't do much harm, and perhaps they even did some good. But I did not have any regular teacher after my sixteenth year.

DUBAL: What then, in your opinion, is the best kind of musical training for a young person?

BRENDEL: Probably to have music at home, to grow up with it. To get extremely capable teachers who do not divide technique from music. This kind of thing may be necessary with singers and violinists because their technical problems are so awkward for a long while. There one has to concentrate simply on fortifying the belly muscles, or coming to terms with the tremendously unnatural situation of holding the violin. But this is not the case with the piano. There should always be a way to begin with the music, to make a student realize that technique is only a tool.

DUBAL: What are the qualities that would reveal themselves to the parents of a child who should have a musical career?

BRENDEL: Certainly, talent; better yet, major talent. But talent in itself is not enough. There must also be such qualities as ambition and real persistence, which reveal themselves fairly early in the child's work. Without this it makes no sense to exploit the talent, even if it is very apparent. In my case, the motivation came from the music itself, and I was fascinated with the piano as an instrument.

DUBAL: Was there anything besides music in your early years?

BRENDEL: When I was in my teens I painted for several years, and I also attended drawing classes.

DUBAL: But then with the prize at the Busoni Competition you must have become much more focused on the music.

BRENDEL: Yes, and this was extremely important for me. It was becoming more and more apparent that I should be a pianist, but the prize was a confirmation. And the recognition was particularly meaningful to my parents, who did not know the musical scene at all, and who were naturally very skeptical about a career which offered no security. I don't blame them for that. One doesn't really know for sure if a pianist can make a lasting kind of success before thirty-five or so.

DUBAL: Yet from early on you were determined to have a pianistic career.

BRENDEL: Yes, I have always had a certain ability to plan ahead. I was ambitious, but never impatient; perhaps because I was so intellectually curious about the music. At twenty I never said, "I have to be famous within the next five years." I realized that I needed time to develop my potential; so I took my career step by step. For me this was certainly the best way to proceed.

DUBAL: In what ways does the intellectual curiosity of a pianist express itself?

BRENDEL: In the constant striving for new musical solutions. The pianist must never be complacent about the solutions he has found in the music—they are never perfect. He must always be looking for new insights. In any piece of music which is worth playing, they are there. I never consider it a burden to work on familiar pieces, not at all! Nor is it a burden to re-record something. This is because I only play music that convinces me. I must believe in the pieces that I play.

DUBAL: As you said, you had no regular teaching after sixteen, but I know you attended some master classes with Edwin Fischer, which you wrote about in your book. You also had a few classes with the famous pianist Edward Steuermann. Do you remember anything in particular about that experience?

BRENDEL: I remember that I played Beethoven's *Hammerklavier Sonata* and the Liszt Sonata for him. He had a wonderful way of teaching which still lives vividly in my memory. He did not like things to be worked out in a slower tempo. Instead he would split up passages into small units, have the student play, let's say, five notes up to tempo, then continue with the next five or six notes—whatever was suitable for that particular phrase. After that, the student had to put the whole thing together in the real tempo.

DUBAL: That sounds very helpful. Slow practice can be very misguided.

BRENDEL: Yes, it can be a mistake to work out something in a tempo that does not really suit the requirements of the music. When I start to work on a piece it is important for me to work out everything—the suitable fingerings and the proper physical movements—in the real tempo in order to give the piece the right character.

DUBAL: We have often heard the phrase "To serve the composer." What does it mean to you?

BRENDEL: I think one can serve the composer's best interests without being his slave. Even if one tries to follow the composer's aims as closely as possible, a gap, which is greater with some composers than with others, will always remain. It is necessary to fill this gap with the help of one's emotions; through one's perception of how a piece of music is put together; by trying to follow the grain of a particular composer's thought. For me, it's always been important to think about the music from the composer's point of view.

DUBAL: And you are a composer yourself.

BRENDEL: I would not call myself a composer, but I have had enough practice in putting things on paper to see some of the difficulties in conveying musical thoughts.

DUBAL: Where do you feel most musicians go astray?

BRENDEL: If there is no clarity of vision, they get to a certain level, but not beyond it.

DUBAL: Yes, physical prowess is only the beginning.

BRENDEL: In some cases it can even be a bit of a hindrance.

DUBAL: How do you mean that?

BRENDEL: If everything comes too easily, if the mechanism is totally effortless, then people tend not to work hard enough, or think hard enough. This can become a very serious problem.

DUBAL: How is your memory?

BRENDEL: It's good, I have a good aural and kinesthetic memory, but my memory is not visual at all. I don't see the score as I play.

DUBAL: Since you are a profoundly analytic musician, when you memorize, do you analyze the names of the harmonic progressions, writing in their numbers and so forth?

BRENDEL: I prefer not to memorize harmonic progressions, because I want to feel them as freshly as possible while I play. Perhaps I am a little bit afraid that knowing them too well intellectually may detract from the spontaneity of my playing. What I like to analyze is the motive connections within a piece.

DUBAL: So you feel that there is a point at which too much academic knowledge will hurt your interpretation.

BRENDEL: That's correct. As I mold my interpretation and conception I play as instinctively as possible; only later do I attempt to understand what I am doing, why I am doing it. Then I start correcting myself whenever necessary, and from that moment on, I am reassessing my findings as often as I can.

DUBAL: May we talk about the role of silence in music? I know it is a topic that interests you.

BRENDEL: Yes, it is a subject which fascinates me. When you go to a hall and see that the public is not able to concentrate, you start to understand immediately how important silence is. It generates attention; it makes music possible; it remains the basis of great music. It is only inferior music which shows no readiness to let silence in. I think all music worthy of our attention needs silence to enliven it. There are pieces that grow out of silence, and there are pieces like Beethoven's last Sonata, Op. 111 in C minor, that lead into silence. And there are those silences within the music, which are as telling as the music itself. Understanding these silences is as important for the performer as the playing of sound itself.

DUBAL: Humor is another aspect of music which has often been misunderstood.

BRENDEL: Oh, yes. For some reason the public and even some performers shy away from music that sounds or seems funny. They think that music has to be something very serious. I have even heard a celebrated performer state that there is no humor in music. This is nonsense.

DUBAL: Perhaps there is some confusion about the definition of humor.

BRENDEL: Yes, that's true. For instance, no two nations mean the same thing when they use the word humor. It is easier to talk about the comical aspects of music, things which make one laugh, the wit, the irony. Look at this aspect of Haydn: he is the paragon of comedy. And when playing Haydn, one should convey this in a way which encourages the public to smile. I wouldn't even mind hearing them laugh.

DUBAL: Mozart also had his real moments of humor.

BRENDEL: Yes, but it is that other kind of humor, very much in the German literary tradition—humor based on tragedy that understands, loves and forgives.

DUBAL: What about Chopin, a composer we do not usually associate with humor?

BRENDEL: There is irony in Chopin's music, and perhaps a certain amount of wit, but not humor or comedy. Chopin was too depressive for that. Beethoven of course has all of these elements. The *Diabelli Variations* alone give the essence of humor, wit and irony in music.

DUBAL: You have recently recorded an album of late Liszt pieces, as well as a new version of the Sonata. And you have played Liszt from the very beginning of your career. What is it that draws you to Liszt?

BRENDEL: For me, one of the most important aspects of Liszt is that he was a musical revolutionary. There are some more conventional pieces where he repeats himself, or gets caught in patterns of diminished seventh chords, but basically he never lost the urge to explore, to find out in which new direction the music would go. And he was completely uncorruptible in pursuing this course, no matter what other people thought. So there is the paradox that the great virtuoso, the great performer who had audiences at his feet like no other performer except Paganini, was, as a composer, independent of the public.

DUBAL: How would you characterize Liszt's later music?

BRENDEL: I would not say that he turned completely away from the public in his later pieces, as I once thought. This is because I have found through playing them frequently in public that they can be communicated very well, especially when they are played in groups to show the variety within this style and the enormous originality of Liszt's mind. They isolate certain factors of newness in music through their departures from tonality, functional harmony and Classical patterns. These pieces have more to do with modern music than with nineteenth-century music. And they reveal Liszt's largesse, his magnanimity. Even the smallest pieces are not miniatures; they are composed on a grand scale. Actually, this compression of ideas reminds me of the late songs of Schubert. Liszt stripped the music down to its essentials; yet I think it's a mistake to see these pieces as primitive. They are highly sophisticated, and they show their sophistication through the colors implied, even if many of them remain in the background.

DUBAL: Debussy and Stravinsky were astonished by the harmonic adventurousness of Liszt's late music. And, of course, the Impressionist movement was anticipated by him.

BRENDEL: This is one of the reasons why I do not play French composers. Liszt anticipated so much of what they did that I'd rather concentrate on his work. Liszt had many faces as a composer, from the mystical to the diabolical. There is so much to explore.

DUBAL: Let's talk about the Liszt Sonata, in which so many of these faces seem to be present. Composed in 1853, and dedicated to Schumann, it is in one monumental movement that is sustained for half an hour. How does one look at such a massive and complex structure?

BRENDEL: One must see the whole piece at once, and also one must have a perspective on the piece as it unfolds, starting with the first bar and ending with the last. But as one starts the piece, one should already perceive the way it ends, even if there are many matters of the moment, of improvisation in between. There is something inevitable about the Liszt Sonata, something that recalls the proceedings of nature, like a seed that flowers in a certain way. This principle of composition is reminiscent of Beethoven. What Beethoven wrote down at the beginning of a sonata, usually in the very first bars, is crucial for the rest of the work. And Liszt understood some of Beethoven's principles of composition better than other Romantics. In the process, he turned the sonata into something completely new. And yet it is a continuation of Beethoven, insofar as the motivic material is compressed in the very beginning. But it is one of the pieces which are hardly ever done justice to. One of the dangers is that it is played too rhapsodically, that it falls apart into episodes; that it becomes a succession of bizarre surprises instead of a symphonic organism with each part leading into the next.

DUBAL: You have recently made a recording of Bach after many years of thinking he wasn't suited to piano performance. What changed your thinking?

BRENDEL: After listening to many performances of Bach on old instruments, I have come to the conclusion that this is not the only way to bring Bach's music to life, and I began to play and record Bach on the modern piano.

DUBAL: Do you still dislike Scarlatti on the piano?

BRENDEL: I must admit that I do, yes. Many years ago I heard Ralph

Kirkpatrick do two all-Scarlatti recitals on the harpsichord in Vienna, and they were so breathtaking—they had such vitality and authenticity and they showed the harpsichord to such advantage—that ever since then I have felt that Scarlatti is tied to the sound of the harpsichord, while with Bach timbre is secondary.

DUBAL: Is Chopin another composer you chose not to play? I haven't heard Chopin from you since you recorded the polonaises many years ago.

BRENDEL: I am not playing him at all, even though I studied quite a number of his works in my early years, and my recording of the polonaises does not make me happy. In my opinion, to do Chopin justice, one would have to specialize, at least I know *I* would have to specialize. Looking back at the tradition of performing since Liszt, I see two basic types of performers: those who mastered a large central European repertory, and those who became Chopin specialists, with a few composers around him. So I had to make a choice, and I'm sure I made the right one. I try to pursue the central European repertory which for me is the mainstream of music. I think hardly anybody would deny that from Bach through Schoenberg most musical matters of importance have, strangely enough, occurred in a geographically confined region, roughly from Hamburg down to Vienna.

DUBAL: Have you sustained your early interest in Busoni's music?

BRENDEL: I have a great admiration for Busoni's later works. In particular, I have played some of his elegies, and I hope to play the Second Sonatina, which is, in my opinion, his finest piano work. It is only eight minutes long, but it requires a tremendous amount of preparation. And recently I played his Toccata, which is one of the most technically difficult works I have ever encountered.

DUBAL: Schubert is one of the composers you are most closely linked with. Why is the public responding to the Schubert sonatas as never before?

BRENDEL: The first reason is that there have been many more performances in the recent past. This was once a relatively unexplored repertory. Of course Schnabel had been a very early pioneer in Schubert performances, but most pianists were daunted by the inordinate length of the sonatas. After World War II the younger artists seized on the opportunity to play this music. These artists became passionately involved in this literature. Length was not a problem for them. Indeed they did not feel any length at all, but simply the necessary expansion of Schubert's compositional style. Also, with the advent of the LP, this music finally became accessible to a wider audience. Another reason has to do with the nature of the music itself. Schubert's sonatas, very much like Mahler's symphonies, do not give the listener a sense of security. For me, Beethoven, a master of the Classic style, always shows the listener where the music goes, and always justifies why it goes there. He also gives the reasons for why it happens as it does. I do not mean that Beethoven is in any way predictable, but that it is his plan to explain himself throughout. In other words, Beethoven is in control. Compositionally, Schubert does not progress this way and neither, in my opinion, does Mahler. They roam: for me there is a feeling in their work of a child lost in a forest, at the mercy of powers which it cannot control. And doesn't this resemble the world we live in now? We are surrounded by problems which do not offer easy solutions, or any solutions at all, as pessimistic as that may sound. The great questioning and poignant modulations within this music seem to have a new relevance in these times.

DUBAL: This certainly is a very interesting perspective; and, historically, Schubert suffered from being defined by Beethoven's concepts of sonata form.

BRENDEL: Which was a great mistake but an understandable one because it was generally believed that Beethoven had taken the sonata form to its final conclusion. Of course, Schubert revered Beethoven's music, but he did not want to imitate him in any way. We now know he was doing something quite different. For instance, the "heavenly lengths" of some of his movements are necessary for Schubert to express himself properly.

DUBAL: Of course, Schubert is not merely the wandering romantic lyricist of popular imagination, but a structural genius in his own right as Beethoven was.

BRENDEL: Yes, he too grappled with the sonata form. For instance, look at a sketch for the "big" A major Sonata, Op. posthumous. It contains the second theme in a much more compressed form than the final version, which benefits enormously from Schubert's additional space. I feel that in some of the early sonatas he does not spend enough time in development sections, elaboration of themes or in certain modulations. But ultimately I think he finally found the forms which were appropriate to his musical temperament.

DUBAL: Musically, we are learning more and more about Schubert, but there are still so many gaps in our knowledge of him as a person.

BRENDEL: But I think I know him a little better since seeing what may be a life mask of him at the Curtis Institute. It is quite unlike any of the portraits we know. It is a sensuous face both in its potential and energy, and it is rather close to Beethoven's. It is a face which to me reveals much more of the essence of his music than any of the portraits I know.

DUBAL: Do you ever feel enslaved by the public?

BRENDEL: No, I don't. But it does happen, of course, that on certain days one doesn't feel very well, or the piano or the hall is depressing. But I have little sympathy for those colleagues who cancel concerts frequently because one cannot really foresee what will happen. On days when I have had a cold or certain things preying on my mind, I have played well. And on days when I have come on stage in a good mood, sometimes the performance goes less well than I would have liked. So one can never say for sure. The only way to find out is to play.

PART TWO
The Beethoven Sonatas

DUBAL: The Beethoven performing tradition is a rich one. For instance, Schnabel was the first to record the sonatas and played them in a cycle in a few cities.

BRENDEL: Yes, there is a long tradition leading up to Schnabel's recording them. People like Eugen d'Albert, for instance, did cycles of the sonatas in the 1890s, and Edouard Risler, a French pianist, did it in France, José Vianna da Motta did it in Lisbon later, and so on, while Sir Charles Hallé was the first to do it in London as early as the 1860s. Of course there were other pianists in this century to follow Schnabel's example like Backhaus and Kempff and Arrau.

DUBAL: As long as we're talking about this performing heritage, let's say a few words about the chief pianists that did contribute to the worldwide knowledge of the Beethoven sonatas. As we see, it didn't happen overnight. Let's begin with the artist who gave the premiere of Beethoven's Fifth Concerto and who studied piano with Beethoven—Carl Czerny, of etude fame.

BRENDEL: Czerny is a very important figure indeed, even for pianists today, because he left such a large volume of comments on Beethoven's piano works. And even if some of those comments are very brief and even if his memory failed him in a few instances, they are still extremely valuable. They are the most precise primary source we have about Beethoven's own ideas.

DUBAL: What about Ignaz Moscheles's importance?

BRENDEL: Moscheles is the second contemporary who left metronome marks for the sonatas. It is actually the markings of Czerny and Moscheles that give us a fairly clear picture of the speeds that were played at Beethoven's time. They are not necessarily Beethoven's own, but there is a consensus in most of the work of Czerny and Moscheles.

DUBAL: Moscheles knew Beethoven and later taught many important pianists at the Leipzig Conservatory. Let's move to Liszt, a titanic force in the dissemination of Beethoven's music.

BRENDEL: Well, Liszt, probably more than anybody else, put Beethoven sonatas into perspective in front of large audiences in the concert hall.

DUBAL: Berlioz said that the Op. 106, the *Hammerklavier,* was an enigma for him until Liszt solved the riddle. With that performance he called Liszt the "pianist of the future."

BRENDEL: Yes, absolutely. In Beethoven's own time there is no record that even one of the sonatas was played in a public concert.

DUBAL: What about Clara Wieck Schumann?

BRENDEL: She played the *Hammerklavier* and the Sonata Op. 111 quite early in her career. Much later, when a young pianist whose name was d'Albert came and played four Beethoven sonatas in one evening, she commented in her diary that this was simply too much! Schumann and Mendelssohn would have agreed. One sonata was then already overwhelming.

DUBAL: So things definitely changed. Soon d'Albert and others would be doing five in an evening, often the last five. Hans von Bülow was the next great exponent of Beethoven.

BRENDEL: Well, as you said, he played the last five sonatas in one concert, not very often, but a few times. His edition was used by Liszt in his classes. Von Bülow himself switched later on to another edition by a Liszt pupil, Carl Klindworth. Von Bülow said that Klindworth's edition was better than his own and was far more authentic.

DUBAL: And the fingerings were probably easier. Von Bülow's were often weird.

BRENDEL: Klindworth's were more practical. He was a very imaginative, romantic pianist. The tempi are usually slower than Czerny's and Moscheles's.

DUBAL: Let's move out of the German-Austrian realm into the great

Russian Anton Rubinstein's contribution. He was the Russian pianist that consistently brought Beethoven to a large public, including America.

BRENDEL: Yes, although he was probably even better known for his playing of Chopin. In Weimar, Rubinstein played the *Moonlight Sonata* and a Liszt pupil came to Liszt to tell him how absolutely fascinated he was by the performance and then Liszt sat down and played the first movement himself for the pupil and the pupil said that it was even better as played by Liszt.

DUBAL: As you mentioned, in 1861 in London, Sir Charles Hallé played them all.

BRENDEL: Yes, he must have been one of those all-around musicians, like Sir George Henschel, who could do nearly everything. He was a musician with a wide musical culture. I cannot imagine that the performances were of the highest standards pianistically, but he certainly did a great deal to make the pieces known.

DUBAL: Then there were d'Albert's contributions. He also made an edition.

BRENDEL: Yes, and he was for the next generation of pianists—Schnabel, Edwin Fischer, Steuermann, Kempff and others—their great inspiration in this repertoire. He must have been the overwhelming player around the turn of the century in central Europe, apart from Busoni.

DUBAL: And what was Busoni's relationship to Beethoven?

BRENDEL: Busoni was not, I believe, quite comfortable with the earlier works. Beethoven was not his favorite composer and he apparently played him in a very personal way. He later reduced his Beethoven repertory to the late sonatas, which many thought to be inimitable. I would like to have heard Busoni in the late sonatas.

DUBAL: Other pianists of that day who made an enormous contribution to Beethoven playing were the Liszt pupils Conrad Ansorge and Frederic Lamond, who made an influential edition of the sonatas.

BRENDEL: In speaking about editions, of course Heinrich Schenker's edition has to be mentioned as the most important, in my opinion. This edition goes back to the sources, thinking in Beethoven's terms, the composer's terms; it puts many things right that have been obscured.

DUBAL: What editions do you use?

BRENDEL: Primarily I use the Schenker and the Henle editions because they are the two editions that attempted at least not to add anything extraneous to Beethoven's intentions. None are perfect for present-day standards, and I am still waiting for one that will incorporate all the different versions of the primary sources and give more information about the dubious points.

DUBAL: You have played all thirty-two Beethoven sonatas in cycle at various times in your career. What are the chief differences in the sonatas of Beethoven and his predecessors, Haydn, Mozart and Dussek, and what about the influence of Clementi on Beethoven?

BRENDEL: Clementi gave Beethoven some ideas. But the mainstream of ideas came from Haydn, with whom Beethoven studied not very successfully, and from Mozart. Beethoven revered both composers throughout his life. I also have to include Bach in this context because there are certain peculiarities in Beethoven's compositions that derive from Bach.

DUBAL: That's very interesting. Very seldom do we hear of that influence on Beethoven.

BRENDEL: The Austrian scholar Erwin Ratz has shown the similarities in Bach's and Beethoven's way of composing. Beethoven's works are always a process. They lead from the first to the last note in such a way that you are guided all the time with the greatest security; there is the feeling that you cannot escape the argument. There is always something forward-leading, forward-looking in his way of composing—much more so than in Haydn or Mozart. There are two technical points characteristic of Beethoven's compositions: one is a method I call foreshortening—a never-ending tightening of the musical argument—and the other is that each of the sonatas constitutes a motivic unity. Each sonata is, in a sense, unified by the use of certain main motives that you may not notice right away, but that subconsciously give you this impression of movements and themes that belong together and that are derived from the same source. This is perhaps a point that has not been investigated enough.

DUBAL: Let's briefly discuss each sonata. No. 1 is in F minor, Op. 2 No. 1 (1795). Beethoven opens with an old-fashioned "Mannheim rocket" theme, but the key of F minor and the storms of the finale seem to inaugurate a new moment in music as well as the dawn of the next century.

BRENDEL: It is interesting to me that the method of foreshortening, of composing under very strict conditions, of leading the music inevitably forward, is already so clearly developed in this sonata—in its first movement in particular. Beethoven's very personal imprint already shows. I do not agree with people who think that in his early works Beethoven was not yet quite himself. I think with all he owed to Haydn and Mozart and some other masters, it is tremendous to see how individual he was from the start.

DUBAL: That's right. Many people forget that the date 1795 means he was twenty-five. Schubert was already composing his greatest works by that age. And Beethoven was a full musical personality by this Op. 2. In the Sonata No. 2 in A major, Op. 2 No. 2 (1795), Beethoven gives us a scherzo instead of the minuet in the third movement. And here he also presents us with a twenty-five-minute work—a huge time scale.

BRENDEL: Yes, I think this symphonic scope was something rather new. Mozart tended toward it more than Haydn, although Haydn did attempt something symphonic in his last, E-flat Sonata. Beethoven continued along these lines, but his textures are much more orchestral, particularly in the next sonata, Op. 2 No. 3. With all its pianistic brilliance, this is a very orchestral piece. I think the modern piano can reproduce its orchestral color better than the pianos of Beethoven's time.

DUBAL: This Sonata No. 3 in C major, Op. 2 No. 3 (1795), is really the most muscular piece of work ever written up until that time. Perhaps it was modeled on Clementi's big C major Sonata.

BRENDEL: I would say even more so on Dussek's C major Sonata. The Op. 2 No. 3 is sometimes underrated. It is full of marvelous musical ideas, full of a wonderful freshness and confidence! The lovely slow movement is a big step from Beethoven's earlier slow movements in Op. 2. It already gives a foretaste of Romanticism.

DUBAL: So here are the first three sonatas, all dedicated to Haydn; they are all in four movements, while not one sonata of Haydn's or indeed of Mozart's is in four movements. So Beethoven is already extending the form. The Sonata No. 4 in E-flat major, Op. 7 (circa 1796–1797) is also in four movements.

BRENDEL: The exposition of Op. 7 is wide-ranging, but the development is extremely short—it's surprisingly short. It modulates into faraway keys.

DUBAL: This sonata is about thirty minutes in length.

BRENDEL: Yes, it is the most extended sonata, aside from the *Hammerklavier*.

DUBAL: And for 1796 it's amazing in size. The Op. 7 is a masterwork, but why is it virtually unknown, not only to the public but to many pianists as well?

BRENDEL: It is a very beautiful piece, but not one that the public readily favors. One of the reasons is that the ending is very lyrical, which is surprising for a work on this scale. Another reason is that the slow movement needs a degree of silence that the audience of a large hall rarely permits. A third reason is that the first movement is extremely difficult. It is technically one of the most demanding pieces Beethoven ever wrote, and therefore often played too slowly.

DUBAL: Let's move on to the Op. 10 sonatas, of 1798. Sonata No. 5 in C minor, Op. 10 No. 1 (1796–1798), is in the key that so many people associate with Beethoven. He seemed at this point to want to compress the sonatas into three movements.

BRENDEL: In the C minor Sonata, the first and last movements are very tightly argued. The middle movement, on the other hand, is one of those serene adagios that only Beethoven could write. From very early on one recognizes Beethoven as the master of the adagio. While Haydn, Mozart and Schubert preferred andantes or allegrettos.

DUBAL: How different the Sonata No. 6 in F major, Op. 10 No. 2 (1796–1798) is. Imagine building a form out of such material as those opening chords.

BRENDEL: It is humorous in the outer movements, and continues the tradition of Haydn in this respect. This is one of the points that I cannot stress enough—Beethoven's humor. I would sorely miss the humor in a Beethoven performance.

DUBAL: Well, in that vein, the Sonata Op. 10 No. 2 has that wonderful false recapitulation in the first movement which is a very subtle stroke, and very few people will hear it at first.

BRENDEL: That's right. There's a good definition of this sonata by Adolph Bernhard Marx, who said the first movement is the present, the second is the future, and the third is the past, as far as the styles go.

DUBAL: There is no slow movement in Op. 10 No. 2—it is replaced with an allegretto movement.

BRENDEL: Yes, he sometimes mixes the traits of *scherzi,* minuets and slow movements.

DUBAL: And there is that very difficult and curious finale, which begins fugally and is also in sonata form.

Brendel: Yes, Marx says it is like a naughty child that plucks an old man's beard.

Dubal: With the Sonata No. 7 in D major, Op. 10 No. 3 (1796–1798), the largest of those Op. 10 sonatas, we're back to a four-movement plan. Probably the high point is the slow movement, which is one of the great slow movements of his early period, wouldn't you say?

Brendel: I would say it is one of the greatest slow movements Beethoven ever wrote. For me, this sonata is the greatest among his earlier works—if one has to make a choice—and one of the most perfect sonatas of the thirty-two.

Dubal: Let's move on to the Sonata No. 8 in C minor, Op. 13 (1798–1799), the *Pathétique*. Perhaps its influence came from the Dussek Sonata in C minor, which had preceded it. But it must have been a revelation when it was first heard.

Brendel: I think that the atmosphere of the *Pathétique* had been preceded by several other works and also by certain things Gluck wrote in his operas. For me, the beginning of the *Pathétique* is close to Gluck's world. And it is a style, of course, that has nothing to do with Tchaikovsky or the nineteenth century.

Dubal: To think that Moscheles and Czerny learned it when they were ten years old. Can you imagine a ten-year-old today learning a brand-new work of such magnitude?

Brendel: No, I can't. I wish we could have a few works of this stature that were as accessible.

Dubal: When you play that work, as did Busoni, do you try and make it sound, as he said, "revolutionary"?

Brendel: Yes, I believe there is something revolutionary in the first movement, but the problem for me is to get the right balance between the two outer movements. It is very easy to have the last movement sound like a postscript or like a piece of music that is not quite of the same quality. I believe that Beethoven had an unfailing sense of equilibrium in his sonatas. They are either wonderfully balanced from beginning to end or, as in the later works, lead to the last movement as to the climax.

Dubal: An interesting aspect of the Sonata No. 9 in E major, Op. 14 No. 1 (circa 1798–1799), is that Beethoven transcribed it for string quartet.

Brendel: He was very proud of his transcription, but actually the original piano sonata is much better. That's why the string quartet is not played more often.

DUBAL: The first movement is very quartet-like in layout.

BRENDEL: Yes, and yet Beethoven had to change certain things when he put it into the quartet configuration. I love both sonatas from Op. 14. They are most sensitive works in pastel colors, and the second contains a great deal of fun.

DUBAL: The first theme of the Sonata No. 10 in G major, Op. 14 No. 2 (circa 1798–1799), has a charm that only Beethoven could have written.

BRENDEL: Yes, we shouldn't forget that he could also be a great charmer. In some of his rondo movements in the earlier sonatas he had his own way of being graceful and seductive.

DUBAL: After five of the last six sonatas in three movements he is back to four movements in the Sonata No. 11 in B-flat major, Op. 22 (1799–1800), and he was very pleased with that work. Do you think that in a way this was the end of a period in his sonata-writing?

BRENDEL: Yes. It is for me. You can feel that he has mastered a certain manner: it comes almost too easily to him.

DUBAL: The Sonata No. 12 in A-flat major, Op. 26 (1800–1801), seemed to have caught the fancy of the early Romantics. In fact, even Chopin, who did not feel close to Beethoven's music, played the first movement. What about this work and its set of opening variations?

BRENDEL: It is a new departure. It does not attempt to be symphonic at all. It goes back to some older models. We must not forget that Mozart also started some of his sonatas with a set of variations and that there are sonatas that do not necessarily contain a movement in sonata form. But the special problem of this sonata is what Edwin Fischer called the "psychological composition." There is a poetic quality about how the movements hang together. One could be completely cynical and see them individually and play the last movement like an etude after the funeral march, but if one takes Beethoven a little more seriously, one will approach the whole work as something coherent.

DUBAL: Von Bülow said in his notes to his edition of this sonata that he didn't care which movement came first in the whole work. So we have changed a great deal in our attitude. The work, of course, contains a funeral march. What do you think about that movement for the burial of a hero, the *Marcia Funebre Sulla Morte d'un Eroe?*

BRENDEL: Well, again, I think it follows a tradition. There is something by an Italian opera composer, Paer, that sounds rather similar. However, to include it in a sonata was unusual enough. It doesn't come quite unprepared, by the way: there is a somber variation in the first movement.

DUBAL: Let's say a few words about the Sonata No. 13 in E-flat major, Op. 27 No. 1 (1800–1801), which is really the neglected sister of the *Moonlight*.

BRENDEL: I've often played it and I admire it very much indeed. It is one of the most original of Beethoven's sonatas, and it already sets some of the patterns for the late works. If you compare it with Op. 101 you will find a few features in common. He called it a "fantasy sonata," and he set out to give a new unity to the movements; they interlock and interact in a way that has not been attempted before, to my knowledge.

DUBAL: The Berlin critic Rellstab is said to be responsible for the subtitle of the Sonata No. 14 in C-sharp minor, Op. 27 No. 2 (1801), the famous *Moonlight*. We know that Beethoven himself thought he had written better sonatas.

BRENDEL: But don't take Beethoven too literally in his comments on his own works. I think it's a wonderful piece, and it is all too easy for a composer to say later on that he's written something better. For instance, he might have spoiled things for some people by saying that his B-flat Piano Concerto, Op. 19, was not very good and that he had written better things since.

DUBAL: Besides the title *Moonlight,* why has that first movement caught on worldwide? It's one of the most beloved pieces ever composed.

BRENDEL: I cannot explain. The form is unique. I think Wagner must have loved it as an unending melody, one of the early cases of that procedure. It is a sort of sonata form, but very well hidden under one consistent mood. And it is one of the great laments that Beethoven wrote, besides the slow movement of Op. 10 No. 3, and that of the *Hammerklavier*.

DUBAL: The Sonata No. 15 in D major, Op. 28 (1801), also has a subtitle that is not by Beethoven: *Pastoral*. Is it because of its comparative lack of drama that this is one of the hardest sonatas to hold together? I must say I see people falling asleep all over the hall when someone tries to play it.

BRENDEL: That's a pity, but I see your point. It is a lyrical piece throughout, and I think the nickname *Pastoral* is well chosen. It takes a lot of imagination and poetic ability on the part of the player to keep the tension. In some ways, it looks back into earlier periods. However, in Op. 31 he has again broken new ground.

DUBAL: In a certain way, the adagio in the Sonata No. 16 in G major, Op. 31 No. 1 (1801–1802), has an old-fashioned quality.

BRENDEL: Yes, it certainly has, but it's like an ironic comment on something old-fashioned. It is actually much more complex than is usually thought. It is a mixture of old-fashioned embellishments and prophetic coloratura. It was written before Rossini's operas came to Vienna. And yet it has very much of an Italian coloratura aria about it. There is a mixture of love and irony that is very strange, and if the player can manage to convey it, it can be very effective.

DUBAL: Yes, and Schubert must have known this finale when he wrote his A major Sonata, Op. posthumous.

BRENDEL: Yes, he modeled the form of the last movement after this finale. The whole sonata, again, is a beautiful example of Beethoven's humor and his liking, sometimes, of the grotesque.

DUBAL: It is very little known, and it is certainly the least-known of that opus number. Now we come to the Sonata No. 17 in D minor, Op. 31 No. 2 (1801–1802), the famous *Tempest,* and this is another unauthorized subtitle. How do you approach this work? It seems to me particularly difficult—even though it has high drama—to bring across.

BRENDEL: There is some difficulty in bringing about what one wants to do with it, yet it shows very clearly what it ought to be. Czerny said about it that it represents musical painting, whereas Op. 31 No. 3 was musical speech. It is interesting to observe the difference. This sonata is like a fresco, a marvelous fresco, and I think it is one of the most perfect sonatas Beethoven ever wrote. In the middle of two absolutely black movements, there is an absolutely white one.

DUBAL: The sonata is a very long one for three movements.

BRENDEL: It depends how fast one plays the finale. It is marked "allegretto," but is sometimes taken slower than Beethoven's contemporaries thought it should go.

DUBAL: You were saying that the first movement of the E-flat Sonata, Op. 7, was so technically difficult. The four-movement Sonata No. 18 in E-flat major, Op. 31 No. 3 (1801–1802), also seems to be very difficult technically.

BRENDEL: Yes, but not quite impossible. It has a brilliance that lends itself more easily to the fingers. Edwin Fischer has likened the piece to a more female psyche while the D minor Sonata is obviously rather masculine.

DUBAL: Yes, and in this E-flat Sonata he has gone back to the minuet again.

BRENDEL: That's right, yes—when Beethoven composed minuets he really meant the old-fashioned minuet character that Haydn and Mozart had sometimes discarded.

DUBAL: Beethoven published no sonatas until the two small ones Op. 49 Nos. 1 and 2, which are No. 19 in G minor and No. 20 in G major, probably composed earlier, in the mid-1790s. Are these little two-movement works in any sense as important as the other thirty?

BRENDEL: Well, I am very far from looking down on these pieces. I think they are beautifully finished, graceful works in which Beethoven comes nearer to Mozart than in any other of the piano sonatas. They are very exposed. Every note is lying bare, so to speak. I admire the pianist who can play them really well.

DUBAL: We move forward to the Sonata No. 21 in C major, Op. 53 (1803–1804), the *Waldstein*. The public never seems to tire of this work, yet the first movement has no really memorable themes, and the introduction to the second-movement rondo is amorphous. Why is it so popular? Is it the virtuosity?

BRENDEL: Yes, it is sometimes mistaken for a virtuoso piece by pianists, but it is so much more than that. There is a new feeling of spacial depth, of a three-dimensional approach toward music in this work. Again, it is very much an *al fresco* piece. It is not necessary for a piece of music to be melodic in order to be a good, memorable and useful piece.

DUBAL: Yes, we spoke before about Op. 2 No. 3, in C major, as being muscular, and this now seems to be even more so.

BRENDEL: I don't find it as muscular as Op. 2 No. 3. There is rhythmic energy and drive, all right, but there is also mystery and atmosphere. When you look at the beginning of the *Waldstein*, it is marked *pianissimo*, something you usually don't hear. The scope of color and expression, the range of keys is wider than in the early works. While the slow movement of the early C major Sonata is in E major, and sounds exotic in the context, the second theme of the *Waldstein* turns up in E major quite naturally.

DUBAL: I find the Sonata No. 22 in F major, Op. 54 (1804), the second sonata Beethoven composed in F major, a real enigma: a rather amazing first movement in the tempo of a minuet and a finale which is like a toccata. It seems such a strange work.

BRENDEL: It is one of the strangest, most original pieces, and it is often underrated. This is a work for connoisseurs, for people who know the famous sonatas very well; then when they listen to this piece they will find that it sets a rule of its own, it is not modeled on forms that you know: it develops its own shape. I have tried to explain what goes on in the first movement in one of my essays. The two themes have been called "*la belle*" and "*la bête*"; it is interesting to see how they act on each other, and that when the themes come back the proportions have changed. There is a real drama going on in the first movement—perhaps more comedy than drama. The second movement is not a toccata at all, it is marked "*allegretto,*" "*dolce*" and "*legato,*" and the beginning is *piano*—but, again, this is something you hardly ever hear. For me it has more of the flowing of water, and many aspects of light, color and liquid dynamics that I associate with it.

DUBAL: That sonata is caught between the great *Waldstein* and possibly the most famous of all, the Sonata No. 23 in F minor, Op. 57 (1804–1805), the *Appassionata*. This seems to be, for the general public, the quintessential Beethoven, the fist to the sky. Of course, all public virtuosos seem to have to play it.

BRENDEL: I can only agree with Beethoven, who thought at the time that it was his greatest sonata. Its greatness lies not only in the stormy temper and in the tragic atmosphere that pervades it but also in its structure. Everything is derived from the ideas of the first two or three lines. It is one of the most concentrated musical structures one can find among the Beethoven sonatas, and one of the best examples of how Beethoven used a few motives to the greatest advantage in order to unify the whole piece.

DUBAL: We are back to two movements with the Sonata No. 24 in F-sharp major, Op. 78 (1809). Beethoven had left the piano sonata for five years, and he returned in a very modest work compared with the tidal wave of the *Appassionata*.

BRENDEL: A lyrical and loving and joyous work. He must have been in a very tender mood. It is dedicated to one of the ladies he admired, Countess Therese von Brunswick. And it is a devil to play.

DUBAL: The Sonata No. 25 in G major, Op. 79 (1809) is a gem in three short movements.

BRENDEL: It is a strange piece. It looks like a footnote on some older compositions, some old-fashioned ways of composing sonatas. A footnote with an ironic light and strange compression, especially in the second movement. Such compression already foreshadows some of the procedures in his late music.

DUBAL: And one can almost hear a Mendelssohn "Song Without Words" in the middle movement.

BRENDEL: Absolutely! Two melancholy ladies accompanied by a lute.

DUBAL: Next in the series is the more famous Sonata No. 26 in E-flat major, Op. 81a (1809–1810), *Les Adieux*. This is a programmatic work, isn't it? It has a story in its turbulent pages.

BRENDEL: Yes, indeed, and not the only one Beethoven wrote; of course we know the *Pastoral Symphony,* and we must not forget that even in some of the later works there are programmatic hints which show that Beethoven was well aware of human situations and psychological reactions when he composed. In this case it was his friend, pupil and patron Archduke Rudolph who inspired him, to whom he has dedicated a number of his greatest works, including the *Hammerklavier Sonata,* the *Missa Solemnis,* the *Emperor Concerto* and so on. There is the departure of Archduke Rudolph in the first movement, his absence in the second movement and his return in the third.

DUBAL: It seems to be a more than unusually treacherous sonata technically.

BRENDEL: I can only agree. Sometimes the lightness of the action of Beethoven's contemporary pianos enabled the player to do things that the modern piano does not easily permit. The last movement is an example. It should be joyous and light and going at a terrific pace, and I congratulate anybody who achieves this nowadays without breaking his or her fingers.

DUBAL: We have arrived at the two-movement Sonata No. 27 in E minor, Op. 90 (1814). Beethoven was going through five fallow and painful years: from 1809 to 1814 he had hardly composed anything. Is this then the inaugural work, perhaps, of Beethoven's so-called third period?

BRENDEL: It is one of the pieces that prepare this period. I would also like to mention the Op. 74 Quartet and the F minor Quartet, Op. 95.

DUBAL: During those years that separated Op. 81a and 90, his hearing had deteriorated badly.

BRENDEL: Yes, and he had a great deal of trouble with his nephew. He tried to be a father to his nephew and keep him away from his mother, with the result that the poor boy attempted suicide.

DUBAL: Eventually Karl did kill himself. And this is the time when Beethoven had Czerny teach him piano. He even told Czerny to give him Cramer etudes.

BRENDEL: In fact, Beethoven provided those Cramer etudes his nephew had to practice with very interesting comments. The "fathering" of his nephew is one of the reasons why he did not compose very much during these years. There were several other reasons. One is that it must have been in his mind to compose works of a magnitude and complexity in the future for which he simply needed a lot of time to lay the groundwork.

DUBAL: And the ground is now prepared, as we move into 1816 and come to the Sonata No. 28 in A major, Op. 101. It is the least-known of the last five sonatas and also seems to me the most enigmatic. The march movement is almost, in a way, ugly.

BRENDEL: You think so?

DUBAL: I love it, but it has a certain element of ugliness to me.

BRENDEL: Maybe it doesn't lend itself to the piano so well. It is very much a string quartet piece, and so is the whole sonata, yet it inspired the Romantics very much: Mendelssohn used it as a model for his Op. 6 Sonata, and the march, I'm sure, gave much inspiration to Schumann; Wagner thought the first movement to be the ideal embodiment of the eternal melody.

DUBAL: And then, of course, we start that great fugal period.

BRENDEL: Yes, it is the first work where the sonata leads toward the last movement as the climax, and that will remain so in the late sonatas.

DUBAL: It's so interesting, and yet it is really not as well-known as the others.

BRENDEL: No. It doesn't communicate as well as the later pieces. But it is a wonderful, basically positive, and energetic piece, not a tortured piece. However, to convey this sense of security, of happiness, is very hard in pianistic terms.

DUBAL: Yes. There is such a rhythmic joy in the fugue.

BRENDEL: I would call it the most difficult sonata to play well.

DUBAL: I have heard that said. Technically it is almost as difficult as the *Hammerklavier*.

Brendel: Yes, in a way even trickier.

Dubal: We are now at that Sonata No. 29 in B-flat major, Op. 106 (1817–1818), the *Hammerklavier.* This is the Mount Everest of the Beethoven literature. If any piece seems to have become legendary, it is the Op. 106. When did you first hear it? What were your reactions? And when did you first learn it?

Brendel: I heard it first played by Backhaus very shortly after the war, and I instantly admired the piece very much. I studied it when I was twenty-one and have played it since a great many times. It was one of the works that did a lot for my career in the long run. Of course it took some decades after Beethoven's death until it was incorporated into the repertoire, and it is still one of those masterpieces that are never quite surmounted.

Dubal: Is this your favorite of all the slow movements of the sonatas?

Brendel: It is the greatest slow movement ever written. And the longest. It depends how slowly you play it, but it is something around eighteen minutes, and I don't think, at least in the piano literature, there is another example of a slow movement sustained so wonderfully and lasting so long. But the whole sonata is, of course, one marvelous unity. It is tremendously complex, yet everything hangs together, everything is justified in its course. In a work of nearly three-quarters of an hour, the economy of the material he uses is absolutely astonishing.

Dubal: We now go to what is certainly one of the most beloved sonatas, No. 30 in E major, Op. 109 (1820). How come this communicates so well—even in a bad performance sometimes? The third movement's variations have such humanity.

Brendel: Yes, they do. The theme alone is so utterly disarming, and the way he makes it return at the end is so moving that nobody could resist it. This sonata is like an angel with a demon in its middle.

Dubal: That's wonderful.

Brendel: This "demon" is not a scherzo. It is sometimes called a scherzo, but it is a sonata movement. The work is actually constructed as two sonata-form movements and one variation movement.

Dubal: As in Op. 101 and 106, he uses fugal writing in the Sonata No. 31 in A-flat major, Op. 110 (1821).

Brendel: Yes—the complexity of the last two movements of ariosos and fugues that return and interlock has Baroque features. Beethoven was not only an innovator in his late years, he also went back to earlier periods of music and took as much as he could from them, transforming the material to serve his purpose. In a way these two interlocking movements are "passion" music: they remind me of Bach's Passions. In the first movement there is a new simplicity, which also comes with the new complexity in the late works, and it's nowhere more simple and lovable than here. The second movement sounds like one of his late *Bagatelles*.

DUBAL: We now come to the ultimate, the last of the sonatas, No. 32 in C minor, Op. 111. It's in two movements, and it was written in 1821–1822, so this covers a span of twenty-seven years of his sonata-writing, beginning with Op. 2 No. 1. Let's say you had never heard any of the sonatas or played them, from Op.2 No. 1 to Op. 111: Would you think of them as written by the same composer?

BRENDEL: The marvelous thing about Beethoven's sonatas is that they are so different, each of them. Even sonatas of the same period can be so unlike each other. That's one of the reasons I love to play the cycle, because there is virtually nothing that repeats itself. The scope of the imagination is so astounding that I would really call it mysterious. It's something one cannot explain by just looking at the person. Beethoven the man had his limitations, and frailties, but as a composer he encompassed and mastered nearly everything that is human. And of course the last sonata is an essence of this humanity; it is a true conclusion of the series. I do not think it was accidental that he stopped composing sonatas at this point. To put two very opposed movements next to each other seems to suggest that he wanted to put his experience in a nutshell, so to speak. There has been no shortage of names to characterize these two movements: samsara and nirvana, the real and the mystical world, the male and the female principle, yin and yang, or rather yang and yin (to remain in the order of movements).

DUBAL: When you program the complete sonatas in seven recitals, how do you arrive at an organic way of programming them?

BRENDEL: With the years, I simply know the pieces better—I know better how they act on each other, and on me. Some problems solved themselves. To put the five late sonatas at the end of recitals was a natural thing to do. To put the *Waldstein* and the *Appassionata* on the two remaining endings also made sense. To start with Op. 2 No. 1 in the cycle and to end with Op. 111 seemed inevitable. To distribute the sonatas in minor keys over the programs proved unnecessary because there are fewer of the minor-key sonatas than those in major. The succession of keys has to be considered—in particular, the avoidance of sonatas in the same key following one another. As a principle, I want to give as much contrast and diversity as possible to each single evening.

Born May 22, 1933, in Denver, Colorado, John Browning made his debut there at the age of ten, playing Mozart's Coronation Concerto. *The family then moved to Los Angeles, where Browning studied with Lee Pattison. At the Juilliard School, he became a scholarship pupil of Rosina Lhevinne. In 1954 he won the Steinway Centennial Award, followed by the Leventritt Award in 1955. In 1956 he came in second to Ashkenazy in the Queen Elisabeth International Competition "by a sixteenth note." His career as a major pianist was launched when, in 1956, he made his New York Philharmonic debut with Mitropoulos. World tours quickly followed. Browning has been one of the busiest concert artists of our time. He gives master classes at the Manhattan School of Music.*

John Browning

KENN DUNCAN

DUBAL: You were always a very hard worker at the piano. Is that still the case?

BROWNING: Yes, I work harder now than ever before.

DUBAL: Can you describe your way of working?

BROWNING: Many people work with tunnel vision. They work on one little section for days and days—or they whiz through the whole work quickly. I learn carefully, conscientiously observing every marking, so I don't have to undo bad habits. I then practice in a middle tempo, not too slow, which is the hardest tempo to practice in. When I feel more or less ready, I play the whole piece straight through, three times in the day, no matter what goes wrong. I try to achieve a large arc, which is what you have to do in a performance. You cannot stop and correct yourself when you are onstage.

DUBAL: I'm told that you're an excellent teacher. Is there particular advice you offer your students?

BROWNING: I think the trouble with most students is that they are emotionally constricted, and this seems to be especially true of our age. Whatever freedom they may have in their lives, it doesn't apply to the music: They play like fourteenth-century nuns. In fact, most fourteenth-century nuns would have had more fire! Above all, I try to get them to loosen up.

DUBAL: What is your objective during a piano lesson?

BROWNING: I listen for their major faults. I listen for rhythmic problems, weak interpretation, faulty pedaling and poor technique. For example, I have one excellent student who constantly pauses before downbeats. But beyond this, I try to get my students out of neutral gear and give them a point of view.

DUBAL: How do you achieve this?

BROWNING: Any number of ways. Sometimes I use insult to get the student angry enough to respond; sometimes I try to coax a kind of sensuality out of them; sometimes I dance and scream and kick and make them laugh; anything to get a message through.

DUBAL: It sounds like it would be amusing to sit in on one of your lessons. . . . Do you assign the Chopin etudes?

BROWNING: Yes, though very few of the kids bring them in on their own. Maybe because, technically, these are *still* the most difficult of the whole etude literature. They're even harder than the Liszt etudes, because you can't fake them. You can't cover your sins by a lot of noise. Every note must sound.

DUBAL: You've recorded both sets of the etudes. Did you study most of them with Rosina Lhevinne?

BROWNING: Some, not all. The eleventh etude in Op. 25, *The Winter Wind,* was one that I did study with her. It was one of her great teaching pieces and, of course, Mr. Lhevinne had recorded it.

DUBAL: And what a recording!

BROWNING: It is fabulous!—in the tradition of Anton Rubinstein. But on my own record, I deviated from at least one aspect of that tradition. I didn't take the last scale two octaves apart as Lhevinne did. I played it as Chopin wrote it.

DUBAL: You have just mentioned Josef Lhevinne. Do you think that technical standards today are as high as they were in his day?

BROWNING: Absolutely not—I fervently believe that technical standards are going down, not up. This is probably because early training in this country is so often sloppy, appallingly bad. Very little repertoire is learned, and then at seventeen or eighteen kids start pushing all of a sudden and by then it's too late to develop an even, clear technique.

DUBAL: Do you find that the technical standard at piano competitions—like the Queen Elisabeth, which you judge—is higher when the Russians come?

BROWNING: Absolutely. If the Russians don't come, the general standards are not nearly as good. One year, at the Queen Elisabeth, we had five Russians in the finals in Brussels—they were all extraordinary. You know, they're ready to give concerts at the age of fifteen—they're truly ready.

DUBAL: Do you enjoy judging the Queen Elisabeth?

BROWNING: Yes. It's wonderful; elegant. You have lunch with the King and Queen of Belgium, and it's all very festive. But it's hard work. And the hardest thing of all is listening to an eighteen- or nineteen-year-old and trying to figure out what he or she will be later on. Will he or she be able to hold up to the pressures? "Does this person have the capacity to turn into a real artist?" is the question I ask myself over and over again, and yet it is impossible to predict how a young talent is going to develop. The hardest thing is to judge the twenty-eight-, twenty-nine-, thirty-year-olds, who are just under the wire as far as the competition cutoff age goes. Their playing is often a bit more mature than that of the eighteen-year-olds but there's always the worry that they have gone as far as they are going to.

DUBAL: What was your early training like?

BROWNING: My parents were both musicians. My mother was a fine pianist and my father was a violinist. When I was ten and eleven I studied with both Lhevinnes in the summers. In California I studied with Lee Pattison and then back to Mrs. Lhevinne at Juilliard. So there was always a high standard for me.

DUBAL: Do you think the high incidence of tendinitis today has to do with poor training?

BROWNING: Yes, it comes from tightness at the keyboard, forcing technique you don't have. It comes from straining—from not knowing how to play the instrument. I really think it's what you do before the age of sixteen that counts most. You cannot develop a major technique after the age of sixteen any more than you can develop an Olympic gymnast at that age. It has to be done from the age of four on.

DUBAL: Can you give me an example of what teachers should be doing in those early years that is generally neglected?

BROWNING: First and foremost: Double notes and more double notes. They show up all the problems. This is the kind of Russian technique that we were taught by Mrs. Lhevinne. Unfortunately mine are not what they should be. I didn't really start working on double notes until I worked regularly with Mrs. Lhevinne at Juilliard.

DUBAL: Some people have deficiencies in their technique no matter how excellent the training.

BROWNING: Yes, very definitely. For example, Ashkenazy probably has the best double-note technique of any living pianist and it is most likely natural with him. But I know that this is something I do not have naturally.

DUBAL: What then are the strongest areas of your technique?

BROWNING: Mainly it is an evenness in my mechanism, an evenness in passagework. I also have a good left hand.

DUBAL: I have to ask the inevitable question: Was Rosina Lhevinne as great a teacher as legend has it?

BROWNING: She was an intuitive teacher and her ears were immaculate. If she didn't like what she heard, she had a very good reason and she was usually right about it. But she really couldn't give you a sense of what to do with the work. I hear her now in her Russian accent: "You know, dear, it is 'your' piece, but you are too near it. Put it away awhile." But she had formidable instincts and, more than anything, she had a natural rubato, a natural roundness in her sound, as all those Russians of her period did. Whether it was Hofmann, Rachmaninoff or Mr. Lhevinne, they all remembered those great final recitals of Anton Rubinstein in Moscow, which set the standard for the way they wanted to play the piano. And though of course Anton Rubinstein never recorded, everybody who was there remembered with an incredible accuracy how he played. All of these people had the same memory of the same concerts.

DUBAL: But in the late twentieth century we are far from Imperial Russia and those playing traditions.

BROWNING: That reminds me of something Mrs. Lhevinne once said: "Today you are all living with this machine noise. You are living in rooms with these square corners. When we were young, there were chandeliers hanging in big elegant rooms with wonderful rococo decorations. Today you live in little boxes with jackhammers splitting our ears. With this kind of environment, how can the young be expected to understand a flexible rhythm?"

DUBAL: Does it mean that music of the past is no longer relevant to us, something we can no longer feel or produce?

BROWNING: I think great art transcends the period in which it was written. And as performers we won't play it the same way as it was played in its own time, and that's fine with me. I don't like the instruments

Beethoven or Chopin had. And I would go so far as to say that Horowitz has even gone beyond the modern piano. I'm sure that ideally he would like something even beyond the piano we know. Today we have people who play wonderful Beethoven and we feel its authenticity because there is an inner reality to a good performance. We don't need an instrument of Beethoven's period to achieve this.

DUBAL: I know you find this "inner reality" in Rachmaninoff's recordings.

BROWNING: I certainly do. When I hear his recording of his transcription of Kreisler's *Liebesfreud,* I literally say, "Will somebody kill me now? I don't want to play the piano again, ever!" But he's the only pianist I feel that way about. And that even includes Mr. Horowitz. I adore Horowitz, and I am dazzled by him. But he does not evoke suicidal feelings in me. Both Rachmaninoff and Kreisler had that thing which nobody has anymore—a type of elegance that seems to have died out. There's a certain kind of humanity in the performance that can bring tears to the eye. It happens very quickly—it can happen in a single phrase.

DUBAL: In addition to Rachmaninoff and Horowitz, are there other pianists whom you admire?

BROWNING: Yes, I have enormous admiration for Myra Hess, for Schnabel, for de Larrocha—all very different kinds of artists.

DUBAL: At concerts, are you usually a good colleague?

BROWNING: Yes, I think so, though I remember one time I wasn't. It must have been over twenty years ago when I trudged to a Hans Richter-Hauser recital at Carnegie Hall during a terrible snowstorm. It was an all-Beethoven program and he started with the *Pathétique Sonata*. After finishing the first movement, he *instantly* started the second movement. For some reason I found this very funny, it just hit me that way. I didn't laugh out loud but my shoulders were shaking, and I was probably making some kind of noise. Suddenly, a little old woman behind me banged on my shoulder and said, "Young man, if you knew what it was like to be up there playing on stage, you wouldn't laugh like that." And I looked at her and whispered back, "Madam, you're absolutely right."

DUBAL: I certainly didn't laugh the last time I heard you on stage. You were giving an absolutely riveting performance of the Barber Concerto—a work which is truly "your piece," which you premiered at the first concert at what is now Avery Fisher Hall at Lincoln Center. I've heard that Barber did not have the final movement ready until several weeks before the premiere.

BROWNING: That's right—he hadn't even started it two weeks before the premiere. So I was literally at the keyboard around the clock during the ten days before the concert. It was hell. I kept having to go up to Mt. Kisco, where Barber lived, to bring back two or three pages of the manuscript at a time.

DUBAL: Why was Barber late?

BROWNING: He just couldn't get an idea for the last movement. I was up there only two Sundays before the premiere with Aaron Copland, who said, "Well, Sam, you've got to come up with something because this poor guy's got to play it, and hopefully by memory." But in despair Sam said, "I just can't get an idea." Miraculously though, the next morning he called me in New York and said, "John, I went to the bathroom this morning, and in the bathroom I got the idea for the last movement!" So out of less-than-heavenly things sometimes inspiration comes.

DUBAL: Creativity knows no bounds. . . . I hope the concerto is dedicated to you for all you went through.

BROWNING: Sam never dedicated anything to the artist who premiered his work.

DUBAL: Besides the world premiere, didn't you play it with George Szell on a tour of the Soviet Union with the Cleveland Orchestra?

BROWNING: Yes, it was on one of the last big State Department tours.

DUBAL: What was it like to work with Szell? He was known to be difficult.

BROWNING: Most people were frightened of him and I was scared to death of him for a while. But I soon realized that if I was prepared and knew what I was doing, even though Mr. Szell might yell at me privately, calling me an idiot or something like that, once we got in front of the orchestra, he would carry me like a baby. You never felt as secure with anybody as you did with Szell. In a New York performance, particularly, you were positive nothing could go wrong, and it never did. I liked him; he seemed to like me. We got along very well.

DUBAL: Did you ever go through solo repertoire with him?

BROWNING: Yes, I once rented a chalet in Switzerland nearby him. I asked him if we could work together. I think he was a little bored up there and to my delight he agreed to work with me for a month. So imagine—four times a week I would get three- and four-hour lessons on all the Beethoven, Mozart and Schubert I wanted. It was incredible. And then after the lesson, he would sit down and play quartets on the the piano, or he would play his own arrangement of Richard Strauss's *Till Eulenspiegel's Merry Pranks.* He had an encyclopedic memory and knowledge. He could isolate on the piano the viola part for a Schubert or Mozart quartet that he hadn't thought of in twenty years. It was Szell who really made me understand the architecture in large-scale works, the kind of "punctuation," as he called it, in a big Schubert sonata or something of that size. Certain things, he would say, are dashes and periods, and commas and semicolons, and new paragraphs and new chapters within a movement. It was an eye-opener.

DUBAL: Do you worry about your hands' being hurt?

BROWNING: Not really. Margot Fonteyn once said to me, "The less we worry about our legs or hands or feet the better, because worrying makes us accident-prone," and I think she is right. Otherwise you can become a raving lunatic.

DUBAL: Have you ever had piano burn-out? Someone once said to me that to be a concert pianist you need two lives: one life to live, and one life to practice.

BROWNING: That's a wonderful way of putting it. How true! It is certainly a monastic life. It can be extremely lonely. Practicing six to eight hours a day takes its toll. Of course there are extraordinary rewards, but one needs nerves of steel to keep at it day after day.

DUBAL: Do the pressures build at mid-life? Did you ever experience what is now called "mid-life crisis"?

BROWNING: I think almost everybody does, usually in their forties. I sure did. I had about five years when I was going through quite an upheaval. I think it happens not only to artists but to women after the childbearing years; to men when they begin to realize that time is getting shorter—that they're on the other side of the hill, and if they don't get it going they're not going to. I think everybody goes through that strange period when the body and mind are both shifting gears. You had traded on certain things which worked automatically, and all of a sudden they don't work. The Maginot Line will no longer protect France. You begin to lose your hair, your body isn't quite the same: certain energies that you took for granted you no longer have. Certain things begin to bore you. You have to make a big shift, an internal shift, and you either come out on top or you come out way down. Fortunately, I think that I've come through it. The secret is reevaluating everything you've ever believed in.

Born July 16, 1928, in Baku, U.S.S.R., Davidovich was a student at the Moscow Conservatory. She shared first prize in the 1949 Chopin International Competition with Halina Czerny-Stefánska. She appeared with the Leningrad Philharmonic for 28 consecutive seasons, and also taught at the Moscow Conservatory. In 1978 she emigrated to the United States. Her quickly sold-out American debut took place at Carnegie Hall in October 1979. She has maintained a tremendous schedule of concerts and recording, and has taught at the Juilliard School since 1982.

Bella Davidovich

Bella Davidovich

DUBAL: What was your early musical life like?

DAVIDOVICH: I grew up in Baku until World War II; it had a very musical atmosphere. I started to study piano at a very early age, and my parents took me to hear the best performers who came in to play with the Baku Philharmonic. My mother and father both worked in the Opera, so I went very frequently to hear opera as well. From my early years on, I retain a very strong memory of the operatic works of the western and Russian repertoire and also of the ballet. In the summer I heard wonderful music, too, because my parents took me to the Caucasus Mountains, where the finest symphony orchestras would come and perform. As I grew I was also fortunate enough to hear the great pianists Lev Oborin, Flier, the young Gilels and so many others, and Heinrich Neuhaus made a great impression on me. My very first teacher in Baku took me to play for Heinrich Neuhaus when I was only ten years old. I played for him, and although I was only a little girl, he said that if they took me to Moscow he would work with me.

DUBAL: Had you known that Neuhaus was the teacher of Gilels and Richter?

DAVIDOVICH: Yes, and he was the teacher of many other fine pianists. He was a very inspired musician. A real artist, with a true artistic nature. Arthur Rubinstein knew him as a young man and when Neuhaus was in the hospital in 1964, Rubinstein came to Russia and he went straight to the hospital to see him.

DUBAL: In Russia today, is there a pianistic culture similar to the one that existed while you were growing up? We see that people like Ginzburg, Flier, Zak, the Neuhauses, Oborin, Goldenweiser and Igumnov, the great Soviet pianists and teachers, are all dead.

DAVIDOVICH: Yes, before my very eyes all these wonderful people disappeared, all died within a few years of each other. Also Sofronitsky, Maria Yudina and Maria Grinberg. They are irreplaceable.

DUBAL: Tell me your impressions of Sofronitsky and Yudina. They were both legendary figures and very mysterious people.

DAVIDOVICH: There is no way one can define Sofronitsky. You can't say he was simply a romantic, or that he was a temperamental player. There's no way to put a frame around him. He was such a unique, individualistic artist and man, completely different from everyone else.

Unfortunately, he was very ill during his last years, when I was living in Moscow. He often wasn't playing. In his last years, he preferred to play in smaller halls, in more intimate surroundings. He was always very nervous before a concert. The first pieces on the program were very shaky. But then, the music gradually became more and more inspired. He played Scriabin as if the composer wrote it just for him. Interestingly, Sofronitsky became Scriabin's son-in-law, many years after the composer's death. Yudina and Sofronitsky both studied with the same teacher, Nikolayev, at the St. Petersburg Conservatory. Shostakovich was also a piano student at the same time. Anyway, Yudina had a very mystical personality and she was a great artist, always very interesting to hear. And she had the courage to play contemporary composers of the West which were forbidden for Soviets. But her fate was not an easy one and she didn't have very good government contacts, not a very good relationship with the government, to say the least, and without such contacts, the career is hard to manage.

DUBAL: What was it like growing up in the Stalinist era?

DAVIDOVICH: I grew up in such a time that after the words "mother" and "father" the next word you had to say was "Stalin." That's how our whole generation grew up, and I am not an exception. It is hideous to think about the monsters that have ruled the world.

DUBAL: You have made a fine career in the West in the few years since you left Russia. What are some of the obvious differences between the musical business here and there?

DAVIDOVICH: In the U.S. I have encountered for the first time a world where sponsors of orchestras or sponsors and managers of artists are very important. I was never exposed to that. Here it depends on individuals or groups of interested people giving money to keep orchestras or concert series alive.

DUBAL: In Russia that doesn't exist?

DAVIDOVICH: No, it doesn't. There is only the government. The government does everything. It's all plain and simple.

DUBAL: What are your feelings about that?

DAVIDOVICH: It's hard for me to say whether it's good or bad, it was all I had known. I have found that in the West when an orchestra goes broke, the musician is out of a job. That doesn't happen in the Soviet Union. In the Soviet Union, they don't have to worry about where to go next. However, if you have such control by the government, then perhaps it can control what sort of music will be played.

DUBAL: And does it happen that way?

DAVIDOVICH: Of course. It's all a very different world. They can tell you what to play, they can plan your programs. Even the name of the orchestra is up to the government. The concept is so different. Here, the Philharmonic, or any orchestra, is simply an orchestra. There, it's an agent of the government; it's a part of the government. So when I was a soloist, I was not a soloist of the Moscow Philharmonic but a soloist of the Moscow State Government Orchestra. It's a whole different situation. It's an organization of the state. The orchestra is literally a political organization. There are people there who monitor the composers we're playing, the soloists we have. What is allowed, what is not. There are no similarities between the Soviet world and here.

DUBAL: Do you miss the Russian audience?

DAVIDOVICH: I love very much the Russian public and, yes, I miss it very much. I already had my public who knew me well. I had a following that always came to my concerts and it was very hard to give that up. The American public is very lucky. They have opportunities to hear the best in the world. In Russia we have a far more limited choice.

DUBAL: Is it difficult for a woman to have a major musical career in the Soviet Union?

DAVIDOVICH: A woman is a woman. She has to be a mother and a wife, and that places a lot of responsibility on her. She has got to travel a lot, the children will have to grow up by themselves. The husband will say, "I don't need a wife who is never here." So it's very difficult, very difficult. I lost my husband twenty-five years ago. He was not just a husband, he was a great friend. We talked the same language. And each of us knew who the other was, what the other stood for. When my son Dmitri was born, and he didn't sleep well at nights, we would both jump to his bed to pick him up. But my husband would say, "I will do it. You save your hands."

DUBAL: Tell me something about how you practice.

DAVIDOVICH: I usually play around three hours a day, though sometimes I end up playing one or two hours more than that. And after each hour I make sure to take a little break, even a little ten-minute one, in order not to lose my level of concentration. But for that hour between the breaks, I am very concentrated. During the break I drink tea, talk on the telephone, I just completely disconnect and do something besides music. But when I work I think about nothing but music. Nothing can disturb me, nothing can distract me. I am listening to myself.

DUBAL: Do you practice hands separately and do you write in all your fingerings, the way so many pianists do?

DAVIDOVICH: No, I never separate hands, and I don't usually write anything into the notes. Occasionally I will put a little sign telling me to pay attention to a certain place in the composition.

DUBAL: Do you memorize during the process of learning?

DAVIDOVICH: Yes, the memorization comes while I practice. I never actually sit down to learn something by heart. It goes in during practice and it stays there. Thank God there are no memory problems!

DUBAL: Do you have perfect pitch?

DAVIDOVICH: Yes, and my husband had it too. But, while my son has very good hearing, he does not have perfect pitch. When I was little, they turned me around with my back to the piano, and they asked me what notes they were playing. I could name all of them and I could even transpose keys.

DUBAL: Is perfect pitch a requirement at the Moscow Conservatory?

DAVIDOVICH: No, it's not required now. It never was. It's not necessary for musicians generally. You just have to have good hearing. Good hearing can always improve.

DUBAL: How do you achieve your pedaling: do you adjust it for different pianos?

DAVIDOVICH: In some pianos the springs are lighter in the pedal, in some they're heavier. Sometimes I will sit and listen to the music in my head, looking at the score without the instrument, and suddenly I might get an idea about the pedaling, and then I will go over to the piano and try it.

DUBAL: Do you find that having small hands is a disadvantage?

DAVIDOVICH: In general, it's a little bit of a problem. When I was small it was clear that my hands would not be big. So sometimes when I need to, I have to adapt the music to my hand. Of course I don't change anything in the score. I think a lot, and use hand positions which make it easier for me. When you have a limitation you work around it.

DUBAL: Who has an ideal hand in your opinion?

DAVIDOVICH: Oh, there are many, but Richter's are especially wonderful.

DUBAL: Are you a good sight-reader?

DAVIDOVICH: Yes. It's because my mother is a very good sight-reader and she used to bring home the operatic scores. I looked at them and I started to play, and I have never stopped reading since.

DUBAL: What is it you reach for musically during a performance?

DAVIDOVICH: I try to have the piano speak. My wish is that when I play my piano it will sing, and for this reason I listen to a lot of vocal music at home. There is a lot for a pianist to learn from good singers, particularly when it comes to phrasing.

DUBAL: Did you get to hear Glenn Gould when he was in Russia?

DAVIDOVICH: I remember very well when Glenn Gould came to us in '57. Nobody knew him then. At the first concert in Moscow there were very few people, a very small public. But it was broadcast on radio. My husband was in the hospital and he listened to the concert from there. When I went to see him the next day, he said to me, "When you get to Leningrad, Glenn Gould will be there. Please stay one more day, you must not miss him, you cannot imagine the concert he gave." And I did stay in Leningrad, and I did go to the concert. In Leningrad you could not get one ticket because after he played in Moscow, everybody was calling Leningrad, saying, "Run to the concert—go to hear Gould." The tickets were gone in a minute. We had never heard such playing.

DUBAL: Did you ever get to hear Rubinstein play? Did he have any impact in Russia?

DAVIDOVICH: In the early Thirties, Rubinstein came to play, and we never forgot his performances. After World War II, when the boundaries opened and Soviet musicians started to go to the West, they began to hear him abroad, and some of them made personal contact with him. My professor, Yakov Flier, came back so elated from meeting him and hearing him. We were all so happy when Rubinstein came back in 1964. All sorts of meetings were arranged with him for students and for musicians. He spoke fantastic Russian. He had so much humor, so much wit in Russian. I didn't get to meet him in Moscow. But in the early Seventies, I flew from Moscow to Amsterdam to play and the manager of the Amsterdam Concertgebouw Orchestra told me, "There are two interesting concerts here today. Fischer-Dieskau is singing in Amsterdam and Rubinstein is playing in Rotterdam. Which one would you like to hear?" Of course I chose Rubinstein. I went to Rotterdam, and I will never forget how happy I was to be there. I applauded so much that the director of the orchestra said, "Tomorrow you have a rehearsal. You are going to hurt your hands." Then I broke my tradition and went backstage to shake hands. The impresario saw me standing on line and she motioned me to come closer, and she brought me to him. There were people around him. He was speaking in French. She introduced me to him in German and when he found out that I was from Russia, he started to speak in perfect Russian. He asked me many questions, and he told me that he had known about me. And he asked me to send his regards to many musicians in Moscow. He remembered his 1964 visit to us very fondly, and wished me all the best success. And I was so happy. He was a man of incredible personal charm and talent.

DUBAL: What do you remember best from that concert?

DAVIDOVICH: The D-flat major Chopin Nocturne which he played for an encore. He must have played it thousands of times before but his interpretation was totally fresh. I myself had had too much of that nocturne. Everybody plays it. But Rubinstein played it so that I felt I had never heard it before. It's hard to find the words for what it was like, but it was as if he was a young man and not eighty years old. It was just amazing that this could be, and I will never forget the experience of hearing that nocturne as if for the first time. It was also a lesson that I never forgot. If when I play I can convey in a familiar piece that startling awareness of freshness to just one person, then I have achieved a great deal as a musician.

Born May 23, 1923, in Barcelona, Spain, de Larrocha first appeared in public at age five and by age nine she had already made a recording of a Chopin waltz and nocturne (issued on the International Piano Archives label in 1976). In 1943 she received the gold medal of the Academia Marshall. She became director of the school in 1959. De Larrocha began making extensive tours of Europe after World War II. In 1955, on her first visit to the U.S., she played with the Los Angeles Philharmonic. She made her New York Philharmonic debut in 1965 with the Mozart Concerto No. 23 in A major, K. 488. De Larrocha has received many honors, including the Harriet Cohen Medal in 1956, the Paderewski Medal in 1961 and the Spanish Order of Civil Merit in 1962.

Alicia de Larrocha

DUBAL: You were raised in a very musical environment, weren't you?

DE LARROCHA: Ah, yes. I remember music around me all my life.

DUBAL: Your mother and aunt studied piano with Granados.

DE LARROCHA: Yes, that's right.

DUBAL: What were the first pieces that you heard?

DE LARROCHA: Well, there was a student at my home that my aunt was teaching, and he was playing the Grieg *To Spring* from the Lyric Pieces. I don't remember, of course—I was two years old, or something like that—but my aunt was always telling me that when her student left I would play the melody and the harmony—more or less—at the piano.

DUBAL: What ears!

DE LARROCHA: Well, it seems that my musical ear was very developed and I could do that easily.

DUBAL: Do you have absolute pitch?

DE LARROCHA: I used to have it. Unfortunately, with age, little by little it's going. Until a few years ago, I could say exactly the notes, chords, intervals, everything. But now, ah, we have to accept the things we don't like, and sometimes I know that I am hearing the pitch a little higher; so I have to figure out and say, Well, I heard a B, so it has to be an A.

DUBAL: How interesting. Did you ever hear the story that Hans von Bülow was very unmusical until nine years of age, when he fell on his head and all of a sudden he had perfect pitch?

DE LARROCHA: Yes. That is a mystery. But my problem is not a mystery. The doctors explain it to me very well.

DUBAL: Your mother stopped playing piano even though she studied with the great Granados, but your aunt continued, and she was a major force in your early career.

DE LARROCHA: Oh, yes, absolutely. I think I owe her everything because when I first wanted to play I was so young that nobody at home wanted me to touch the piano. They were afraid I would ruin it. But, finally, she saw that I really wanted very badly to play, and she decided to start me. I was practicing as a baby of three years old and she was right there next to me. She was everything to me. Even when I went to my teacher, Frank Marshall, she was always in the class so she would know what he wanted, and then she would make me practice. It was a fantastic thing.

DUBAL: So it was your aunt who really gave you that environment. She taught at the Frank Marshall Academy, didn't she?

DE LARROCHA: Yes, all her life. She started with Granados, but then when he died she continued on at the academy until her own death not long ago.

DUBAL: When you came to Frank Marshall then, how old were you?

DE LARROCHA: A little over three.

DUBAL: Did he actually start working with you that early?

DE LARROCHA: He didn't want to. He refused at first, saying, "No, impossible. I can't teach her; she's too young." But it seems that I was very, very stubborn, and one day I went with my aunt to hear someone who was playing at the academy, and I went to him and I said, "I want to play, and you have to teach me." I don't know if it was just because he thought it was charming, but he took me on.

DUBAL: That's amazing because very few people will take a child that young. What kind of teacher was he, and what kind of man was he?

DE LARROCHA: He was extremely conscientious as a teacher, and as a human being he was like a father. He took me in as a baby. He and his wife were a couple without children and I was really like their child. It was sort of a combination of a very strict and severe teacher and a wonderful father. So in one way I felt absolutely at home. I used to spend the whole day at the academy. I would be playing all over—every piano in the academy. And I was also playing with toys. So I remember the academy not only for music but for the atmosphere—it was like my home. But he never took one cent. Never. And, of course, my family was not well off. We were four children, and my mother and father worked very hard, and when I got scholarship money from a little competition in Barcelona, Marshall didn't want to accept it. He gave it to my family—to my father. He was absolutely . . . well, those people you find very seldom.

DUBAL: Yes, very seldom indeed. Marshall was inspired deeply by Granados, who died tragically in 1916 when his ship was torpedoed by a German U-boat. Wasn't he returning to Spain after playing for President Wilson at the White House and he was only 49 years old?

DE LARROCHA: Yes, Granados was our composer; we felt very close ties with him. But I have to say that I didn't play Granados until I was a teenager. Of course, I played the little pieces he wrote for children in a Romantic style like Schumann, but they had nothing to do with Spanish music, you know. They were written for children, and they were very good for me. But I didn't play the real Granados until after our revolution, when I was sixteen years old.

DUBAL: When you grew up did you hear things about this composer as a man, as a pianist?

DE LARROCHA: Yes, of course. Through my mother, my aunt, my teacher and Granados's daughter—we are very close friends. So I always heard curious anecdotes. He was a very sensitive, very romantic man, with big eyes and . . . well, you know that kind of man in that period of history. Very romantic, very sensitive, and poetic—yes, and a very good-looking man. *Very* good-looking. Beautiful eyes. So he had many, many romances and many, many women fell in love with him. And, I wouldn't say my mother was really in love with him, but she had some admiration and something for him that was very strong.

DUBAL: So he was an entrancing individual.

DE LARROCHA: Yes. And when my father took my mother as his fiancée, my mother, of course, still had this admiration for her teacher. And since Granados had this reputation, my father didn't like it very much.

DUBAL: Was Granados married?

DE LARROCHA: Yes, of course, with children and everything. But, you know, Spanish men, they are a little jealous and don't like very much those things. And my mother told me several times, especially when she was old, "You know how I loved your father. But there is one thing I'll never forget and will never forgive him. In a moment of rage and jealousy, your father ripped up the photo Granados dedicated to me. And this is something I never will forgive him."

DUBAL: As a child, when you were growing up with Marshall—and Marshall died in 1959, I believe, so he lived long enough to see your career flower—who were the composers you were most fond of from four years old to ten, let's say?

DE LARROCHA: We started with Bach and Mozart, of course. And then a little Scarlatti and then a little Schumann. That was the favorite of Granados—he loved Schumann. Schumann and Scarlatti. But Schumann was also our favorite composer at school.

DUBAL: Did Marshall give you Czerny or Hanon?

DE LARROCHA: Ah, yes. But since my hands were so small, you can imagine . . .

DUBAL: Especially at four years old.

DE LARROCHA: Yes, if they are small now, you can imagine what they were at four years old. So, what Frank Marshall did, which I think was fantastic, was to adapt exercises to my capabilities. So I played some Czerny, but other Czerny I couldn't play. And Frank Marshall wrote for me some other things the way he wanted them for me. For instance, there were some extension exercises he wrote for me especially.

DUBAL: So he was quite a teacher, he really thought about how to adapt things for your growth.

DE LARROCHA: Absolutely.

DUBAL: You were a child prodigy, but you weren't pushed out onto the stage, were you?

DE LARROCHA: Fortunately, I wasn't.

DUBAL: Was this because your parents were aware of its dangers?

DE LARROCHA: Yes, since Mother was a musician and so were my two aunts, they understood very well what the marketplace was. The only thing they cared about was that I loved music and that it was my life. They were happy because I was happy. They never thought about concerts, but little by little I started, just as a test, once a year before a small audience. We never, never thought about it from the point of view of money—even though the family was not well off. In the beginning, I always played for nothing. I never had money from playing concerts.

DUBAL: When you played your first concerto with Enrique Fernández Arbós, was there no money for that either?

DE LARROCHA: No money at all, unfortunately.

DUBAL: Were you excited to play with an orchestra behind you?

DE LARROCHA: I was eleven, and of course I was very, very excited. I still feel on my face the kiss he gave me because he had a beard. I was excited. Yes, very much. I played the Mozart *Coronation Concerto*.

DUBAL: What happened during the Spanish Revolution? Did Marshall continue to teach you?

DE LARROCHA: No, he had to leave—it was dangerous. So my aunt would listen to me. I was already a teenager at the time, and you know teenagers want to be independent, so she just listened and coached more than taught. I was mainly by myself. I did a little composition at that time—silly things. Just for my pleasure. Some songs and some little pieces.

DUBAL: Do you have any remembrances, impressions of life in Spain during the revolution years?

DE LARROCHA: I remember that we had nothing to eat and that it was very hard for my parents. Terrible things happen in revolutions, in wars. It is a very difficult life.

DUBAL: Are you a political person?

DE LARROCHA: Absolutely not!

DUBAL: You say that emphatically.

DE LARROCHA: I hate politics. It makes me sick to hear people even talking about politics.

DUBAL: And how come?

DE LARROCHA: In my opinion politicians just spend their lives criticizing one another and wanting to be at the top and doing nasty things to other people. They are selfish, and, well, I don't like it, I don't like it!

DUBAL: Historically speaking, there have not been many women pianists of your stature. Do you have any thoughts on the idea of a woman's career in music? For instance, Leschetizky once said he did not want to take any more women on as students because they all get married and give up the piano. You have had a full life, and yet you do not seem to have sacrificed your career in any way.

DE LARROCHA: I think it was a matter of luck. Luck, because I never did anything to get all the things I have. And I fell in love, and I got married. I did not think about whether it was good or bad for my music. That's all. And it happens that my late husband was a fantastic husband, and *he* was the one who was pushing *me.* Many things I didn't want to do because of my children. I wanted to stay at home with my babies, and he was really the one who helped me with the home problems and the children's problems—even musical problems, because I am quite a lazy person, and there are programs to think about and letters to write. He always did those things. It's just luck. And then there were people who were interested in me—I don't know why—but things were coming my way. I was just surprised—surprised, that's all.

DUBAL: Are you still surprised at the great career?

DE LARROCHA: Absolutely!

DUBAL: Do you see it as a responsibility? Even though you say you are lazy, your husband, who was obviously a very unusual man, undoubtedly thought that you had something very important to offer. But have you ever felt an *obligation* to play?

DE LARROCHA: No, if I play it's because it is something I need for myself.

DUBAL: When you say that you're lazy, I understand that you don't have time to write letters, but are you telling me that you're lazy about playing the piano or your daily practicing?

DE LARROCHA: That, no! When my life is normal I cannot stay away from the piano for even one day. For other things I am not lazy either. But to write letters and decide about programs is different. It's not exactly that I'm lazy; it's that I sometimes think nothing is possible. I think, "What can I play? This I can't play. This is too difficult. I've already played that." They are my own problems, and my husband knew so well the repertoire—he was a musician also, a pianist. So many times he made things easier by helping me with programs. He would show me a program and say, "What about this? You didn't play this," or "You didn't play that." He was fantastic.

DUBAL: This sounds like a very unusual relationship: The fact that your husband was a pianist, and that he was obviously not in competition with you, that he was only interested in your career.

DE LARROCHA: When we met each other he was a student pianist, and we used to play two pianos together until we got married. Then we decided, because we needed money, that he would teach, and so he taught at the Frank Marshall School until about ten years ago, when he got very sick. And all that time he took care of everything in my work.

DUBAL: And yet it must have been difficult at times to be a mother, a wife and an artist with an international career.

DE LARROCHA: Unfortunately I never felt like a good mother or a good wife, I've never felt like a good anything, because doing many things means you're not doing any one of them right.

DUBAL: So you feel something is always sacrificed?

DE LARROCHA: Absolutely; and that is why it is so difficult for women. Many people ask me, "Why is it so difficult for women to have a career?" And that is the reason, because our position in social life and our responsibilities are very, very big and very important, and we have so many responsibilities.

DUBAL: And you believe that you have failed in some ways in your responsibilities as a mother?

DE LARROCHA: Yes, I've been a very bad mother. I left my son when he was one month old. I went to South America to play concerts. And I haven't been with my children enough to raise them, to educate them. That is something a mother has to do.

DUBAL: I understand. But perhaps the time you have spent with your husband and your family was of special quality. Have you ever thought of that?

DE LARROCHA: No, I don't know. It is very difficult.

DUBAL: I think you're a woman who is very hard on herself.

DE LARROCHA: Just realistic.

DUBAL: But I understand what you're saying. There has been quite a price paid for the career. For instance, traveling itself is a monumentally difficult situation, isn't it?

DE LARROCHA: Especially nowadays.

DUBAL: Many pianists have not been able to continue the tours.

DE LARROCHA: It is hard. And there are always unexpected things, like being caught in a place you've never been before. It's very strange.

DUBAL: And yet you don't seem to resent this, you just seem to accept what comes.

DE LARROCHA: Well, what can I do? At times I used to get mad, but now I think it's useless, and I just accept it, that's all.

DUBAL: You are not a pianist who has come through the competition route. What are your thoughts about that kind of career-building?

DE LARROCHA: In my day there was no such thing as a big competition. It so happens that I wasn't looking for one, but even people who were could not find one. Maybe because there was nowhere near the number of performers that there are today. Or because it was not quite so difficult to get work, in general. These days musicians think of competitions as one of the only ways to get in. I don't think it is a good way, sometimes, because many artists win competitions, and then they fizzle out. But at least they get their names heard for a while, and they get the possibilities of concerts. For me, though, it is difficult to understand. I am from another period, another time—completely different. Also, the feelings and the reactions of the people were different in my time.

DUBAL: What do you mean by the feelings and reactions? To music? To people?

DE LARROCHA: To everything. It is difficult to explain in English. The human feelings now are a little bit colder. And life is seen much more realistically. Everything has to be done quicker and faster, and you have trouble with everything, so your feelings are thwarted.

DUBAL: How sad that is.

DE LARROCHA: It is. And it's in art and everything. Beauty, love, real love, family love—many, many things are different. There is no time. You are going somewhere, and you have to rush. There is no time. For people my age, we already have our feeling of security, but for the young people who are starting their lives nowadays it is really difficult. They have to fight just to make a living, and art and sensitivity are suffering. You can imagine how different it was when artists traveled by boat and spent two weeks in one place. They had time to think about many, many things. Now you go on the Concorde, and in three hours you play somewhere, and you come right back. How is this possible physically, spiritually or emotionally?

DUBAL: How do you protect yourself from this numbness?

DE LARROCHA: Fortunately, when I play, I forget all that.

DUBAL: You're immersed in the music?

DE LARROCHA: Yes, it surrounds me. And if the instrument is good and the acoustics are good, that is my compensation.

DUBAL: What about the fact that you have to play a certain number of concertos every year? Do you get bored with certain works of the repertoire? Do you ever feel, "If I ever have to play this again I'll die"?

DE LARROCHA: Yes, I think this, but it doesn't happen when I'm playing—it only happens when I'm *thinking* about it.

DUBAL: What are the circumstances that enable you to immerse yourself in the music when you are performing?

DE LARROCHA: This is a real mystery. I've talked about it many times, and really I don't find any explanation. The only possible explanation is acoustics. That helps enormously. Even if I am terribly tired or not in a good mood or not really well-prepared and worried about the concert, if the acoustics sound beautiful, little by little, I come to myself again and I forget. And sometimes it's just the opposite: I can really feel like playing and I start and it doesn't go, it doesn't sound right. Then I say to myself, "What are you doing here? Why don't you go home? And, you people, you should go home too."

DUBAL: Are you nervous before recitals and concerts?

DE LARROCHA: Yes, but not always, not every time. It depends on what I'm playing and the circumstances. But sometimes I think, "Why isn't there an earthquake or fire or something so I don't have to play?"

DUBAL: And how does noise affect your nervous system?

DE LARROCHA: The human being gets used to anything; finally we get used to it. But what really bothers me is when I am waiting in an airport, when my mind is filled with music, and I'm hearing what I am going to play, and I'm practicing, every note, every phrase, every harmony, practicing my left hand, and then I hear that background music in the airports—even on the planes! It's terrible because I can't concentrate.

DUBAL: Do you have time to read with the schedule you keep?

DE LARROCHA: Well, I love biographies, especially musicians' biographies.

DUBAL: Do you like painting?

DE LARROCHA: Yes, I like the Impressionists. But *our* painter, Goya, is my favorite. We had a lot of great painters. We had Velásquez. But the genius and the imagination of Goya was really astonishing. The ideas he had were fantastic.

DUBAL: Have you ever had a secret wish to be something other than a pianist—a dancer, a singer or even a bullfighter?

DE LARROCHA: You know, music was always the first thing for me, but I had when I was young a real vocation for nursing and medical things, like surgery. I was fascinated with surgery. I have many close friends who are surgeons. And I have been present for many operations. They used to tell me if they had an interesting operation, and I used to go. And I would stand right next to the surgeon. I was there for my husband's operation and my daughter's, my teacher's wife, my mother-in-law's operation—right next to the doctor. Now it's forbidden. But in that time I was there. It fascinated me because, after all, it requires such great virtuosity and intelligence. And the hands—the way they work is fascinating.

DUBAL: Yes, there are certainly great similarities between the control required of a surgeon's hand and that required of a pianist. Are there composers that are uncomfortable for your hand?

DE LARROCHA: Of course. Especially big extensions in Brahms, Liszt and Rachmaninoff.

DUBAL: Even though your hands are small, you have played some of the most difficult literature, like the Rachmaninoff Third, the Brahms Second Concerto, the *Iberia,* and there seem to be no technical problems.

DE LARROCHA: That is because I look creatively at the text and distribute things to make it more comfortable. That is what I have always done. Otherwise with my size hands, I could not have played them. But the most important thing for me is, first, to know what the meaning of the music is, and then, to find a way to bring it out.

DUBAL: I think your physical limitation has helped you to work at a piece of music creatively.

DE LARROCHA: Yes, I think every pianist has his own problems in one way or another, and should do what I'm doing—adapting fingerings and changing things for more possibilities—because it is in favor of the music. Why should you be fighting and struggling if the music isn't coming out?

DUBAL: What is more comfortable for the hand: Albéniz's *Iberia* or the *Goyescas* of Granados?

DE LARROCHA: They are so different. *Goyescas* is very difficult but it requires a different technique. You have to adapt your technique for *Goyescas* and forget *Goyescas* when you go to *Iberia.* But in a way, perhaps, *Goyescas* is more pianistic. Granados was a great, great pianist and it was easy for him to play. Albéniz, at the time he was writing *Iberia,* was not playing, so it is more intellectual.

DUBAL: How do you memorize?

DE LARROCHA: This is another thing that was once very easy and little by little has gotten more difficult. First, I sight-read and then I look at the structure of the work and work on the fingering and write it in. I used to play without writing it in but now I have to do that. Then I memorize the piece from a visual point of view; and then the harmonies. In a sonata, for instance, first you have the exposition, then the development, then the recapitulation, and so you have a union, a connection you can build on.

DUBAL: How do you accomplish the gigantic sound you are capable of? Your chords ring in such an extraordinary way.

DE LARROCHA: Well, I think it's not the volume but the intensity and the proportions of the playing. The proportions can make us hear fortissimo when it is not really so.

DUBAL: You play Scarlatti, Soler and Bach on the piano. Did you ever feel that the harpsichord was a better instrument for that music?

DE LARROCHA: That instrument was beautiful when there was nothing else, but I'm sure if Bach were around now he would be very, very happy with the big concert-grand.

DUBAL: In other words, you're not likely to start playing Mozart on a fortepiano?

DE LARROCHA: The fortepiano was very nice for the salon or the living room and in parlors. But it is impossible today because of the dimensions of the concert hall.

DUBAL: Do you have a big concerto repertoire?

DE LARROCHA: No, no, I don't. Everything about me is small.

DUBAL: Then how do you feel about playing concertos?

DE LARROCHA: It depends. If I am playing with a conductor and we understand each other it is a very pleasant occasion. But that seldom happens. I think it was Rudolf Serkin who once said he preferred things to be his own fault—so I, too, prefer to do my own wrong things.

DUBAL: When you were growing up, what records did you get to hear?

DE LARROCHA: Mostly Rubinstein. He was my idol.

DUBAL: Rubinstein was always a hero in Spain.

DE LARROCHA: He started his career there.

DUBAL: He could play Spanish music with great flair.

DE LARROCHA: Yes, and he was the very first pianist to play Spanish music all over the world. He started with Albéniz's *Navarra.*

DUBAL: They would scream *"Navarra! Navarra!"* Did you know Rubinstein well? I know he loved your playing.

DE LARROCHA: Well, I first met him many, many years ago, and the last time I saw him was June of 1981. I went to see him in Geneva, Switzerland, where he was making his home.

DUBAL: How was he at that time?

DE LARROCHA: Well, his mind was amazing. He was alert, he knew everything. He was up-to-date on what was going on, who was playing. He was enjoying those little cassettes. He had thousands of cassettes and records. We talked for a couple of hours, and it was amazing the way he remembered everything; and he had a fantastic sense of humor until the very end.

DUBAL: What advice would you give to parents of a child with a musical gift?

DE LARROCHA: I'm very much against advising for a career. I would say if the child is really gifted to encourage him to work as much as possible, to love what he is doing and forget about the career. If it comes, it comes.

DUBAL: You're against planning too much in life?

DE LARROCHA: In everything. I am a person who lives for the day I am living. By the moment.

FRANK E. SCHRAMM III

Born September 27, 1945, in Shanghai, Dichter was a student of the well-known teacher Aube Tzerko in Los Angeles, and later, of Rosina Lhevinne at the Juilliard School. At Juilliard he was awarded the Josef Lhevinne Scholarship. In 1968 he received the Silver Medal at the Tchaikovsky Competition, where he was a favorite with Russian audiences. Ever since, Dichter has made numerous tours throughout the U.S., the Soviet Union, the Middle East, the Far East and Europe, appearing in recital and with virtually every major orchestra in the world.

Misha Dichter

DUBAL: How did it happen that you were born in China?

DICHTER: My parents were Polish refugees who fled Poland in '39, by way of the trans-Siberian railroad. Like so many others, they waited out the war in Shanghai. These were horrible years for them.

DUBAL: When did you decide that you wanted to be a concert pianist?

DICHTER: When I was about fourteen or fifteen I started thinking that playing concerts would be a wonderful way of life. Of course, this was after many years of practicing.

DUBAL: Who was your first important teacher?

DICHTER: After studying for six years, I went to Aube Tzerko, who literally started me from scratch. The first thing he said was "Your hand position is not good," and then he gave me scales, arpeggios and other exercises. For one year I endured that boredom. This was difficult for me, as I had already been playing repertoire I love—I felt I was back to zero. But I soon realized the point of it all.

DUBAL: Yes, years later you have a major career which takes you all over the world. But has the touring gotten tedious?

DICHTER: For me, there is always some kind of pleasure. For instance, if the city is not wonderful, maybe the orchestra is; or there is an excellent piano. And now there is even a way to fight off Muzak. I've discovered those little travel cassette players that block out that dreadful sound. I no longer have to listen to the stewardess telling me for the thousandth time where to find the oxygen masks.

DUBAL: While on tour, how do you pass the time? Do you ever keep a diary, for instance?

DICHTER: I do keep a diary, but it is in the form of drawings. If something funny happens with a conductor, or in an airport, I record these anecdotes in sketches.

DUBAL: Can you be particular about the instruments you play when you are touring?

DICHTER: I certainly can! The person sitting in the hall has no idea how many trials I've had with the tuner that day. At times I've had parts of the piano strewn all over the stage ten minutes before the recital, knowing the public is there to be seated. Something was not quite right with the pedal, the regulation or the voicing.

DUBAL: What is the nature of the relationship between the pianist and the piano-technician?

DICHTER: It is usually adversarial. Lots of times I feel like cursing the instrument, and the technician says, "Is everything all right," and I ask him if he's kidding. "Can't you hear the problems with the voicing, and don't you hear that rattle?" Then the negotiations begin.

DUBAL: Have you played in places where the piano was so wonderful that you hated to leave it?

DICHTER: Almost never . . . though recently, while making a recording in Switzerland, there was an instrument which was a revelation to me. It was the piano of my dreams. I cannot tell you how I hated to leave that instrument. It was like leaving a wonderful friend I might never see again.

DUBAL: Do you still practice a great many hours a day?

DICHTER: Yes indeed, when I'm home. That's when I learn new material. For me, it's very difficult to do this on the road. At home, I'm up with the children at seven in the morning. I have coffee and I am at the piano by eight. Before I know it, it's six o'clock and time for dinner.

DUBAL: That sounds like an exhausting and compulsive day.

DICHTER: But for me it's enjoyable; even if it is a little compulsive. Particularly when I'm working on something new, I have a fierce desire for mastery. As you know, in practicing, one thing leads to another.

DUBAL: Don't you have back problems from sitting on a bench for such a long stretch?

DICHTER: I couldn't do it on a concert bench because my back would go out. I need the support of a straight-backed chair, and I've also analyzed what muscles come into play and how not to strain them.

DUBAL: Do you worry about memory lapses, as so many pianists do?

DICHTER: Basically, I've eliminated that problem through my own theory of memorization. Of course I'm not going to tell you that I will never have a memory slip, but I have conquered the horrible anxiety that so many pianists suffer from.

DUBAL: Yet doesn't it seem unfair that only pianists have the tradition of memorizing their music? If not for Liszt and Clara Schumann, who thought it more romantic to play from memory, this might not be a requirement.

Dichter: Not at all. I find I really don't study those pieces that I'm not obliged to play from memory, such as chamber music, as well as the works I have to memorize. For instance, good memorization forces me to know why a certain G flat appears at measure 105.

Dubal: Do you suppose that pianists of the nineteenth century played as well as those of today?

Dichter: Thanks to better teaching and the high standards of the conservatories, pianists of today reach a level of technical competence which would probably have astonished most pianists up to 1830. After that, Chopin and Liszt led the way to the Impressionists and the Russian school, with their increasing technical demands.

Dubal: What do you hear when you listen to recordings made early in the century?

Dichter: A tremendous difference in style. When listening to an early recording with left-hand-before-right-hand executions, and things like that which were commonplace then, I just have to smile.

Dubal: You have often complained about inferior conducting.

Dichter: In my opinion, conducting is one of the last bastions of quackery in the music world. Suddenly someone who may not even play an instrument well is telling the violin section what to do. Of course, with major orchestras, this is not the case. When a conductor is wonderful, it can be the most gratifying thing in the world to play a concerto.

Dubal: Are there some composers that fit your hand better than others?

Dichter: Yes, because I have a large hand, Liszt works very well for me, and even the thickest configurations of Rachmaninoff, or Brahms, in his chordal writing, suit my hand. In fact, when I play Brahms, I sense that our hands must have been similar. My wife, Cipa, who has a very fine-boned hand, plays Scarlatti with ease, while I'm like an elephant on egg shells with that music.

Dubal: You have a big, rounded piano sound. How is it accomplished?

Dichter: It is a function of the weight with which I strike the key. Let's face it, though: The piano is not a legato instrument. Therefore you must simulate a legato by complete calculation. It's all an illusion.

Dubal: Which pianists had the greatest impact on your development as a musician?

Dichter: Horowitz and Schnabel made an incalculable impact on me as a child. I can still remember my first exposure to the Horowitz sound; while Schnabel, in his recordings of the Beethoven sonatas, had a profound impact on my concept of structure. And Schnabel's interpretations are timeless.

DUBAL: Wasn't Rubinstein one of your idols as well?

DICHTER: Oh, I adored Rubinstein, but he came a little later for me. How I miss seeing him strut onstage, and giving that little tug to his lapels, before starting a glorious polonaise of Chopin. He made so many pieces his own that I sometimes hesitate to play them myself.

DUBAL: Did you ever have the opportunity to meet Rubinstein?

DICHTER: Yes, several years ago we did a television film together in Paris. I remember playing Schubert for him—he loved the Schubert sonatas.

DUBAL: Speaking of Schubert, I recently heard you play the Schubert B-flat Sonata.

DICHTER: Yes, and each time I play the first chord of it I think, "My God, am I actually getting to play this piece again? It's such a privilege." It's completely inspired. All you can do is hold your breath, and hold back tears in the development section. The whole world is in that music.

DUBAL: That almost sounds religious.

DICHTER: Yes, for me it is a religious experience to listen to Schnabel's recording of the Schubert B-flat.

DUBAL: Have you ever found satisfaction in pianists outside the classical tradition?

DICHTER: I am floored by the piano playing of the late Art Tatum. I just can't get enough of his records.

DUBAL: I think Horowitz also admired Tatum.

DICHTER: How that man could improvise! What harmonic imagination! Classically trained musicians have almost completely lost the art of improvisation. Ironically, Tatum may be in a more direct line of descent from Bach than we are. They could both improvise an eight-part fugue if they had to.

DUBAL: Do you ever compose?

DICHTER: Yes, and I took it seriously until I was about sixteen or seventeen, and I completed the first movement of a piano concerto, which meant a great deal to me. I had a very romantic image of the composer, walking in the Vienna Woods, communing with nature. But the music composed during my time hardly lent itself to this vision. I became inhibited, time passed quickly, and my concert career began to take form.

Born June 7, 1934, in Rheims, France, Entremont first received lessons from his mother and then, at the age of eight, was taken to Paris for study. At twelve he entered the Paris Conservatoire, where he studied with the celebrated pianist Jean Doyen. His official debut took place in Barcelona in 1951. In 1953 he won the Marguerite Long–Jacques Thibaud Competition. Entremont made his American debut at the National Gallery in Washington in 1953. His honors include the Netherlands' Edison Award and the Harriet Cohen Medal; he is also a Knight of the French Legion of Honor and has been awarded four Grand Prix du Disques. The city of Philadelphia, because of his annual performances with the Philadelphia Orchestra, made him Good Will Ambassador—the first nonresident to be so honored. A former president of the Ravel Academy in Saint-Jean-de-Luz, Entremont is the music director and permanent conductor of the Vienna Chamber Orchestra and the music director of the New Orleans Philharmonic.

Philippe Entremont

DUBAL: Harold Schonberg said that most French pianists incline toward elegance, facility, a shallow tone and fast tempos. Marguerite Long, your own teacher, described her school as "lucid, precise, slender." Yet I don't see your piano playing as typically French by these descriptions. Is there a French style in piano playing anymore?

ENTREMONT: I think that Schonberg's description of the French school is still accurate for some but I can give a lot of examples of great French pianists who don't at all fit that description. The greatest one of all, Alfred Cortot, was very French, and yet he doesn't in any way fit that description of the French school. And truly, you are right about me, because I don't think I fit that description either.

DUBAL: You have a big tone.

ENTREMONT: Yes, I think so, and I think I fare better in larger halls than in small halls. Which is fine for me today, since I'm more likely to play in big halls than in smaller ones. Ultimately, having a big sound is not so much a question of power, but of having a sound that carries.

DUBAL: A moment ago you said the greatest of all French pianists was Cortot, which I find very provocative. Wouldn't Cortot's playing be condemned if he played today? Wouldn't it be considered too extravagant, even sloppy?

ENTREMONT: Of course I understand what you say. But I am more fascinated by some of the old recordings of Cortot than by most of what I hear on recordings made today. Today's recordings tend to be extremely well-executed—I use the word "executed" on purpose, because sometimes it is a deadly execution—with a kind of cool perfection, and a good sound. But there is an antiseptic quality about them. Even in the realm of tempi: people are not playing as fast as they used to play years ago. They have to be reasonable, middle-of-the-road, instantly intelligible, never disturbing. I find this somewhat distressing. Pianists are not willing to take the risks they once did.

DUBAL: Is today's playing a reaction to the musical extravagance of the past?

ENTREMONT: Yes, pianists once went to extremes, so we now have the complete reverse. But some of the playing today is extremely boring. I can go to a concert and hear beautiful playing, very well balanced with beautiful sound, and there's no doubt that I am captivated by the perfection of what I hear. But when I wake up the following morning, most of what I heard the night before has not stayed with me. But that would not happen with a pianist like Cortot—even his mistakes were fabulous! Nobody has ever played the Chopin etudes the way Cortot played them. They are so immense, so gigantic. Once when I was in Yugoslavia playing a concert, I heard them on the radio in my hotel room. I was beside myself, absolutely spellbound by the courage of his playing, the nonconformity, the fabulous drive—the poetry of the music was airborne. Where is playing like that today? I could listen to those etudes every day of my life.

DUBAL: Did you ever meet Cortot?

ENTREMONT: Yes, but very briefly; I was from another "school," so to speak. My teacher was Marguerite Long, at the Conservatoire, and Cortot was the founder of his own school. So I was strongly dissuaded from going to the other place.

DUBAL: Was Long a powerful influence on your life?

ENTREMONT: Not really. But I'm very grateful for a lot of things she gave me. She was very demanding. They were teaching then in a way that would be impossible today. "You do it my way. Period!" But I was very opinionated, so we had a lot of conflict. We had some heroic fights. I was very interested in the Russian school and she was not at all. It got so bad that we separated when I was seventeen years old. And I didn't see Marguerite Long again until I was twenty-seven. We reconciled, but then she died two years later.

DUBAL: Did you take anything in particular from your lessons with her?

ENTREMONT: I think she was especially marvelous with Fauré. I learned a lot about sound with her, about Fauré, about the way of playing him. She also played Debussy very well. She knew him and played for him. She knew Ravel, too. She had given the premiere of *Le Tombeau de Couperin* as well as the Concerto in G. She was a remarkable pianist. Even at a very late age, she had what I call beautiful fingers.

DUBAL: She made a wonderful recording of the Concerto in G with Ravel conducting.

ENTREMONT: That's right. But strangely enough, she always refused to teach me the work; there was never a mention of my playing the Concerto in G. She told me, "That is *my* concerto." And she was extremely upset when I played it later on. She always said to me, "You have played my concerto *many* times."

DUBAL: So there was a little rivalry. Do you think that's typical of musicians?

ENTREMONT: No, I don't think so. For instance, the violinists are very close to one another.

DUBAL: In your judgment, is a French musician likely to play the French literature better than a musician of another nationality?

ENTREMONT: No, I'm not one to wave the nationalistic banner too much. Though we are exposed to this kind of music at a very early age. I was exposed to Ravel, Debussy, Fauré, Satie when I was very, very young, and this is definitely a help.

DUBAL: What can you tell us about your Debussy-playing?

ENTREMONT: The way I play Debussy can change from day to day because there is so much room in Debussy; it depends on the mood I am in. I can have a very heroic Debussy one day and a very subdued Debussy the next. But today it is not fashionable to play Debussy Impressionistically. A clean Debussy, with all the bones exposed, is now what is typically heard. I am not too pleased about that.

DUBAL: Do you feel as I do that Fauré has not received the recognition he is due?

ENTREMONT: Fauré is a wonderful composer, but he doesn't carry at all in a big hall. Nor is he a salon composer. This is the problem. The ideal situation is to play Fauré in a smallish hall like the Salle Gaveau in Paris. It can be marvelous. Otherwise it all evaporates.

DUBAL: Since you play worldwide, who is the most-played French composer in your experience?

ENTREMONT: I think the biggest export is Ravel, there's no doubt, followed by Debussy. Ravel is the pre-eminent internationally known French composer today. He is played and loved all over the world. And Ravel is aging extremely well. There was a time when it was said that he was imitating Debussy, but there's nothing further from the truth. And over the years we have seen Ravel eclipsing Debussy in performances. This is due to the fact that he has written some incredible orchestral masterpieces—the *Bolero, La Valse, Daphnis and Chloé,* the concerti. The brilliance of his orchestration is awesome: he was the most brilliant orchestrator of all time.

DUBAL: And, of course, the *Gaspard de la Nuit* is one of the great pieces of pianistic scoring. Every pianist attempts *Gaspard.*

ENTREMONT: Yes, if you can play *Gaspard,* you "pass the exam," so to speak.

DUBAL: You recorded the Concerto and the Capriccio of Stravinsky, which he conducted himself. What was it like to work with Stravinsky?

ENTREMONT: When you work with somebody like Stravinsky, you cannot escape a feeling of awe; you are so overwhelmed with respect and deference that you are not really yourself. I'm not sure that it is always good to know the composer—you have to keep some illusions sometimes.

DUBAL: You have recorded an immense concerto literature. Did you learn these concertos early?

ENTREMONT: At the beginning of my career, I was asked to make many recordings, especially of concerti. This forced me to build a very large repertoire and I am very grateful for that now. As a conductor I get to see the repertoire of my colleagues, and I am sometimes appalled at how small it is. And they all play the same thing. They always have the same six concerti.

DUBAL: Do you ever tell these colleagues that this is not good for music?

ENTREMONT: Yes, but I don't think they care that much. They just want to play their Tchaikovsky First Concerto, not knowing or caring that he also wrote two others which are delightful.

DUBAL: What happened to the great French piano industry now that Pleyel, Erard and Gaveau are gone?

ENTREMONT: It doesn't exist anymore, sad to say. I think, again, it's a reflection of the times. There was a time when the French were buying pianos the way the Japanese are buying them today. Everyone had to buy a piano. But after World War II it was a difficult time, especially in Europe, and the money wasn't there to buy instruments. The war killed the French piano industry and it was never able to be revived.

DUBAL: Do you think the electronics industry has hurt the piano industry in some ways?

ENTREMONT: Yes, the record industry made the amateur musician lazy. Instead of being forced to play music themselves, it became very easy to put a recording on the machine. I am convinced of this—I would have done the same thing. Besides, people today don't have time as they once had. People do not take the time to live anymore. We now have television. People are looking at "The Thorn Birds." I was giving a concert the other day, and my God, everyone was in such a hurry to get home to see the end of this TV series. It's just dreadful. Nor do people read as much as they once did. Everything is sports and beer.

DUBAL: Since people are more oriented toward listening than playing these days, has the concert audience expanded?

ENTREMONT: Yes, I think the audience is growing and that's good. It is part of entertainment. The same way people like to see a good baseball or football team, they like to hear good piano playing. If you consider the number of pianists who are playing today, and who are making big careers, the field is certainly bigger than it was fifty years ago. There is more opportunity than there has ever been in the piano world.

DUBAL: And yet there are also many schools of music with hundreds of graduates coming out each year with nowhere to go.

ENTREMONT: Yes, that is the irony.

DUBAL: As a result of this problem, would you discourage many young people from entering conservatories? Would you encourage them to play for their own pleasure, instead?

ENTREMONT: I would try to discourage all but the very gifted from going to the conservatory today, because the competition is very fierce. Though I happen to think the spirit of competition in the music schools is too strong. Everyone is concerned with outdoing everyone else, and this is at the expense of the music. We are not making music-lovers in music schools today. Most of them remind me of General Motors more than anything else. They are only interested in the product. If I have to say something to young musicians, I would say, Don't always learn the piano—learn another instrument. For instance, there is a real shortage of good string players today. We are desperate for good string players in orchestras today. There's nothing wrong with being an orchestra musician. If you love music, this can be a really terrific career. There are too many piano students. What are they going to do later on? They are like rabbits proliferating.

DUBAL: How does one sustain a career?

ENTREMONT: There are so many things involved—talent, patronage, luck. If young artists in the conservatory realized what they were up against, I am sure they would do something else, right away. Because the average piano student at the conservatory has about as much chance of becoming an internationally known pianist as being the President of the United States.

DUBAL: As a pianist who conducts a great deal, do you find that your conducting interferes with your playing?

ENTREMONT: No, I am very fortunate. That was one of my concerns in the beginning. I had some muscular problems in the early stage of my career as a conductor. But that has disappeared entirely. After conducting a two-hour concert, even on a day when I have two rehearsals, I can sit down and play without any problem.

DUBAL: Have you ever been bored by the piano? What made you want to conduct?

ENTREMONT: No, no, I was never bored, but in my case, the piano led me to the orchestra. The piano is the most wonderful instrument. You can play ten notes together because you have ten fingers. And the range of the keyboard is immense.

DUBAL: Indeed, it is higher and lower than the orchestra's range.

ENTREMONT: Yes, this is absolutely amazing. I think pianists are very well equipped to be conductors, though it is very fashionable to say that a pianist cannot be a great conductor. My goodness, just look at the list of pianists who are conductors: Karajan, George Szell, Bernstein and Solti are all pianists.

DUBAL: And, of course Liszt, Mendelssohn and von Bülow were among the first modern conductors.

ENTREMONT: That's right. Pianists are generally excellent musicians, probably due to the large repertoire. Composers often express themselves best through their piano or chamber music.

DUBAL: Can you give me some very quick impressions of the music of a few composers: Chopin, Schumann, Ravel, Scriabin?

ENTREMONT: Chopin is generally difficult. Schumann can be very weird and awkward technically. I hate the finales of Schumann. His dotted rhythms drive me crazy. I think his rhythmic obsession is part of his madness. Ravel pushed the technique of the piano to the limit, and yet his music is never unplayable.

DUBAL: What about Scriabin, a composer I believe you never play?

ENTREMONT: There you touch a very sore subject. He's the only composer I can't stand. I never could. For me, his work is sick. I can't take it.

DUBAL: Yet his fellow countryman Rachmaninoff is a favorite of yours.

ENTREMONT: Rachmaninoff is fabulous. So well-written, so grand, and yet so easily dismissed. I think we are very unfair to Rachmaninoff. I remember a conversation I had with Zino Francescatti a very long time ago. I told him I tired of playing the Rachmaninoff concertos. And Zino said, "Don't ever say that. We violinists would be so glad to have had a violin concerto by Rachmaninoff."

DUBAL: How do you react to Prokofiev's piano music?

ENTREMONT: I think it's wild. Very exciting, witty, notey.

DUBAL: Too many notes?

ENTREMONT: It wouldn't hurt to drop a few. I think his piano works are extremely well written, but extremely difficult.

DUBAL: And what is your opinion of Bartók?

ENTREMONT: He is wonderful—maybe the best composer of the twentieth century.

DUBAL: Who is the pianist who influenced you most?

ENTREMONT: I think Rubinstein, because I had the possibility to hear him when I was young. I have always been very close to Rubinstein's playing because of his enthusiasm and his grand style, which was not always careful, but never indifferent. He had an extraordinary *joie de vivre*. Here was a man in love with what he was doing. His death made me very sad.

DUBAL: The other great pianist we lost recently was Glenn Gould.

ENTREMONT: Yes, Glenn's death was so very tragic . . . I loved his sound. It was a very particular sound, and his finger articulation was remarkable—it could not be imitated. He was unique, a phenomenon, one of a kind. Among the young musicians of today there is too much imitation. I recently asked a young French pianist who came to see me about her conception of interpretation. She very frankly replied by saying that she listened to a lot of recordings, and if a phrase pleased her from Brendel she would take it and try to do what he does, and if a phrase pleased her from Weissenberg she would take it and try to do the same. This means she has nothing to say. You cannot be successful at imitation; it is the death of music. Music must be an expression of your own feelings. Your interpretation has to be your own. You can't worry about what people say, whether they are friends or newspaper critics.

DUBAL: Do newspaper critics contribute anything to the vitality of concert life?

ENTREMONT: That is a very difficult question to answer. I do not think it is an easy thing to be a music critic. I feel sorry for them most of the time. They are not liked by the artists, or even by their readers most of the time. Nor are the readers today as influenced by the critics as they once were. Often, after I read the reviews of a concert I've been to I've said, "My God, could we have been in the same hall?" I have gotten extremely good reviews for concerts that I was not too keen on; and extremely bad reviews for concerts that I thought went very well. This used to make me furious. But now I have reached an age where it doesn't mean anything to me. If they are not happy, too bad for them.

DUBAL: How do you feel about playing in countries whose governments you disapprove of?

ENTREMONT: I have always said that if I had to stop playing in countries of whose government I am critical I would be all but unemployed.

DUBAL: In other words, artists should have no territory except art. They should be citizens of the world.

ENTREMONT: Yes, the best peace movement is through art. Let us exchange artists instead of threats. Music, truly, is the international language of peace.

DUBAL: How do the pressures of your concert schedule affect your personal life?

ENTREMONT: To be a pianist involves many sacrifices, but they have to be made. I am very grateful to have been blessed with a talent, and I have an obligation to it. But the joy that I get from what I do is extraordinary. I never think of it as work. It's true, my schedule affects my private life, but nothing is perfect. People think the life of a touring musician is glamorous. They don't realize the enormous amount of work involved, the incredible toll on the nerves. You have to have nerves of steel to succeed today. Because of jet travel we are expected to be on stage almost every night. This can be exhausting. But let me tell you, the only fun we have, and the only joy we have, is when we are on stage.

DUBAL: So the stage becomes your home.

ENTREMONT: Yes, it is where I belong.

Born February 11, 1912, in Napajedlá, Moravia, Firkušný toured Europe as a concert pianist from 1928 to 1938, playing his U.S. debut at Town Hall in 1938. He has played throughout the U.S. with every major orchestra, and has toured South and Central America, Australia, New Zealand, Israel and Japan. He has had a lifelong interest in Czech music—from Dussek to Martinů; and has become the pre-eminent Czech pianist of the century. He is on the faculty of the Juilliard School.

Rudolf Firkušný

DUBAL: How old were you when you went to study with the great composer Leoš Janáček?

FIRKUŠNÝ: I was exactly five years old when I met him and he was about sixty.

DUBAL: Only five?

FIRKUŠNÝ: Yes, only five. When my father died my mother decided to move to Brno, the biggest city in Moravia. I was only three years old at that time but I had already started to flirt with the piano, though in a very simple, not knowledgeable way. But when we came to Brno I was desperately eager to find a teacher who would teach me. Nobody wanted to accept me because they thought I was much too young, and so they told my mother I should wait until I went to school. So I learned on my own. Soon, though, I found one teacher who taught me some elementary things, but after a few lessons I wasn't satisfied with him so I left and continued to play my own way. I remembered what I heard in the Sunday concerts, the little bands in the parks. I went home and improvised a bit from what came in my mind. Soon the word went around that there is this little boy in town who had some talent.

DUBAL: Was there nobody musical in your family?

FIRKUŠNÝ: Nobody. My mother was not musical, so she didn't know what to do with me. But soon someone said to her, "Look, it seems that this boy has true talent, and I think somebody should hear him and decide if this is so. I will arrange for him to meet Janáček." My mother was a little bit worried because Janáček had a reputation for being a very impatient and often difficult man, and so it was with real trepidation that we went to Mr. Janáček. And do you know what? He was wonderful. I loved him from the moment I walked in the room. I still see it like it was yesterday. He gave me a very tough examination, playing all kinds of very complicated chords, which I immediately named. Then he touched my head and felt around the contours of my skull.

DUBAL: Was he a phrenologist?

FIRKUŠNÝ: Yes, he believed that there was a particular formation of the head for a musical disposition. And then he said, "Now, play for me." So I played. And I had the nerve to play my own version of the little chorus from his opera *Jenůfa*—from the last act, when the girls are singing before the marriage. I think he was touched by this naive gesture. Then I played the Eighth *Slavonic Dance* by Dvořák, in my own way. To that Janáček said, "My boy, it is fine, but . . ." and he went to the piano and played it three or four times faster than I had, which is the way it should have been played. He then told my mother, "If you trust me, and if you will do exactly what I have in my mind, I will take the responsibility of guiding his education." He then found a piano teacher for me, and he himself taught me elementary theory and composition. He also insisted that I receive a general education. That was one of the conditions; the other was that I not be exploited as a child prodigy. And so we started to have this wonderful relationship. I think he had a special affection for me, because he lost his son when he was a baby and his daughter also. He had the most extraordinary patience with me. He was terribly kind, and he never looked down on me. There was never baby talk; it was always to the point. And of course with the passing years, the relationship became deeper and more interesting.

DUBAL: It sounds like Janáček was your spiritual father.

FIRKUŠNÝ: I would say he was. He even helped me get some means of support for my education—we were not well off financially. I have recently received from Czechoslovakia some letters he wrote in my behalf, of which I am very proud—letters recommending me for some stipends and so forth. Janáček and I had a wonderful relationship which lasted practically until his death. I saw him for the last time in June of 1928 and he died in August.

DUBAL: When did you begin studying with Vilém Kurz, the most famous piano teacher in Czechoslovakia?

FIRKUŠNÝ: When I was around seven or eight, Janáček told me, "I don't think it would be such a good idea for you to go to Kurz now, you should study with his wife first. She is also a very fine piano teacher, who teaches the same way he does. I feel this would be better for you now because a woman has more feeling and understanding than a man." And God knows, he was very right. Kurz, however, was supervising me from the beginning. So I was actually working with both of them, but only later did I become 100 percent a student of Kurz. He was an excellent teacher who understood the mechanics of the piano, but he was also a very difficult and demanding man—sometimes not so helpful psychologically. When I started to develop my own personality, he couldn't accept it. He was too much the professor. It had to be done his way, or it was no good. So we finally parted.

DUBAL: What was it like to study with Schnabel?

FIRKUŠNÝ: Schnabel was a completely different experience, though I must say that when I came to him, I was already a so-called finished product. The lessons were really discussions of music—it was a completely different approach. Kurz wanted to teach you how to play the instrument, and this he did very well. But Schnabel opened up wonderful new possibilities for me with respect to the music itself. And one didn't need to always agree with everything he said. He encouraged me to think for myself in new and different ways.

DUBAL: When you were growing up in Moravia, which pianist first showed you what the piano was capable of?

FIRKUŠNÝ: I had heard many great pianists such as Emil von Sauer, who possessed great charm and elegance in his playing. But hearing Rachmaninoff for the first time was a tremendous discovery for me; then I knew what the piano could do. He was such a strong personality as an artist that somehow everything he played was quite different from what we had known before. The same was true when Horowitz came to Prague for the first time. Again I realized what could be achieved on the piano—it was a revelation.

DUBAL: The first time I ever heard you play was in Cleveland with George Szell, in the Beethoven Fourth Concerto. When did you first meet him?

FIRKUŠNÝ: Shortly after Hitler took over in Germany, I had decided to study with Artur Schnabel, who had left Germany for Italy, where he continued his classes. There I met George Szell, but there was little opportunity to talk. So you can imagine my surprise when, back in Prague, Szell telephoned and asked me if I would play with him the Dvořák Concerto. I told him, "But Mr. Szell, you've never heard me play!" He answered, "What Schnabel told me about you is good enough for me." Of course I was thrilled. And so we played, and from the very first moment we established a wonderful kind of musical relationship.

DUBAL: Did you become personal friends?

FIRKUŠNÝ: He was a wonderful friend to me through the years. I very often turned to him for advice and ideas. People were sometimes frightened of him because he was so uncompromising and hard on himself. And he expected the same from others. But personally, I never found him difficult in a way that would be considered unpleasant. If he liked you, one could only benefit from knowing him, and of course making music with him was a tremendous inspiration. Also, he would never say, at least with me, "Unless you do it my way, it's wrong."

DUBAL: How does one retain individuality and respect for the composer at the same time?

FIRKUŠNÝ: I think that every interpreter has full rights, unless the artist does something which is absolutely contrary to the composer's wishes. As Bruno Walter once said to me, the performer must drive the music the way Misha drove his sled in *The Brothers Karamazov* when he said, "Now I am driving!" In fact, I think composers are often ambivalent about their own intentions. And I do not think they cling so dearly to every dot and dash of the score as we think they do. I remember Janáček would like something one way one day, and the next day he would say, "No, I think I would like it done this way!" I also studied composition with Josef Suk, who was also a member of the Bohemian String Quartet. One day the quartet was to play for Brahms one of his works, and Brahms detected their nervousness. Just as they were preparing to play Brahms said, "It's already too fast!" This somehow broke the spell, and after that all went well. When they were finished they asked him for his suggestions, but he would only say, "No, my friends, just keep playing as beautifully as you just have." So you see, composers are not all so terribly harsh on the performers.

DUBAL: Certainly composers are not always the best interpreters of their own music.

FIRKUŠNÝ: That's right. I remember doing the premiere of the Howard Hanson Piano Concerto with Hanson conducting. It was fine, but later when I played it with Stokowski, I was amazed at the magic he brought to the score, something the composer could not manage.

DUBAL: As a performer, do you find that there is a gap between what you realize musically onstage and off?

FIRKUŠNÝ: Music lives by its performance, not by recording, because a recording is always the same, no matter how wonderful it is—it doesn't change. But live performance is ever-changing, sometimes better, sometimes not so good. But it lives. For me, I don't always feel I am getting across what I am aiming for while on stage. It's more difficult to play for the public. I think Arthur Rubinstein was different there. You felt that it gave him joy to create on stage. In my case, it is easier to get what I am after when I play for myself. But whenever we play we are reaching for the untouchable.

DUBAL: Are you able to get what you want in recording?

FIRKUŠNÝ: With recordings, sometimes you feel sorry that you have to leave something as it is, which you may not like years or even months later. So you try to play correctly, so at the very least you are not ashamed of the results.

DUBAL: Is there any music that you love that does not fit your hand?

FIRKUŠNÝ: Oh, yes, definitely. I love many composers which I don't play at all—Scriabin for example. My hands are just too small for his music. I can only take a tenth, and not always comfortably.

DUBAL: You have long been a champion of the late Czech composer Bohuslav Martinů. On a recent New York recital, you played his massive *Fantasy Toccata*.

FIRKUŠNÝ: It is a good piece, yes?

DUBAL: Excellent. Why is this composer not quite given his due?

FIRKUŠNÝ: Personally, I feel Martinů was a wonderful composer, but perhaps he wrote too much. He left us a tremendous number of compositions but not all of them are of the same caliber, although they are all beautifully crafted.

DUBAL: Another Czech composer whose piano music is seldom heard is Smetana.

FIRKUŠNÝ: Yes, and it's very odd because it's so pianistic; such beautiful music. Do you know Smetana's operas? People claim they are naive, but many operas are naive. I think the music is beautiful and should be heard.

DUBAL: Do you think concerts have the same importance today as they did before records and radio?

FIRKUŠNÝ: Unfortunately, art is no longer sacred. When I was growing up, the concert was something very special. It was a tremendously important affair, almost like a holiday. We would live in anticipation of this great event. But today we can go home and listen to everything Beethoven or Chopin ever wrote with no effort at all. If we are not careful, music can lose its meaning.

Born July 23, 1928, in San Francisco, California, Fleisher gave his first public recital at the age of six. When he was ten, Schnabel heard him and was so impressed that he broke his rule of never accepting pupils under sixteen. In 1943 he made his official San Francisco Symphony debut under Pierre Monteux and in 1944 he made his New York Philharmonic debut. At the age of twenty-four he won the prestigious Queen Elisabeth of Belgium Competition. He gave the New York premiere of the Leon Kirchner Concerto, which had been written for him, in 1964. Later that year, his right hand became inoperative. However, he continued to play left-hand works, and embarked on a rather extensive conducting career, becoming associate conductor of the Baltimore Symphony in 1973. For many years Fleisher has taught at the Peabody Conservatory in Baltimore, Maryland.

Leon Fleisher

DUBAL: When did you come to the piano?

FLEISHER: When my parents bought an upright piano for my older brother, who was four and a half years older. I was the one who seemed to have an aptitude for it, though.

DUBAL: Were you a child prodigy?

FLEISHER: I suppose so. But I had very good early teaching. I studied with Alfred Hertz, who was the conductor of the San Francisco Symphony before Monteux. Hertz created the WPA orchestra there in the mid-Thirties.

DUBAL: Did he engage you to play with him?

FLEISHER: Yes. I was eight years old when I did some school concerts with the WPA orchestra. From the first second up there with the orchestra, it was sheer exhilaration. Oh, I loved it—that give and take.

DUBAL: What were the first concerti that you played?

FLEISHER: The Beethoven Second, the Mendelssohn G minor and, oh, yes, the seldom-played G major Konzertstück of Schumann.

DUBAL: Who was the most famous pianist to come to San Francisco when you were a child?

FLEISHER: I remember, when I was six or seven, Rachmaninoff came to San Francisco for a recital. When the program was over, my mother rushed me backstage. I think she felt that if you touched such a genius, some of it would rub off. So here I was backstage, as Rachmaninoff began giving encores. I remember being quite astounded that he walked from the wings of the stage to the piano and back very slowly and deliberately, but the moment he was offstage he moved very quickly. That made a big impression on me. Suddenly, in between encores, he came over to me, he peered way down at me and asked, "Are you a pianist?" And I looked up at this Empire State Building of a figure, and I nodded my head. He then shook his head and said, "Bad business."

DUBAL: He was probably fed up with the endless travel and inconvenience. Once at a train station a friend of his asked, "When will you be home?" He pointed at the railroad car and answered dejectedly, "This is my home."

FLEISHER: Yes, it can get to you, year in and year out. It's terribly stressful to go from one imperfect situation to another, lousy piano, noisy audiences, drafts—you name it. It's not your typical job.

DUBAL: During those early years did you come to the attention of Monteux?

FLEISHER: Oh, yes, and Monteux and Hertz both felt that my next step was to study with Artur Schnabel. It was actually Hertz who contacted Schnabel on my behalf.

DUBAL: You were certainly very young to be studying with one of the great musicians of the century.

FLEISHER: Yes, imagine I came to him when I was nine years old, and worked with him for ten years. I was terribly lucky.

DUBAL: Did anyone else ever have that much contact with him?

FLEISHER: I think there were a few who had almost the same exposure. Possibly Claude Frank saw him even more, and also Leonard Shure.

DUBAL: Being so young, did you usually understand what Schnabel was getting at?

FLEISHER: In the beginning I didn't know what was going on in an intellectual way. But over the years, his sound, his thoughts and his reverence and love for great music seeped in. It all remains with me as a standard to constantly subscribe to and reach for. Being with Schnabel was the most profound experience imaginable. He had a kind of cosmic passion.

DUBAL: How did he treat his young student?

FLEISHER: Wonderfully—for me he had a kind of fatherly image; he had beautiful twinkling blue eyes. He loved to smile and he was always playing word games. He was full of humor, wit and joy.

DUBAL: Schnabel certainly changed the way a lot of musicians thought about music.

FLEISHER: I think so, and very deeply, too. Probably Schnabel and Toscanini were two of the most important influences on performing in this century. They counteracted that horrible nineteenth-century trend in which the performer became more important than the music. If the score said *piano* and the player wanted to play it *forte,* then he played it *forte,* and so forth. Both Schnabel and Toscanini brought back fidelity to the text. Not just a dry fidelity, but an alive, impassioned re-creation, in which the reality of the text becomes your base of operation.

DUBAL: To think that Schnabel was once branded by some as cold and cerebral.

FLEISHER: Yes, that would be a total misunderstanding of him. But there were people who brushed him aside and labeled him a dry intellectual player.

DUBAL: Today when we listen to a Schnabel record we are awed by his overwhelming passion. How ears can change!

FLEISHER: Yes, they can. . . .

DUBAL: What in his discography immediately comes to mind?

FLEISHER: This moment I'm thinking of a late recording, the A minor Mozart Sonata. How did he achieve the warmth, fullness and passion in that first movement, without for a second breaking the incredibly fine framework of the Mozartian texture and style? Another record of his I love is much older, the Bach *Italian Concerto*. In the slow movement Schnabel achieves wonders of human re-creation. It is absolutely unbelievable, the vision of it. How he manifested it all in sound, the way he brought it all into being. Words are a very poor thing for such a description. But there are those who can pick up a bunch of black dots on a piece of paper and inspire the world.

DUBAL: Did Schnabel ever speak to you about the interpreter's place or mission?

FLEISHER: Schnabel likened the function of the interpreter-performer to that of the Alpine mountain guide: "He's indispensable in getting you to the top of the mountain, but only so you can enjoy the view."

DUBAL: Can the word "genius" be applied to a pianist or other re-creative artist?

FLEISHER: Yes, there are some who possess that quality within the realm of re-creation. The rare artist with the clarity of vision and individuality that Schnabel, Glenn Gould or Lipatti had.

DUBAL: Poulenc called Lipatti an artist of "divine spirituality."

FLEISHER: He had a vision, and his conceptions always proved inevitable. I never felt that Lipatti went through agonies of indecision, that he thought "I'll try it this way for a while, and if it doesn't work, I'll do it another way." Lipatti's music-making went so directly and unequivocally to the heart of the music.

DUBAL: How did William Kapell affect you? His intensity always thrilled me.

FLEISHER: Without question Willy was the greatest pianistic talent this country ever produced. His raw talent was awesome. He had little time on this earth, but very few used it like he did. He started out with the big success pieces, like the Khatchaturian, Rachmaninoff and Prokofiev concertos, but at the end he was coming around to Schubert's posthumous sonatas.

DUBAL: Kapell died at thirty-one, while Rubinstein, who also loved Kapell's playing, lived to ninety-six. Was there ever a career in any performing art to compare with his?

FLEISHER: No, nothing like it. He was a figure of enormous hope, though he was not truly focused until he was around forty-five, when he really began to be the artist he would become. He was a man of elegance, refinement and yet boldness of spirit and nobility of heart. A modern giant.

DUBAL: When did you first encounter George Szell, whose concerto performances with you have become legendary?

FLEISHER: I was twelve or thirteen when I received as a birthday present the Brahms D minor, recorded by Schnabel with Szell conducting. It just knocked me out! Soon I started fantasizing that someday I would play with Szell. He had become to me a kind of Norse god figure. Then one day in 1942, maybe '43, I was at a concert in New York. Schnabel was there and called me over to introduce me to a man with the palest blue eyes behind silver-rimmed glasses. Those eyes just pierced you. Schnabel then said, "I want you to meet George Szell." I had kept alive my fantasy of playing with him and, lo and behold, when I was seventeen or eighteen I was engaged to play at Ravinia. It was the Brahms D minor and Szell was to be the conductor. That was one of my great experiences. Later, I was his very first soloist when he took over the Cleveland Orchestra in 1947. We did the Schumann Concerto.

DUBAL: For more than eighteen years a muscular problem in your right hand has kept you away from the two-hand repertory. It must have been a glorious moment when last season you played the Franck *Symphonic Variations*.

FLEISHER: It was a great joy. But in a sense it was like walking on egg shells, terrifying and exhilarating at once. I was only at about 60 percent of what I need to be and want to be. I'm still not ready to go at it regularly. When it happens, it'll happen. In the meantime, my doctors, I feel, are doing great things.

DUBAL: I'm sure you are tired of people saying, "When are you going to play the *Emperor Concerto* again?"

FLEISHER: No, not really, because *I* think in those terms, so it's not surprising that others might think or ask that, too.

DUBAL: You don't seem to be the least bit bitter at having been deprived of the full use of your hands.

FLEISHER: Not being able to play with two hands has had a terribly profound affect on my life in many fundamental ways. But fortunately I was able to get into conducting, and through that I've had some of the most gratifying experiences of my life. I've learned enormously about music through conducting. If you allow it to, good can come out of most any situation.

DUBAL: Have you been frustrated at not being able to learn some of the works you hadn't gotten to?

FLEISHER: Oh, yes, but, in a way, that's been compensated for by teaching, which keeps me in touch with these works all the time.

DUBAL: Emerson said "Art is a jealous mistress." Have you ever felt tied down or captive to the piano's demands?

FLEISHER: Yes, I have. Besides the problems of delving to the heart of the music, there is the constant problem of reproducing it at a consistently acceptable professional level. Which means keeping your muscles and technical mechanism in good enough order to do some very extraordinary things. That takes great blocks of time.

DUBAL: You were the first American to win the Queen Elisabeth Competition in 1952. Are competitions today different from what they were then?

FLEISHER: In '52 they made a difference. But like all things that catch the public's attention, they have become overworked. In the Fifties, there were only about half a dozen major international competitions, and they had real importance. Today every other street corner has a piano competition taking place. This diminishes their significance and of course it makes it difficult for the young people who still think of the competition as the golden door. It just isn't anymore. But back in 1952, it helped me enormously.

DUBAL: There are now more pianists than ever. How does this affect your thinking about teaching?

FLEISHER: I must take the point of view that we are there to explore the music. Because if I worried for each one of them about their future I think I wouldn't be able to teach.

DUBAL: Do you think pianists are generally the best musicians among instrumentalists?

FLEISHER: It might be dangerous to say that, but I think there might be a grain of truth in it, simply from the point of view that the pianist is really the only instrumentalist that is forced to look at music vertically as well as horizontally.

DUBAL: Do you think there are any differences between the playing of men and women?

FLEISHER: No, no difference at all. I was talking with somebody at a party recently and when I mentioned the Beethoven Fourth Concerto, this person said that it was a "lady's concerto."

DUBAL: Yes, that's often been said about the Schumann Concerto, too. Also, that the Brahms B-flat is for men. If Myra Hess, who played it so massively, ever heard that, I imagine she would have been enraged.

FLEISHER: It is all absolute nonsense.

DUBAL: What is essential in the environment of a gifted young person?

FLEISHER: Exposure to creativity in all fields.

DUBAL: That puts the less wealthy at a disadvantage, doesn't it?

FLEISHER: Perhaps, but I think access to the arts is easier than ever before. One can be exposed to great music twenty-four hours a day on radio if one chooses.

DUBAL: Yes, but isn't discipline harder to achieve in the young in this age of instant communication and stimulation?

FLEISHER: It certainly is. Discipline, after exposure and encouragement, is the most important thing for the young. The greatest freedom comes from discipline. That's the really difficult thing to get across to the young and gifted person whose sensibility is on the surface, flapping in the breeze. The gifted young people want to react, and follow their feelings, and that's fine. But there must be a kind of shape to their experience. It's got to be something more than a willful, chaotic impulse.

DUBAL: I was just thinking about your *Brahms-Handel Variations,* which certainly are not willful or chaotic. It's a fantastic recording. Did you always relate to that score?

FLEISHER: There are pieces you relate to instantly, that you have no real questions or doubts about. Sure, you experiment with this or that detail, but basically you know what you want to do with it. Then there are other pieces that are just so elusive and frustrating at first that all you can do is live through the problems. Only that way can you eventually arrive at an acceptable solution. After you've suffered through these pieces, in a few years, perhaps, the light shines. Then of course you wonder, "Why didn't I see this long ago?"

DUBAL: I'm afraid the light doesn't shine often enough on contemporary music for many performers. It's so often neglected. But you have been involved with it as both pianist and conductor.

FLEISHER: I've had great satisfaction from my involvement with the Theatre Chamber Players of the Kennedy Center, where we've given at least 60 percent of our programs to contemporary music. I feel we have an absolute obligation to look at the music of today and to present that part of it which seems convincing. Even some that doesn't completely convince us on every level the way a Beethoven sonata would, but that we feel has something, some spark of originality and conviction, and maybe even staying power.

DUBAL: But so many performers feel locked out of it. They say it's too difficult, not worth the effort or unattractive to the public.

FLEISHER: To me such responses are lazy. Too difficult? What about the *Hammerklavier Sonata?* That's *very* difficult; and it takes years of preparation before you can go out and play it in some small town where the critics may never have heard it before.

DUBAL: What is the function of the critic, in your opinion?

FLEISHER: When musical criticism began it was a very important and valuable thing—the composers themselves were writing about the direction the music was taking.

DUBAL: Yes, Weber, Schumann, Berlioz, Debussy were all great critics, along with the latest in that noble line, Virgil Thomson.

FLEISHER: Yes, they were splendid. Today most critics are former gardening or fashion editors.

DUBAL: How do you feel about people bringing scores to a concert?

FLEISHER: I don't like it. It's distracting. I really don't think they hear the music at all. All they hear is slower, faster, louder or softer. They're not really listening. They have no comprehensive musical or spiritual experience.

DUBAL: What does art do for us?

FLEISHER: It takes us out of ourselves into a dimension of higher awareness. It is a way of connecting with the universe, with that which is beyond.

Born in Toronto, Canada, September 25, 1932, Glenn Gould, who died in Toronto on October 4, 1982, was the greatest Canadian pianist in history. He studied with Alberto Guerrero at the Royal Conservatory of Music in Toronto and graduated at the age of twelve, the youngest student ever to do so. He made his official debut with the Toronto Symphony at thirteen. Gould played his first U.S. recital in Washington, D.C., January 2, 1955, to sensational press, then made his New York debut at Town Hall three weeks later. Glenn Gould's first continental tour of the U.S. took place in 1956–1957, followed in 1957 by his European debut with the Berlin Philharmonic under Herbert von Karajan. At the age of thirty-two he left the concert stage, never to return; but he continued to record prolifically, leaving ninety LPs. A flood of articles, interviews, and radio and television documentaries are also a part of his legacy.

Glenn Gould

Glenn Gould

DON HUNSTEIN/COURTESY OF CBS RECORDS

DUBAL: It seems many pianists are compulsive practicers but as afraid of approaching the piano as they are of leaving it. You have stated that you do not necessarily "practice" the piano. Do you separate the idea of practice from the idea of playing?

GOULD: Well, quite frankly I'm at a loss to understand the compulsiveness that accompanies the notion of practice—that—in effect, most view as an appropriate relationship to the instrument. I've talked about this frequently, to be sure, and I'm in some considerable danger of repeating myself, but to me the relationship to the piano—to any instrument, really, but I can only speak of the piano with first-hand authority—which involves some sort of tactile servitude, which demands six or eight or ten hours a day of kinetic contact, which seems to need, for example, backstage pianos at the ready so that, presumably, one can reassure oneself that one's relationship to the instrument remains secure before one walks on stage is simply beyond my ken. I couldn't even begin to emphasize how far from my own experience—my own belief—if you like—such a relationship really is.

Let me tell you a story. When I was a child, I was profoundly mystified by the fact that most of the editions, even the best ones, in circulation at that time—Bischoff's Bach, say, or Schnabel's Beethoven—contained, among other indulgences, fingerings. I would look at those fingerings, even try them out on occasion, and find that they rarely corresponded to what I had been doing or wanted to do. And I was always amazed that people were actually paid to sit there and add extraneous, perhaps erroneous (and in many cases mischievous) data to a fugue or a sonata.

Well, I still am, I can't really get over it. For me, a fingering is something which springs spontaneously to mind when one looks at a score, and is altered, if at all, when a shift of emphasis alters the way of looking at the score.

I've had occasion to relay this astonishment to various people—usually in conversations such as this—and I've always sensed from interlocutors, at the very least, a tacit skepticism, something along the lines of "Why don't you tell us another whopper?"

Well, over those years, and despite my insistence that I had never, to the best of my recollection, entered a fingering of any kind in a score, I began to doubt the story myself. I began to wonder if perhaps it wasn't just a little too good to be true (or too negligible, depending on your point of view). Well, anyway, about six months ago I came across a cache of scores and various memorabilia from my teens and pre-teens. And one of the earliest was the score from which I learned the Fourth Beethoven Concerto—the first concerto I ever played with orchestra.

It wasn't actually the first concerto that I ever learned—that was the Mozart *Coronation*—but, as I say, it provided the material for my orchestra debut. That took place when I was thirteen.

Well, the score was dog-eared beyond the aspirations of even the most bedraggled mutt. Any number of pages had been ripped and spliced with Scotch Tape, and there were a number of mysterious six-figure codes written in the margins and on the front and back covers. These puzzled me at first, until I remembered that in those days Toronto had not yet expanded to seven-digit telephone numbers and that these were, in fact, the home phones of classmates and school friends.

Anyway, I looked through it—every page—and it was a spooky experience. Quite frankly, I'd not have been surprised to find maybe a half dozen fingerings, presumably in troublesome spots, or perhaps a few descriptive words of admonition inspired by my teacher's comments. You know the sort of thing one sees in students' and sometimes even in professionals' scores: "Move gently forward, ritard gracefully, become suddenly agitated, ethereal calm"—all that sort of nonsense.

Well, there was nothing, not a word, not a fingering, no sign, apart from the clipped pages and the Scotch Tape and the phone numbers, to show that that score had ever been visited by human hand, and this, mind you, was a score that had played a very important part in my early life—a score that I probably spent more hours practicing—if you can call playing along with Schnabel's records with Frederick Stock and the Chicago Symphony practicing—than any work of comparable size before or since.

Well, I've delivered myself of this anecdote only because it perhaps suggests that my notion of how to go about practicing the piano always was a bit unorthodox. What was less unorthodox in those days was the amount of time I actually spent at the instrument per day. I never set myself time limits or anything (other than those limits imposed by the fact that I was going to school, and homework had to be accommodated, too) but it feels like something on the order of three hours a day or so would not be an exaggeration. Frankly, I don't know how I stood it, but it was the only period in my life when I had what might be thought of as a relatively regular and, by my standards, rigorous practice schedule—not surprising, really, in view of the fact that that was when one was forming a repertoire and going through new pieces for the first time.

Now, to bring matters up to date. These days and throughout my professional life, indeed, I've practiced only on an if-, as- and when-needed basis, and only for the purpose of consolidating a conception of a score—never for the sake of contact with the instrument per se. I'll give you an example. The most recent recording I've made as of the date of this interview is the Brahms Op. 10—the four ballades. I recorded them three weeks ago in New York. It happens that I'd never played them before—not even sight-read them—and, apart from the "*Edward*" Ballade, the first one in the set, the one a good many of my conservatory colleagues used to essay, I'd never even heard them played until I decided to record them (what that says about my playing of piano repertoire I'll leave for you to decide).

Now, as it happens, I made that decision about two months before the recording was done and for approximately the next six weeks I studied the score from time to time, and developed a very clear conception of how I wanted to approach the ballades. I found the last one, for example, particularly difficult, particularly hard to get a handle on. It's very beautiful in its way—hymnal almost, and what endears it to me is that it is one of those relatively few works where Brahms lets his imagination—a sort of stream-of-consciousness process really—prevail over his sense of design, of architecture. But for that very reason it's difficult to bring off. I did feel at last that I had found an acceptable tempo. But as for playing them, I spent only the last two weeks at the keyboard and, unlike the experiences of my youth, which I'm now hazy about, I can tell you almost exactly how much time I spent because, in recent years, I've taken to clocking myself at the piano—no sense in overdoing things and all that. Anyway, as is customary for me before a recording session, it averaged one hour a day. There were a couple of occasions when I doubled that because I perhaps had to be absent for an editing session, or whatever, on the following day, but that one hour gave me the opportunity to play through the ballades twice on each occasion (they're almost exactly half an hour in length) and think about the conceptual changes I wanted to make.

Now, those conceptual changes were reinforced, needless to say, by running the ballades through in my head many dozens of times when driving along in the car or conducting them in my studio. It's amazing—the least time spent was during the practice period as well as during the six weeks or so prior to the recording. Anyway, the recording sessions have now been over for three weeks and I haven't touched a piano since then. Moreover, at the moment I'm into a period of editing and mixing and other extra-pianistic, if not necessarily extra-musical, endeavors, and I don't plan to record again for approximately two months—more Brahms—the rhapsodies. When I do, in due course the whole process will begin again and I fully expect to cap the last fortnight of that period with one-hour-a-day forays to the keyboard.

DUBAL: Do you realize that this sounds quite unbelievable?

GOULD: I do. I realize that it is contrary to common experience, but it's the truth.

DUBAL: And when you go back to the instrument after all that time, after six weeks, or eight weeks, or whatever it may be, you don't find that the fingers simply refuse to cooperate at first, that it takes a certain number of days just to reestablish coordination?

GOULD: On the contrary, when I do go back I probably play better than at any other time, purely in a physical sense, because the image, the mental image, which governs what one does is normally at that point at its strongest and its most precise because of the fact that it has not been exposed to the keyboard, and it has not, therefore, been distracted from the purity of its conception, of one's ideal relationship to the keyboard.

I'll give you a further bit of evidence for that, if you like. When I record, I deliberately cut off all contact with the piano about forty-eight hours in advance of the first session, and when I arrive at the studio I never touch the piano until the engineers are ready and somebody announces, "Take One." There are exceptions to that of course—if the piano has been under repairs, surgery of some kind—I have to find out in what way it has been changed and compensate accordingly, and for that matter make certain alterations in my coordinative allowances. But otherwise I stay as far from it as possible and, as a consequence, "Take One" is very often the best thing we do because the mental image is at that point strongest and least subject to contradiction by the reality of an improperly adjusted instrument, or whatever.

DUBAL: But this presupposes that one has a very specific and very secure conception of what is involved in playing the piano.

GOULD: Oh, absolutely. It presupposes that at some point, one has hit upon precisely the coordinates that are involved and then frozen them, stored them in such a way that one can summon them at any time. What it all comes down to is that one does not play the piano with one's fingers, one plays the piano with one's mind. If you have a clear image of what you want to do, there's no reason it should ever need reinforcement. If you don't, all the fine Czerny studies and Hanon exercises in the world aren't going to help you.

CHRISTIAN STEINER

Born October 14, 1928, in New York City, Graffman studied at the Curtis Institute from age seven and made his debut with Ormandy and the Philadelphia Orchestra at eighteen. In 1948 he won the Leventritt Competition. After a year in Europe on a Fulbright Fellowship, he returned to the U.S. to study with Horowitz and in the summers with Rudolf Serkin at the Marlboro Festival. For more than thirty years Graffman has been touring the world. He has recorded with the New York, Philadelphia, Cleveland, Boston and Chicago orchestras. His autobiography, I Really Should Be Practicing, *appeared in 1981. Graffman is on the faculty of the Curtis Institute and the Manhattan School of Music. During the last several years a hand ailment has curtailed his performing career.*

Gary Graffman

DUBAL: When you were in Kiev during your Russian tours, did you think about Horowitz and the great tradition of Russian pianists?

GRAFFMAN: Yes, I certainly did. I remember on a very hot Sunday morning after photographing the balcony of a building in which my mother spent part of her childhood, I walked past the Kiev Conservatory. All the windows were open, and I simultaneously heard pouring out of them the Rachmaninoff Third Concerto and Balakirev's *Islamey,* the *Appassionata Sonata* and the Chopin etudes, everything at once. And at that moment I thought of Horowitz. Horowitz is Russian; he spent his youth there. At that minute I felt at home.

DUBAL: Did you come from a musical family?

GRAFFMAN: My father was a violin student of the great Leopold Auer at the St. Petersburg Conservatory. I knew the whole violin repertoire by the time I was four. In my father's generation, and even in mine, to be a musician was something of great importance, and also a way to get out of the ghetto. Although there was anti-Semitism, if a Jewish child from Vilna, Odessa or wherever was very, very talented, nobody would really stand in his way. He could end up studying in St. Petersburg or Moscow, where Jews were ordinarily not allowed to live. That was the one way for the Jewish child to do better than the parent. The parent would be a tailor and the son a violinist.

DUBAL: Once the great wave of piano playing came from Central and Eastern Europe; today it comes from the Orient.

GRAFFMAN: Yes, Tokyo and Seoul and Taiwan, and the next group is going to come from mainland China.

DUBAL: From my teaching at Juilliard, I find that the Asian students are among the most highly motivated.

GRAFFMAN: Yes, they work day and night, and they're killing themselves. They're even more motivated than the eastern European pianists were. They shame their families if they don't do their best. At the last two Curtis auditions, there were about one hundred applicants and only five places. Of those five, four were Asians.

DUBAL: Curtis is where your teacher Isabelle Vengerova taught.

GRAFFMAN: Yes, she was a student of Leschetizky, and one of the great teachers of the Russian tradition.

DUBAL: One often hears about the Leschetizky method. Was that Vengerova's method?

GRAFFMAN: No, it wasn't. Methods are usually made up by the less talented students of a great teacher.

DUBAL: Speaking of the great Russian tradition, you also studied with Vladimir Horowitz. Did he ever discuss hand position with you?

GRAFFMAN: No, it was never discussed. He never commented on such non-musical things as my hand position or the way I would sit at the piano. But he showed me how he would practice things himself. When working on the Tchaikovsky B-flat minor Concerto he said, "Let me show you how I practice octaves. This works."

DUBAL: What did Horowitz tell you about pedaling?

GRAFFMAN: Horowitz is a master of pedaling in the large hall. When I played for him in his living room he asked me if I would be pedaling differently in Carnegie Hall. He then demonstrated certain pedalings that he felt appropriate to a big hall, especially the blending of harmonies. And I remember saying to him, "It sounds like the tonic and dominant are practically on the same pedal." "Yes," he replied, "but this only happens in the living room, not in the great hall."

DUBAL: Pedaling is certainly one of the trickiest aspects of piano playing.

GRAFFMAN: That's right. The variables are many. First of all, it depends on the piano—each is a different animal. Each piano reacts differently when you rest your right foot on the pedal. So you must be careful that you are not activating the mechanism by inadvertently resting on it. But with other pianos that are regulated differently or even incorrectly, you have to push the pedal three-quarters of the way down before anything even happens. Most pedaling is not a question of putting it all the way down and taking it all the way up, but it is somewhere in the middle, and that's where we get half-pedalings, three-quarter pedalings and all the blendings in between that make for the mysteriousness and individuality of pedaling.

DUBAL: I once asked Arthur Loesser, "How do you pedal?" and he said, "With my ear!"

GRAFFMAN: Loesser was absolutely right. In the final analysis, the ears have to tell you what to do.

DUBAL: The title of your autobiography, *I Really Should Be Practicing,* says so much about the pianist's dilemma. There never seems to be enough time to learn the repertoire.

GRAFFMAN: Yes, there is always something new to learn and this goes on while one is rethinking and repolishing works that you've played all your life. Some pieces demand an eternity and all we have is a lifetime. How many times has it happened that I have been learning a Mozart concerto while thinking of the ones that I still haven't played. And then, all of a sudden, out of the music case fall Fauré nocturnes, which I hadn't even thought of for ten years. I put them on the piano and say, "My God, how is it that I've never played more than one of these?"

DUBAL: In your case, with the injury to your right hand, this must have been a particularly excruciating source of frustration. Is your physical therapy achieving good results?

GRAFFMAN: Yes, it is, but unfortunately it's a slow process and I lost a lot of time by not going to the right doctors right away. In the beginning, no one bothered to examine my hand or watch me at the piano. They thought I had some kind of serious neurological disorder. I'm now being treated by doctors at Massachusetts General Hospital who are becoming specialists in the hand problems of pianists.

DUBAL: It sounds a bit like sports medicine.

GRAFFMAN: It is something like that, and a formal study is finally being made about the varied problems pianists can have with their hands. Each month more and more is learned, and what has been learned from my experience will undoubtedly help others.

DUBAL: Why do you think most pianists suffer problems in the right hand?

GRAFFMAN: I think it is because most music written since Bach has the melody in the top voice, most of the time, that is; and the top voice is played by the right hand. And on the piano, this takes place at the second octave above middle C, which is the weakest part of the piano. So from the age of six you're practicing six hours a day on the weakest part of the piano with the weakest part of your right hand: it's not hard to see how you can get inflammation of the extensors, usually involving the fourth and fifth finger of the right hand.

DUBAL: And, of course, there is lots of hard-hitting, bad practice that goes on with many pianists, too.

GRAFFMAN: Absolutely. Striking the key in a particular way or sitting in a peculiar way can have devastating results.

DUBAL: Can you pinpoint the actual moment when your problem began?

GRAFFMAN: Yes. Most people cannot, but I am almost sure about when it all started. I was playing the First Tchaikovsky Concerto with the Berlin Philharmonic and the piano didn't have enough sound. And the orchestra was playing particularly loud that night. I remember being frustrated and angry at these circumstances, and the instant I hit the piano with my fourth finger I knew it was wrong. It felt like a sprain—a "baseball finger"—and it healed in four or five weeks. But soon, in my playing, I started compensating without realizing it. I started playing octaves using the thumb and third finger. I guess I began doing this so gradually that I had no pain, and in my case the octaves came out fantastically well because the third finger is so strong. So this became a habit. And the relationship between the flexors and extensors went completely haywire. Some muscles became hyper—too strong, actually—and others atrophied—became very weak. So this is my present condition, and it certainly can be frustrating not to be able to play both Brahms concertos when you know you can play them. And nobody knows if my therapy will totally succeed or not.

DUBAL: Though you're probably playing more than you ever expected, with the left hand alone. I recently heard you in the Ravel Concerto for the Left Hand.

GRAFFMAN: Yes, and I am now looking into the rest of the left-hand repertoire. I've started to play the Prokofiev Concerto, which is quite a marvel. Did you know there are also two works for left hand by Richard Strauss? And there's a very beautiful piece by Benjamin Britten called *Diversions*. There are also five works by Franz Schmidt that I know of—three chamber works and two works for piano and orchestra, one being a concerto and the other a set of variations on a theme by Beethoven. The concerto is discussed in the concerto volume of Donald Francis Tovey's *Essays in Musical Analysis*. And a few months back there was a great surprise—out of the blue, two works by Korngold were sent to me, a concerto and a chamber work, and I think the concerto is going to be a terrific piece.

DUBAL: And was the Korngold commissioned by Paul Wittgenstein, the pianist who lost his arm in World War I, as were the Ravel and the Prokofiev?

GRAFFMAN: Yes, it was. Most everything for piano and orchestra from that period was commissioned by Wittgenstein, except Janáček's Capriccio for Piano and Orchestra.

DUBAL: Which is a tragic and marvelous work. . . . What about the solo literature for left hand?

GRAFFMAN: Well, there is a whole series by Reger, as well as six charming etudes by Saint-Saëns. Also, do you know Blumenfeld's devilishly difficult left-hand etude?

DUBAL: Oh, yes, it was often played by Simon Barère, who recorded it.

GRAFFMAN: And, of course, there are the two glorious pieces by Scriabin, the Op. 9 Prelude and Nocturne, which he himself wrote when he injured his right hand. And although I haven't gone into them yet, Godowsky has made transcriptions of twenty or so of the Chopin etudes for the left hand alone, as well as some original works, too. And as long as we're discussing this repertoire, I should also mention the Reinecke Sonata and the Brahms transcription of the Bach Chaconne.

DUBAL: Going back to the two-hand solo literature, what are your thoughts on the *Brahms-Paganini Variations,* which you have recorded?

GRAFFMAN: It is surely the *tour de force* of the Brahms solo literature. It is written for a large hand, though, and mine are a little smaller than average, so I had to work terribly hard on the first two variations of Book I, which are not necessarily the most difficult parts of the work, but for my hands they were. The *Brahms-Paganini Variations* is a pianist's work—only a pianist can understand the tortures. It is much harder than it sounds. I really wonder if Brahms himself could actually play it. Fortunately, in public it's impossible to prevent an audience from applauding after Book I, so you're given a rest. Thank God!

DUBAL: Another piece of legendary difficulty that you have recorded is Balakirev's *Islamey*.

GRAFFMAN: *Islamey* takes only eight minutes, but in the time it takes to learn it, you could learn three Beethoven sonatas.

DUBAL: How did you come to it?

GRAFFMAN: My friend Schuyler Chapin, who was at Columbia Records at the time, told me to look into it, that it was a piece that would suit me very well. And so I did. But one should only play *Islamey* if you have a feeling for Russian music. As a work of piano scoring, it is sensational.

DUBAL: What constitutes a good audience piece from your point of view?

GRAFFMAN: Liszt had a great instinct for writing for the audience. A work like *La Campanella,* even in a terrible performance, brings the house down. I should know: I've played that piece in concert literally hundreds of times. If I tried to leave it out they'd shout "*Campanella!*" And think of the two Liszt concertos. A great performance of a Brahms concerto will make the audience responsive, but all it takes is a mediocre performance of a Liszt concerto to elicit the same response.

DUBAL: Do you have any advice about repertoire for young students?

GRAFFMAN: Most definitely. They should learn as early as possible the Chopin etudes. When I was about twelve, my father made me practice the etudes hands separately, at whatever tempo I could manage. He had me practice them all this way over the course of a few years, as part of my exercises. Then suddenly, when I was in my middle teens, almost without knowing how it happened, I knew all the Chopin etudes without ever planning to learn them.

DUBAL: Who were some of the pianists of your generation whom you admire?

GRAFFMAN: Three men, all of whom died young, come to mind. Julius Katchen, William Kapell and Glenn Gould. Katchen was an extremely close friend, and I loved his playing very much. He recorded a huge amount of repertoire, but the complete piano works of Brahms remain in the mind most of all. The Brahms recordings are a great legacy of his. For Kapell, every performance was an event—every one. He was one of the most honest individuals I had ever known, sometimes brutally so, and this honesty translated into a passionate integrity in his playing. He was very difficult to please, and the more success he had, the more he drove himself. As for Gould, I will never forget his debut in Town Hall. I went to the recital with Eugene Istomin and we were amazed; we weren't expecting to hear a fully developed original. After the concert, we were introduced to him at a party that Mrs. Leventritt gave for him, and there we told him about the impact he'd had on us. He then said, looking at both of us as if we were from another planet, "I know you. You play Chopin!" For some reason I remember that on that night he only drank milk. In the late Fifties, Gould and I had many dinners together. Once, when we were both making our Berlin debuts, we were at a French restaurant and I ordered escargots. When it was brought to the table I said to him in jest, "I hope this doesn't offend you." He answered in utter seriousness: "That's perfectly all right, I'll look in the other direction!" Although we did not see each other in later years, I always had a warm spot for him. How could one not?

DUBAL: It's often said today that playing has become homogeneous. That there is little imaginative playing anymore.

GRAFFMAN: I don't think that's necessarily true. There's an enormous amount of imaginative playing today, and the differences are subtle. Usually, those who complain about standardization are the ones who cannot discern the subtleties. The failing is in them, not in the people they're listening to.

Born in Kiev, Russia, October 1, 1903, Horowitz had his early training with Sergei Tarnowsky. On January 12, 1928, he made his American debut with the Tchaikovsky B-flat minor Concerto. Annual recitals in the U.S. followed, as well as tremendous success throughout Europe. From 1936 to 1939 he did not play publicly, but during the war years he maintained a furious concert schedule throughout the U.S. In 1949 in Havana, Cuba, he gave the world premiere of the Barber Piano Sonata, which was composed for him. Horowitz again was absent from the concert stage from 1953 to 1965. On May 9, 1965, he made one of the great comebacks in concert history. To mark the fiftieth anniversary of his American debut, he performed the Third Rachmaninoff Concerto with Eugene Ormandy and the New York Philharmonic in 1978. It was his first concerto appearance in twenty-five years. Horowitz has been given innumerable honors, and his recordings have been among the best-known of any artist's in history. Throughout his career, Horowitz has made many sparkling arrangements and transcriptions, the most famous being Sousa's "The Stars and Stripes Forever."

Vladimir Horo

PETER FINK/COURTESY OF CBS RECORDS

DUBAL: Who was your most important teacher?

HOROWITZ: I studied with Felix Blumenfeld, who had studied piano with Anton Rubinstein and composition with Tchaikovsky. Felix, my professor, wrote some good piano music and was also a very good conductor. He was the right hand of Anton Rubinstein, and although Rubinstein died before I was born and never recorded, when I was growing up in Russia, Anton Rubinstein was a magic name. Blumenfeld knew his playing by heart, from every angle.

DUBAL: Was Blumenfeld a good pianist?

HOROWITZ: Yes, but when I came to Blumenfeld, he was paralyzed on the right side. He couldn't play very much. You know, Szymanowski, the composer, was his nephew, and another nephew was Heinrich Neuhaus, who was a great teacher.

DUBAL: And, of course, Neuhaus taught Richter and Gilels.

HOROWITZ: Yes, he did, and many others. He played a lot of Scriabin, too. I was good friends with him, and we gave concerts together on two pianos. Neuhaus and I would play music of Wagner transcribed for two pianos.

DUBAL: Will you tell me a little about your early years?

HOROWITZ: Yes, I will. My father was a leading engineer and a very successful man. I came from a cultured family. We had a fine library and I was able to read all the classics, and every kind of music was accessible to me. My father had only one brother, who was a pianist and musicologist, and also the critic of the main paper in Kharkov. And, most important, my uncle was a pupil of Scriabin. He graduated from the Moscow Conservatory, where Scriabin taught. He had received the silver medal, but he should have received the gold medal. The judges giving the awards were anti-Semitic. Scriabin was so angry about this that he left his teaching post at the conservatory. Later, Scriabin and my uncle became the greatest friends and when I was living in Kiev, my uncle said to Scriabin, "I have a nephew who is very talented and you should hear him if you have time." Then Scriabin came to Kiev to give a recital (by the way, he played there premieres of the Seventh, Eighth and Ninth Sonatas—music of his late period). He was staying in a private house, and he made an appointment to hear me there at three o'clock, just four hours before his concert. He was terribly nervous because of the recital before him. Anyhow, I came there with my mother, and I played two or three pieces for him—a little bit of Chopin, the *Melodie* of Paderewski, and I think something of Borodin. I was about eleven, I don't remember exactly. So after I played, he took my mother outside and he told her, "Your son will be a great pianist, but please, let him be an overall cultured man, and make him understand not only music, but other important aspects of life. There are the arts of painting, of philosophy, of literature. Only then will he be an all-around musician." Then Scriabin said to my mother, "But a pianist he will definitely be." That is the story of when I played for Scriabin. You know, his opinion was very important to us; he was a very intellectual person.

DUBAL: Of course, you are also very close to Scriabin's music. Between the time of his death in 1915, when his music suffered an eclipse, and until the recent Scriabin revival, you have been the main force in Scriabin playing.

HOROWITZ: I helped, but there were other pianists who played Scriabin, though mostly in Russia. Vladimir Sofronitsky did much for him.

DUBAL: How would you describe Scriabin's music?

HOROWITZ: Scriabin is a mystic composer. His music is super-sensuous, super-romantic and super-mysterious. Everything is *super;* it is all a little bit overboard. You know, I play the Tenth Sonata. It is a fantastic sonata, one of his finest works, but for the public it is still very difficult. I have recorded four of the ten sonatas, Nos. 3, 5, 9 and 10. But I think Nos. 5 and 9 are the most popular with the public.

DUBAL: Yes, and you chose to play the Fifth Sonata at the Met, at the first piano recital ever given at the Metropolitan Opera House at Lincoln Center, and the recording from it is electrifying.

HOROWITZ: The recording is very good; we did a good job. No. 9 I recorded twice, but the second recording is better. I feel it much differently in the second recording, which takes nine minutes. The first one is in six minutes: too fast.

DUBAL: Are the Scriabin sonatas among the most difficult sonatas in the piano literature?

HOROWITZ: From the point of view of spiritual and emotional values, they are. They are also very difficult to read on the page. His notation is complicated, especially in the Seventh and Eighth Sonatas.

DUBAL: Did you always want to be a pianist?

Horowitz: No, when I was twelve or thirteen years old, I was more interested in composition than piano. After the revolution in 1917 I had to concentrate on the piano, where I knew I could eventually make a living. We lost absolutely everything. In twenty-four hours all we had was lost. *Everything!* We still don't understand how big was that revolution. It changed the whole world. Everything was different as a result of the Russian Revolution. When I write my memoirs, I will tell more of these times.

Dubal: After the revolution, you played a great deal. And in Leningrad you gave eleven programs without ever repeating a single work! When did you leave Russia?

Horowitz: In 1925. I came to Berlin; my first success was in Germany. And I went to concerts from morning to night. I heard Richard Strauss conduct, I was friends with everybody. I remember that I played the *Fantasy of Figaro* of Liszt-Busoni in my second recital in Berlin. Schnabel was at the concert. I was very friendly with Schnabel. At the recital, I played lots of Chopin and other good works. Afterwards, he came to me and said, "Oh, very good." I said, "Maestro, you never play pieces like the Liszt-Busoni transcription." "My God," he said, "I have only so much time to learn Bach, I don't have time for *that* kind of music." I looked at him and said, "You know, maestro, I do the opposite. I play this music, but I still have time for Bach." I was at that time around 23.

Dubal: What was the atmosphere in Germany at that time?

Horowitz: Although I was successful there, I remember writing home, telling my mother there's a kind of *Götterdämmerung* going on in Europe.

Dubal: How right you were. You also had a great success in Hamburg, and right after that you conquered Paris. You were booked to play two recitals in small halls, but the triumph was so spectacular that you ended up playing five recitals, the last one at the Paris Opéra.

Horowitz: Yes, I was liked there very much.

Dubal: What were the circumstances of your American debut?

Horowitz: In 1928, Arthur Judson, the American concert manager, heard me in Paris, and signed me for a United States concert tour. I made my debut at Carnegie Hall in the Tchaikovsky Concerto No. 1. On that night Thomas Beecham, who conducted, was making his American debut also. I chose the Tchaikovsky because I knew that I could make such a wild sound, and I could play it with such speed and noise. I very much wanted to have a big success in the United States.

DUBAL: And that you certainly did. According to *The New York Times,* "The piano smoked at the keys," and during most of the intermission, the audience continued to applaud and called you back to the stage.

HOROWITZ: Yes, I wanted to eat the public alive; to drive them completely crazy. Subconsciously, it was in order not to go back to Europe.

DUBAL: But Beecham's tempi were too relaxed for you, so in the last movement you took the horse by the reins.

HOROWITZ: That's absolutely right; I knew I had to go ahead. So in my mind I said, "Well, my Englishman, my Lord, I am from Kiev, and I'll give you something." And so I started to make the octaves faster and very wild.

DUBAL: How did it feel when you arrived in New York to find so many celebrated pianists?

HOROWITZ: It was wonderful! Everybody here was playing to sold-out houses—Rachmaninoff, Paderewski, Hofmann, Iturbi, Novaes, Schnabel, Lhevinne, Myra Hess, Gieseking, Friedman, Backhaus. It was an amazing time, and they were all there at my debut. They liked me right away, and I became friendly with everybody.

DUBAL: Was Rachmaninoff at the Tchaikovsky performance?

HOROWITZ: Yes, but he was not happy.

DUBAL: Why?

HOROWITZ: He said to me, "Your octaves are the fastest and loudest, but I must tell you, it was *not* musical. It was not necessary." So I explained to him why I did it, and he began laughing and laughing. But Rachmaninoff could always find something to complain about in any performance. Or he would like something that nobody else liked. For instance, he was crazy about the ending of the *Dante Symphony* of Liszt. He would be in tears at the ending when the chorus comes in.

DUBAL: How interesting. That's the worst part of it.

HOROWITZ: Yes, yes. I tell you, he could be funny about such things.

DUBAL: Did you meet Rachmaninoff soon after you arrived in New York?

HOROWITZ: In fact, I arrived in New York, and the second day I was in his apartment. Rachmaninoff had asked the Steinway firm to have me visit him when I came. In Europe, he had heard from Fritz Kreisler that "some young Russian plays your Third Concerto and the Tchaikovsky

Concerto like nothing I ever heard, and you have to meet him." And so I came to Rachmaninoff, and it took five minutes and we were friends. In ten minutes, he was playing for me.

DUBAL: What did he play?

HOROWITZ: He played the *Fairy Tale* in E minor of Medtner, which had just been published. He liked Medtner very much. I liked him too, and used to play some of his music. Rachmaninoff then asked me to go to the famous Steinway basement, where he accompanied me on his Third Piano Concerto.

DUBAL: And Rachmaninoff was astonished. He said that you swallowed the work whole. Would you say that the Third Rachmaninoff is the most difficult concerto in the literature?

HOROWITZ: Yes, maybe it is. I have made three recordings of it, but the first one I don't count. It was on 78s, with Albert Coates conducting. They gave me only one hour and a half, and I couldn't do what I wanted in such a short time.

DUBAL: Well, many people treasure that recording, even above the other two. Getting back to Rachmaninoff, is it true that he never smiled, and that on the concert stage he was a stone?

HOROWITZ: With me he always smiled, especially when I imitated the Russian singers for him. He laughed at that. Yes, he could laugh, but he only liked a few people. He was not a gregarious person and he didn't mix well. I once said to him, "Mr. Rachmaninoff, you never give interviews. A new generation will be very much interested in your views on music and literature, and on life in general. Nobody knows what you think about other composers." So he looked at me with a very severe face and said, "Mr. Horowitz, I must tell you something. I was brought up never to lie, and I *cannot* tell the truth." I told this story to President Carter.

DUBAL: Did the President like the story?

HOROWITZ: No!

DUBAL: Rachmaninoff was a tremendous musician as well as composer. Isn't there an old Russian proverb that says one cannot hunt two rabbits at the same time?

HOROWITZ: Yes. In fact, Rachmaninoff said to me many times, "I am hunting three animals, but I don't know if I have even caught one." But he was a first-class composer, he was a first-class conductor. You know, he conducted the opera in Moscow. And, of course, he was a wonderful pianist. He was offered the conducting post of the Boston Symphony before Koussevitzky came.

DUBAL: So many pianists today are trying their hand at conducting.

HOROWITZ: Yes, but Rachmaninoff said, "Those people who think they can conduct and play the piano are wrong, because all the muscles used are completely different."

DUBAL: It seems that Rachmaninoff remains very close to you to this very day. You continue to record him and your latest recording of the Rachmaninoff Third with Ormandy has been enormously successful.

HOROWITZ: You're right, Rachmaninoff is very special to me, and I'm glad that my recording of the Third Concerto has been well received. But I also love his Second Sonata, and I've been playing that recently. I like my second recording of it on RCA better than the one I made in the 1960s for Columbia. It's different.

DUBAL: That Second Sonata in B-flat minor was published in 1913. But didn't Rachmaninoff, thinking it was too long, make a condensed version later on?

HOROWITZ: Exactly. But I told Rachmaninoff that I thought it was too condensed, and so he told me to "put what you think best of both versions together." So I did, and Rachmaninoff approved.

DUBAL: Another Russian composer you have played quite a bit is Prokofiev; and I believe you premiered several Prokofiev sonatas in America.

HOROWITZ: Yes, the Sixth, Seventh and Eighth.

DUBAL: Those are called the War Sonatas.

HOROWITZ: That's right. The Sixth was composed just before World War II. I was the first to play it here. The Seventh and Eighth, I played at the Russian Consulate, during the war. Many musicians came to the consulate. They all wanted to hear the new sonatas. In the first rows were Stokowski, Bruno Walter, Toscanini, the young Bernstein, all the critics and many American composers, like Barber and Copland. A little later, after the war, I made a recording of the Seventh Sonata, and I sent a copy to Prokofiev. In return, he sent me a copy of the music with a very generous inscription, "To the miraculous pianist from the composer."

DUBAL: One of your most celebrated performances of the Russian literature is Mussorgsky's *Pictures at an Exhibition,* in which you altered the composer's text. That took courage, because a pianist is very much open to criticism if he dares tamper with an established masterpiece.

HOROWITZ: Yes, they criticized me very much. Some critics said, "He is putting graffiti on Mussorgsky's music," and things like that. Well, I don't give a damn. I'm not ashamed of it. I am proud of the transcription, I did a good job, and I think perhaps I played it very well.

DUBAL: Why did you make those changes?

HOROWITZ: Because I felt that the *Pictures* had to be brought forward, they were too introverted, and this was perhaps because Mussorgsky was a little bit of a dilettante, and he was not really a pianist. I doubled things, changed some octaves. You know, the piano is a very funny instrument. You have to know it well. Everything counts because you can hear it all—it is exposed. Take Beethoven's Ninth Symphony for example. There are all those people who want the text exactly as written, you cannot change a note. If you do, they think you have committed a crime, even though nobody really hears it. Believe me, Mahler or even Toscanini changed things here and there, for reinforcement or clarity, and nobody heard it. But on the piano, if you change one note, everybody hears it. I only make changes to make a good sound, to improve awkward writing, or to fulfill the composer's intentions.

DUBAL: Which is very much in the great tradition of Liszt, a composer who is very close to you.

HOROWITZ: Yes, but Liszt has to be selected very carefully, because he has written lots of inferior music, along with lots of beautiful music. We have to look very, very carefully at his work. But I understand Liszt very well. He was a terribly important figure in the history of the piano.

DUBAL: Yes, Liszt revolutionized the world of concert-going. Before him a pianist would only play a few solos. The program needed variety—singers, a quartet, a harpist—it was thought too boring to listen to just the solo piano. But in 1839, Liszt gave the first solo recital. He said, "The concert is me."

HOROWITZ: Yes, he was a phenomenal man. I think Liszt is the *greatest* piano virtuoso in history. It was Liszt who really had the best understanding of what the piano could do. He was a formidable musician. He knew everything and could play it by heart. He was absolutely god-like. I knew only one person who met him, the composer Glazunov.

DUBAL: What did Glazunov say? Was Liszt a brilliant conversationalist?

HOROWITZ: Yes, brilliant, but more, much more. He said that every word was like an apparition.

DUBAL: Yes, Liszt was the piano's great cavalier and he produced fantastic pupils, never taking any money for his lessons. He helped everyone around him.

HOROWITZ: Yes, he helped everybody, including Wagner, but some people were skeptical of this. I once had a discussion with Toscanini, who said that all those good deeds must have been a pose, that Liszt was not sincere. I said that even if it was a pose, it was a good one. I don't care what his reasons were, he did it. He did many generous things in his lifetime.

DUBAL: Naturally, many people envied and criticized Liszt because he was so magnificent.

HOROWITZ: An example of this was the young Berlin music critic who tried very hard to put Liszt down. He said he was just a dilettante, that he was neither a good composer nor a good pianist, nor a good conductor. He tried to destroy the greatest pianist who has ever lived. Imagine! So some of Liszt's pupils came to him and begged him to publicly respond. So Liszt promised he would and he wrote: "I am very happy that you don't like my music. You are right, and I don't protest at all. I am very happy that through my name I could help you to be noticed." I think this is a beautiful story.

DUBAL: You have recorded the Liszt Sonata, several of the Hungarian Rhapsodies, the *Vallée d'Obermann,* the Second Ballade, *Funérailles* and much else of Liszt's. Did you ever play the concerti?

HOROWITZ: Ah, the A major, No. 2. I play it, but I have never recorded it. I must tell you that I am a terrible man. I always want to change just a little bit the ending, and a little of the orchestration, too.

DUBAL: In your recording of the *Mephisto Waltz* you did some interesting things.

HOROWITZ: Yes, I did perform operations on that piece.

DUBAL: It's a demonic performance.

HOROWITZ: At my age I should be an angel with no more demons, but I discovered that I still have some *demonica.* So I played it at concerts, and we recorded it.

DUBAL: What did your *Mephisto* operations consist of?

HOROWITZ: Well, you know, I was never satisfied with the Liszt transcription on the piano of his own orchestral version, so I looked to the Busoni transcription of the Liszt orchestral score. Some parts of the Busoni are better than the Liszt, so I decided to extract the best from each, and that is what I did. I think the mixture is a good one.

DUBAL: Yes, it is; I've heard your recording of it. And even though it comes from a public performance, I noticed that you left in a few wrong notes.

HOROWITZ: I must take chances. If there is a wrong note, I leave it. You have to have one or two, because if you play very carefully, it can become academic. It must never be a bore.

DUBAL: When speaking of Liszt, I think of his contemporary Chopin. Chopin, the poet of the piano, whose works you have recorded so extensively.

HOROWITZ: Imagine! He never weighed more than ninety-odd pounds. Near the end of his life he was so weak that when something was written triple *forte,* he could only play it *mezzo piano.* Perhaps that is why there is a legend of Chopin as a delicate, ethereal pianist. But on paper he was never ninety pounds.

DUBAL: Yes, he was really a lion, a very determined man.

HOROWITZ: Chopin contributed tremendously to our understanding of the piano; he is the composer for the piano only.

DUBAL: Chopin's etudes certainly added another dimension to piano technique.

HOROWITZ: Yes, and they are very difficult, especially on the modern piano. If Chopin were here today, he would change many things to suit today's instruments. Of that I'm sure.

DUBAL: Which are Chopin's greatest works for you?

HOROWITZ: They tend to be the smaller works. Of the mazurkas, each one is better than the next. They are pure gold. Some nocturnes, too, are very beautiful, though they can suffer from a little bit of over-ornamentation, I think. But Chopin can express in three pages so much. A Shostakovich or Miaskovsky symphony can last for an hour and they sometimes don't say anything. Of course, the ballades are very serious and poetic. They are very great works.

DUBAL: I know you greatly admire the polonaises.

HOROWITZ: Yes, and I love the big *Polonaise-Fantaisie.* I once wrote a paragraph for my Chopin record on the Polonaise Op. 53, which I would like to quote: "I think that this polonaise reflects the fury of the Polish under the yoke of Czarist domination. Chopin was a fierce Polish patriot himself, and his patriotic feeling thundered through this music, which is like a call to arms. It is also proud, majestic, heroic, chivalrous and in the grand manner. It is indeed a polonaise for all seasons and all oppressed lands—a polonaise for the millions of men and women who still hold dear the free human spirit."

DUBAL: You always played a lot of Schumann, but with each year, you seem to gravitate even more to him.

HOROWITZ: I love him. I love him very much. You see, Schumann for me is *the* Romantic composer. Schumann goes straight to the music, and he is very idiomatic for the piano, too.

DUBAL: Schumann is creative every moment.

HOROWITZ: Always creative; there is something new in him always. There is something that touches me very deeply. I have recorded a lot of him. *Kreisleriana* is not a bad record. The Fantasy I played in my comeback in '65. I think also the *Humoresque* is a terrific piece, and should be much better known.

DUBAL: You also recorded the Toccata twice, a work of fearsome double-note technique.

HOROWITZ: Ah, the Toccata—a very good work, but a little bit uncomfortable for the hand. It is usually played too fast; one doesn't have to play it so fast.

DUBAL: Did you ever hear Simon Barère play it?

HOROWITZ: Yes, he was a pianist who had a tremendous technique. I once said to him, "Simon, you play the Toccata a little bit too fast." You know his answer? "Oh, I can play it even faster!"

DUBAL: You continue to play Scarlatti, especially in the last twenty years or so.

HOROWITZ: Yes, and I became friends with Ralph Kirkpatrick, the harpsichordist who made his own edition, a tremendous research.

DUBAL: Many pianists now leave Scarlatti to the harpsichordists.

HOROWITZ: I know, but the harpsichord cannot achieve the continuity of tone that the piano can. On the piano, I still try to play the music in the framework of Scarlatti's period, yet I never want to imitate the harpsichord; I only want to show the public how the music sounds on the piano.

DUBAL: Still, the harpsichordists get upset when pianists play the sonatas, saying the music sounds better on the original instruments.

HOROWITZ: Yes, the harpsichordists always say that. But I think this is because we can do a little bit more. You know, the most interesting thing is that they are more noisy than we are. The harpsichord can produce tremendous noise. But when we produce a little bit of noise, we are criticized right away.

DUBAL: I know exactly what you mean. But there is no more pleasurable literature than those 550 Scarlatti sonatas.

HOROWITZ: I agree. Let me read to you Scarlatti's own preface to the few sonatas that were published in his lifetime:
"Dear Reader,

Whether you be dilettante or professor, do not expect any profound learning, but rather, an ingenious jesting with art to accommodate you to the mastery of the harpsichord. Neither consideration of interest nor of ambition, but obedience alone spurred me on to publish these pieces. If they prove agreeable to you, then only more gladly will I obey other commands to favor you with more simple and various styles. Therefore, show yourself more human than critical, and thus you will increase your own pleasure."

That means, if you don't criticize the music, you will feel better. I love that!

DUBAL: It seems to me that the nineteenth-century Romantics didn't understand Scarlatti very well.

HOROWITZ: You are right. Chopin said, "People criticize me when I give my pupils Scarlatti to play, but they don't understand that one day he will be in the concert programs of every pianist."

DUBAL: Let's turn to another Italian-born composer, "the father of the pianoforte" according to the inscription on his tombstone at Westminster Abbey.

HOROWITZ: You are speaking of Clementi, born in Italy, before Mozart, in 1752, and taken to England as a boy. By the way, I recently discovered that his mother was German; she was Swiss-German. Her name was Kaiser.

DUBAL: When did you discover Clementi? I know your recordings of several of the sonatas made many pianists curious about them.

HOROWITZ: Yes, the Clementi sonatas have been absent from the concert repertoire too long. They are pianistically wonderful and very prophetic of many things. Schirmer's had for years published two volumes of them, but not necessarily the best ones. Then Mrs. Horowitz went to Italy, and she found first editions of the sonatas. So many were never again published. I have twelve volumes. There are about 68 of them. Clementi was very important for the piano. He was the real beginning. As you say, he was the piano's father. He gave up the harpsichord, toured on the piano. He even manufactured pianos.

DUBAL: Yes, he did everything.

HOROWITZ: He sure did, perhaps even too much. He also taught, and Beethoven was tremendously influenced by him. They even have some passages which are exactly the same. Clementi is very original, very strong, and his formal sonatas are completely schematic. And you know, I find his music very Romantic, extremely Romantic sometimes.

DUBAL: Do you still practice a great many hours a day, and do you think that scale and arpeggio practice is necessary?

HOROWITZ: Oh, I cannot play more than two hours a day, not more, and I don't play scales or exercises.

DUBAL: You don't need it?

HOROWITZ: No, I need it, but I am lazy. I have other more important things to do. I do not want to get tired.

DUBAL: Do you think many pianists, especially young pianists, compulsively over-practice—practice too much and think too little?

HOROWITZ: They may think, but often they think the wrong way. Just to remember music one must think. And pianists are not stupid. But they practice and practice, and repeat passages and parts a hundred times over. Then they go on the stage, and repeat them for the hundred-and-first time. And you hear it that way. You feel it. But performance must be more than just the next repetition; it must live and breathe. Too often the pianist thinks, "Oh, I must not miss one passage." They think it is so important to play all the notes. Maybe that attitude comes from recordings, or radio—from some machine—because that microphone hears things you can't hear on stage; it's more powerful than our ear drums. But, on stage, you have to take chances to make the music really live.

DUBAL: And yet you consider recording an important process.

HOROWITZ: Yes, I do. It's important for a good knowledge of music. One can find and explore so many things on records. Even if I dislike the interpretation, I can come to know the music easily. I can have all the music I want to hear. But there is always for me something missing. The record is a remembrance; it is a postcard. When you go somewhere, you see a beautiful landscape—it's beautiful—or a sunset—such colors—you will see it that way once, and you go buy a postcard to bring home and remember what you saw. This is what happens when you buy a recording of a concert. But probably in some years to come, there will be improvements that enable you to see the performer, feel closer. For me it is very important to see the performer.

DUBAL: A fine piano is very important too, wouldn't you say?

HOROWITZ: It can't ever be good enough. You know, when I arrived in Berlin in 1925, I didn't know which piano to play. There were then maybe eight or nine important piano makers. So I went to Weber, to Bluethner, Bösendorfer, Steinweg, to Bechstein—everywhere, and then to Steinway. And when I played the Steinway in Berlin, I said, "That's my piano." Since that time, I am the only artist of Steinway that never played another piano, no matter what country I am playing in. Maybe in Paris, Rubinstein played a Gaveau, or Paderewski played Erard. But for over fifty-five years or more, I play the Steinway. And the Steinway piano of today I think is improved in some respects. Its action was once too heavy. The most important thing for me is that the piano has beautiful continuity of sound, that it be a singing instrument, not a detached instrument. The notes must sing like the bel canto singing of the eighteenth and nineteenth century. I try to sing on the piano. If I don't have a great instrument, I cannot do it. And for me, to sing is necessary.

DUBAL: Many people think that just having a good instrument is enough.

HOROWITZ: Ah, not at all. There are thousands of parts. You should take care of a piano like you should take care of yourself. It needs voicing and regulating. For me, I need to have my piano go with me, just like the violinist takes his own instrument. And I'm an old trouper. I already know a little bit about the mechanism of the piano, and I can tell the piano technician what I want. There are, of course, so many things to take into account: some halls have difficult acoustics, the piano has to be properly centered on the stage, sometimes deeper or closer. But every acoustic is different. I spend hours on these things. After all, I have to give my best. If I charge for tickets, it must be the best I can do. But sometimes, if I don't do as well as I want, it's not always my fault; it may be that the acoustic is very bad. But I will never return to that hall again. They could give me a million dollars, but I will not return if I cannot play my best for the public.

Born November 26, 1925, in New York City, Istomin made his debut in 1943, after winning the Leventritt Award, with the New York Philharmonic, playing the Brahms Second Piano Concerto. Soon he was appearing with major conductors of the world. Besides his solo career, Istomin has been involved with one of the most celebrated chamber groups of our time, the Istomin, Rose, Stern Trio.

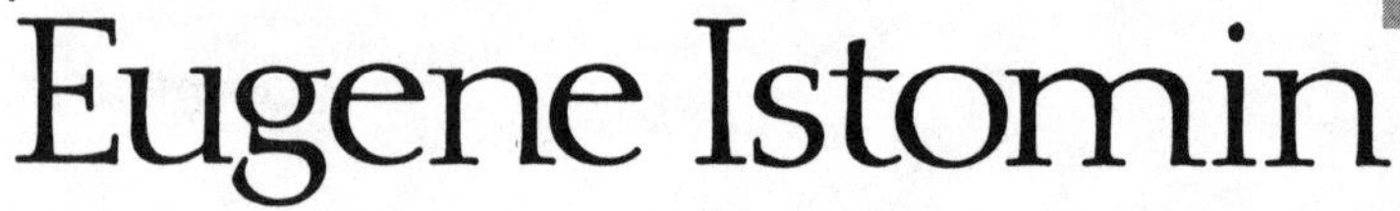

FRITZ HENLE

DUBAL: Your family background was Russian.

ISTOMIN: Yes, my parents were Russian émigrés. My first musical authorities were Russian as well. As a child I was fortunate in studying with one of Liszt's favorite pupils, Alexander Siloti.

DUBAL: Who became a very important figure in Russia.

ISTOMIN: He was a wonderful human being. After the tragedy of the revolution in Russia, he had some bad times, but eventually managed to come to New York. He lived at the famous Hotel Ansonia on Seventy-third and Broadway, and taught a whole generation of pianists at the Juilliard School.

DUBAL: How old were you when you were brought to him?

ISTOMIN: Only six years old. I wasn't ready for his teaching. He played four-hands with me, joked around, played games. His daughter Kyriena was the one who gave me a day-to-day tutoring. Actually, in that household I was sort of a grandchild.

DUBAL: In that environment, you must have been developing quickly.

ISTOMIN: Yes, but Siloti was against an immediate career for me. Fortunately, my parents were in agreement with him. Siloti had seen too much exploitation of children.

DUBAL: Siloti was Rachmaninoff's cousin and teacher. Did you ever get to meet him?

ISTOMIN: Once Kyriena took me over to Rachmaninoff's house. After the customary baby-hugging I was asked to play. Can you imagine, if it had been ten years later I would have passed out!

DUBAL: What did you play for the master?

ISTOMIN: The little Beethoven Sonata Op. 49 in G major. I was perfectly uninhibited and blithely played away for my reward of a candy and a kiss. But later Rachmaninoff said to Kyriena, "Are you giving him technique?" As if to say, all this musicality is very good but what about his fingers?

DUBAL: As you grew up, did you hear Rachmaninoff often in public?

ISTOMIN: I managed to hear him quite a few times. No doubt he was the best pianist I ever heard. His was more than incredible virtuosity. It was more than musical; there was an overpowering eloquence that came from his tone and the depth of feeling he projected. His face looked like a mask as he played, an Asiatic mask; he didn't move. He hulked over the instrument, but the instrument was flesh and what came out was intoxicating and heartbreaking. Both. Yes, those are the words. But you know, he played very fast, terribly fast at times, sometimes too fast. Today his music is frequently played too slowly. So there you are.

DUBAL: Let's go back to your training. How did Rudolf Serkin enter the picture?

ISTOMIN: My father, following the traditions of Peter the Great, decided that after my Russian beginnings a German influence, a disciplined and grounded education, would be best for me. And he set his sights on Rudolf Serkin, Viennese-trained, with his reputation as a musician's musician, as the optimum goal for my training. So in April of 1939 while Serkin was still in Europe, Isabelle Vengerova, David Saperton and other faculty accepted me as a student at the Curtis Institute in Philadelphia under Serkin's tutelage. I was thirteen when he first set his eyes on my chubby countenance.

DUBAL: What were your early impressions of Serkin?

ISTOMIN: He was thirty-six years old when I entered his life. He was very nervous, impatient, hiding a volcano under near-pathological shyness. At that time he was already revered, but not yet a big box-office star. It was not until Toscanini launched him with the New York Philharmonic that Serkin's prestige soared in America. At that time, Horowitz and he were good friends, and I think Serkin's pianism profited from close observation of Horowitz's phenomenal pianistic power. Nobody understood big-scale piano playing better than Horowitz. Nobody enlarged the scale of his own playing as Serkin did in the 1930s. He proved you could alternate chamber-music mastery with "fire-eating" virtuosity. In those few years he became a paradigm and mentor for the entire younger generation.

DUBAL: What was he like as a teacher?

ISTOMIN: He was very severe on himself and equally severe on his students. I think especially so with me because he considered me the most gifted of his class of six.

DUBAL: As a student, did you need that much severity?

ISTOMIN: Perhaps not. At that time Serkin had little experience with teaching; he tended to dump so many of his own problems onto me. He would say to me, only half in jest, "You should play this work better than me." I would answer, "How can you expect me to play this that well?" He seemed to forget that I was only a teenager. "Oh, no, on the contrary," Serkin would say, "I have no talent—*you* have talent. You should play it better!" Of course this sort of thing was perfectly ridiculous. Nobody can be more talented than Rudolf Serkin; and we all knew it even then. He had an unconditional reverence for the composers he played, and his struggle to get the composer's meaning was fierce. Of all the musicians I've ever known, it was Serkin who was the most intensely unbending in this way. "Better to fall on your face in honest striving than to have a cheap success." To Serkin, the devil was Leopold Stokowski, and in Serkin's greatest rages, he would look at me and mutter under his breath, "You will become a Stokowski."

Studying with Serkin was sublime, but dangerous too. Serkin was my hero and my self-excoriating "conscience."

DUBAL: Did Serkin's emphasis on the central European composers engender a kind of elitism?

ISTOMIN: Yes, I was steered by Serkin to the great central European masters: they became my first priority–they still are. Nevertheless, there was an adolescent one-upmanship that callow Serkin pupils tended to develop. The ethos was "Avoid easy successes, tackle the more meaty stuff. The Tchaikovsky Concerto will get you more noisy bravos, but the Beethoven Fourth is far more nutritious for growing talent than the Russian or French composers."

DUBAL: Of course the result is that you are typecast as a pianist of the Germanic repertoire even though I've heard you in bravura performances of the Tchaikovsky Concerto.

ISTOMIN: Unfortunately, you are correct. I recently played the Rachmaninoff Fourth with Rostropovich, but the truth is that I've become pigeonholed. Ironically, Virgil Thomson said of one of my earliest recitals that I was like a child when playing Beethoven and Schumann but that when I got to Ravel's *Gaspard de la Nuit* I was a consummate master. However, through the years, the French and Russian connection simply disappeared from my public image, even though my recording of the Rachmaninoff Second with Ormandy has been my most successful record.

DUBAL: Who besides Serkin and Rachmaninoff had a formative influence on you?

ISTOMIN: Arthur Rubinstein. As a child it was Rubinstein I tried to emulate.

DUBAL: What were the qualities you tried to emulate?

ISTOMIN: There was something in the rise and fall of his phrasing that captivated me. There was something in the way he articulated the fioriture in Chopin. His sense of phrasing simply addicted me—even in stylistically suspect rubatos that he would use in a Mozart concerto. Socrates certainly was right about the essence of learning being remembering what one knew even before awareness.

DUBAL: It sounds like Rubinstein touched your deepest musical nerve.

ISTOMIN: Oh, yes, indeed, deeper than Serkin, because Serkin's lessons were acquired. Rubinstein's voice felt like a part of my own. His music-making had that same immediate intimacy that I had encountered when I first made music with Casals.

DUBAL: During that growing-up period, did you also encounter the playing of Schnabel, who was twenty-one years Serkin's senior?

ISTOMIN: Did I! He was another of my heroes. He was the musical guru of the time.

DUBAL: How did Serkin feel about him—the other servant of the "nutritious" literature, as you called it?

ISTOMIN: Serkin definitely admired him as a great musician, but had contempt for his technical sloppiness. Then again, Schnabel had contempt for technical accuracy. During concerts he often went far beyond the quota of wrong notes, loftily disposing of technical challenges by looking above and beyond them to the grand line of structure. After all, what do a few botched bars matter on the ascent to Olympus? Serkin thought, however, this was not a good example for youth to follow. And I think he was right.

DUBAL: You haven't mentioned Horowitz as one of your heroes.

ISTOMIN: Horowitz is the most hair-raising pianist in history. Even as he draws out unimagined colors from the instrument, there's an electrical intensity which is irresistible. But being hair-raising is not my top priority.

DUBAL: Were pianists your only mentors?

ISTOMIN: No, they didn't have to be pianists. There was something I absorbed from Casals, Heifetz and Toscanini. Each of them had something I needed for my music-making, and like a sponge, I absorbed it all.

DUBAL: You are not speaking of imitation, are you?

ISTOMIN: No, what's alien is rejected and what's compatible is assimilated, even if only a single gesture.

DUBAL: Do you consider yourself a good teacher?

ISTOMIN: No, because I get impatient and bored with anything less than first-rate talent. Real teaching is an art unto itself.

DUBAL: You intrigued me with the phrase "real teaching." What does that mean? Anton Rubinstein said there are no great teachers, only great students.

ISTOMIN: The real art of teaching is active, and creative. This type of teaching shows a student how to do this or that. Such teaching is a must with more limited talents. With important talent, however, each must have his own evolution, his own course. For the gifted, the teacher is to be devoured, a nipple to be suckled upon.

DUBAL: What happens when a pianist asks for your teaching? Do you make yourself available?

ISTOMIN: I don't know any artist who hasn't made himself or herself available. It'll be the rare person that says, "Go away!" to the aspiring artist. After all, you never know if an important talent is coming your way.

DUBAL: Yes, there is a fine tradition among pianists of nurturing the next generation. But if the person coming for your advice is not talented enough for a career, how do you handle the situation?

ISTOMIN: I tell them that if they're not as talented as, say, Murray Perahia or Daniel Barenboim or Jean-Bernard Pommier, they're in a lot of trouble. "It's a hard world, and you've got some stiff competition."

DUBAL: Are you telling them to get out of the profession?

ISTOMIN: I am often reminded of Rilke's admonition to the young poet to ask himself in the stillest instant of the night whether he would perish without his work, and if the poet replies, "No, I could, if need be, live without it"—then for heaven's sake stop! The sacrifice is too great. Go sailing, go to the moon, but don't make art your life's work.

DUBAL: Obviously art has high meaning for you.

ISTOMIN: To me, it is the highest activity possible. Whether it's painting or poetry, music or dance, this is the very best thing that we are capable of—also the most demanding.

DUBAL: What makes art better than sports, science or politics?

ISTOMIN: Art has to do with the mind and the spirit, the reaching beyond the physical and material, even the explicable. You can't really describe a phrase in Mozart or Beethoven, or a line in a great drawing. It proves the existence of a dimension that's more dense, and yet simpler. If you have for even a moment experienced that reality, you have felt an aspect of God.

DUBAL: As someone who has been in contact with the public for decades, how do you feel about the level of culture today?

ISTOMIN: My guess is that more people truly cared about the arts up to World War I than do now. Since then we have certainly made great leaps forward towards "equalizing society." Everyone is a consumer of culture today. We have a plethora of projects to "popularize" the arts. But the public worships celebrity, not art. We live in an affluent society, those of us, that is, in the "free world." The people have power; their opinions count; their prejudices count; and their failure to develop sensibility counts. Totalitarian governments impose their gross values brutally. What if we discover that we are freely choosing similar ones? Instead of using our inalienable right to reach our potential, we use it to seek quick thrills or artificial serenity. I'm afraid the egalitarian ideals are congenial to mediocrity, and we are living in a time when individuality is more threatened than it has ever been.

DUBAL: You feel this deeply, our era scares you.

ISTOMIN: You bet it does, because the truly cultured and refined elements in society appear to be fulfilling an Orwellian prophecy and going underground. The media marketplace is *Big Brother.* Will it sell? the question. The sold-out sign is our icon.

DUBAL: Would you say that artistically, you live in another time?

ISTOMIN: Musically, I live mostly in the eighteenth and nineteenth centuries, with an occasional foray into the early twentieth century.

DUBAL: Do you ever feel anachronistic musically?

ISTOMIN: I don't know whether it's the music that makes me an anachronism, or whether it's my being an anachronism that gives me a particular aptitude for the music.

COURTESY OF ICM

Born March 24, 1928, Janis is a native of McKeesport, Pennsylvania. After hearing him play, Josef Lhevinne urged his parents to send him to New York for study. He made his official debut in the Rachmaninoff Second Concerto on February 20, 1944. He later studied with Horowitz. Janis made his Carnegie Hall debut in 1948. He soon found himself playing in Moscow, Lisbon, Paris and Stockholm. He became one of the most sought-after pianists in the world. During the last fifteen years he has played much less frequently in public and has not recorded, but he has taught, and made a film about Chopin.

Byron Janis

Byron Janis

DUBAL: You were the first of a small group of young pianists to have studied with Horowitz. When did that happen and what was your earlier experience?

JANIS: Well, in a way the great Horowitz discovered me when I was sixteen. I had been working for years with Adele Marcus, who gave me a tremendous foundation. She worked with me twice a week. She was herself a student of Josef Lhevinne, whom I studied with as a child. I was also working with Rosina Lhevinne at the time. I had moved from Pittsburgh to New York to study with them, so I was immersed in the Russian style of playing, a style which strives for color and high virtuosity as well. At the age of sixteen I was to play the Rachmaninoff Second Concerto with the Pittsburgh Symphony, and another Russian was to become part of my life—Horowitz.

DUBAL: Who was conducting the concert?

JANIS: None other than Lorin Maazel, who was at the time fifteen years old. Horowitz, who had just played in Pittsburgh, came to my concert. He came backstage and said, "Good." I was greatly excited. He also said that he would like me to call him and play for him at his home. This happened, and I began a four-year period of study with him, which was invaluable for me as a pianist.

DUBAL: During those years wasn't Horowitz constantly playing concerts?

JANIS: Oh, absolutely. His concert tours were endless and it was all train travel then. But one cannot imagine the kind of commitment Horowitz had. I would often travel with him and Mrs. Horowitz, so the lessons went uninterrupted. I became like a son, a part of the family. We all went on vacations together. Sometimes I had lessons at his father-in-law's house in Riverdale. This was not just a father-in-law, it was Toscanini himself.

DUBAL: How did he teach?

JANIS: Well, Horowitz certainly had no "method." There was tremendous experimentation, trial and error. Indeed, he had never taught before and he was learning himself. Horowitz is a great cataloguer of ideas. In a sense he needed me creatively. Through these sessions he was himself spurred on to new ideas, especially musical ones. One cannot properly imagine the creative imagination of an artist like Horowitz. He understands the instrument's insides, and at certain times in his life he needed a pupil to bring out things he needed to articulate. You know, the endless concert schedule can leave you dry, and teaching is a unique form of giving.

DUBAL: What music did he give you to work on?

JANIS: Horowitz brought me to the grand Romantic repertoire. I added the Third Rachmaninoff Concerto to my diet. He wanted me to think big, to project big and to realize that the world's large concert halls were not ordinary rooms. Pianists spend too little time in judging a hall's properties. In a hall if you sit on the left side, the right side or in the balcony, you get three different sounds. Horowitz understood, he still does, the acoustic of a hall perhaps better than anyone.

DUBAL: Did he play for you?

JANIS: It was a never-ending stream of music. He just loved to play for you. He was never selfish, never stinted. And what a reader!

DUBAL: Was there anything harmful about such an intense relationship?

JANIS: Of course. During that time, I was growing up. I was becoming too imitative under the powerful force of his personality and musicality. I'm convinced that I had to stop being with him. I was unconsciously becoming a copy. There was no doubt that Horowitz was first attracted to my playing because he felt something of his own in it. The four years were enough. I needed my time. I received a lot of publicity by being Horowitz's pupil—some helped, some didn't. But I didn't need to enter competitions, that's for sure. Success came early for me.

DUBAL: Who are the other pianists that you have most admired?

JANIS: For me one of the most magical pianists was Cortot, who had many shortcomings, and in the U.S. we tend to make shortcomings too important. Cortot tended to slide around a lot, had memory lapses and was not always in good shape, but my God, there was something there! There was an essence, and he captured it. His Chopin and Schumann are unbelievably beautiful. He is the best of French poetic style, but with a true depth.

DUBAL: Did you feel close to Rubinstein's playing?

JANIS: Yes, I considered him a truly great artist. He was very much in touch with the joy of music, and for that reason he was probably the most universally loved pianist of all. There was a naturalism about his playing which was absolutely beautiful.

DUBAL: Who was your favorite concerto collaborator?

JANIS: I adored Fritz Reiner—he and I had an amazing musical rapport. I don't know how to describe it, but when we got out on stage, it was like riding a wave. He was a real virtuoso.

DUBAL: How did you come to play in Russia?

JANIS: I was the first American pianist sent in the cultural exchange back in 1960. I also went back in 1962.

DUBAL: You had great success in Russia; you captured their imagination. Was it because you were an American pianist and they didn't realize an American could play with your kind of sweep in the Grand Romantic repertory?

JANIS: I think so. Perhaps they detected something of my Slavic soul, because I am of Russian-Polish descent. Then again, I was thought of primarily as an American; I was "the enemy."

DUBAL: Yes, that was at the height of the Cold War.

JANIS: That's right. Two years before, when Van Cliburn unexpectedly won the Tchaikovsky Competition in Moscow, the Russian propaganda was very strong. The Russians considered it a fluke that an American won their competition because up until that time America was considered a cultural wasteland. Then I came along and had this success, and that was really upsetting to many officials. Indeed, the official box was always empty at my concerts. But the public was really extraordinary, and there was a tremendous rapport between us. The Russians are a special public. It's a public that will react to a single phrase within the piece. You can actually hear them sigh in a Chopin nocturne. Anyway, when it became apparent that I was having a success, Llewellyn Thompson, our ambassador at the time, came back at intermission and told me how thrilled he was. He would no longer have to listen to the Russians telling him that America has no pianists.

DUBAL: Do you have any desire to go back to Russia?

JANIS: I would love to play for the Russian public again, but there are so many problems involved in playing there. It's so exhausting and bureaucratic. Everything is made extremely problematical. One wonders if it's worth it.

DUBAL: Do you feel that pianists today tend to lack a vocal style in their playing? Horowitz adored Battistini; Chopin talked about singers constantly; Rachmaninoff loved the basso Chaliapin; Arthur Rubinstein was influenced by Emmy Destinn.

JANIS: I think, generally speaking, piano teachers today place less emphasis on thinking vocally. When I worked with Horowitz he was always talking of singers and going to the Toscanini rehearsals, where every other word out of his mouth was "Canta, canta, canta." Of course, it's one thing to say something, another thing to do it. At a master class I recently gave, some of the students were playing a mazurka of Chopin, and it was percussion playing, not vocal playing. So I said, "Do you have a good singer around here somewhere?" They got one, and I asked her to hum the theme. I remembered that the soprano Pauline Viardot-Garcia, a close friend of Chopin's, often sang along with him when he was playing mazurkas. Anyway, I had this young woman vocalize the melody, and these students were absolutely astonished at the difference in the feeling and the breathing. It offered them another dimension. Today's young pianists sort of pretend at doing it, but they seldom really sing. I adore Rachmaninoff and Josef Hofmann recordings. Listen to *them* sing; that's what it's about. That's how the pianist makes the audience remember the playing. Look at Paderewski—who did not have the greatest technical equipment. Yet, he is remembered because he sang. He didn't have such a career just because of his golden hair—listen to the best of his recordings. He sang with his heart, which gave him the most glorious melting tone.

DUBAL: And that is what the audience really seems to want.

JANIS: I think so, but they are not getting it often enough. And when the piano does not sing it is the most boring instrument in the world.

DUBAL: Someone said that it can be as impersonal as a butler.

JANIS: Yes, listen to it when it's accompanying a violin or a cello. Listen to how dull it often sounds, while the violin comes out with an incredibly lyrical sound. But, in the records that Rachmaninoff and Kreisler made together you don't hear that. Rachmaninoff treats the piano just as vocally as Kreisler does his violin. This is because Rachmaninoff does not think of himself as an accompanist. He and Kreisler are both singers. Chamber players should study their recording of the Grieg C minor Sonata. Rachmaninoff's recordings are even more wonderful as time goes on.

DUBAL: Tell us something about your approach to performance.

JANIS: Before each performance I think it's very important to practice to the point where you feel that your technique and concept of the pieces you will be playing are ready. But then you have to let it all go and perform and create on stage, as though you hadn't practiced. Surprise yourself and listen, because if you don't listen, you're not going to play for the hall. It's more important to be spontaneous than to strive for perfection. I think "perfection" is a very destructive concept and comparison is deadly. We must stop trying to make today's performance like yesterday's. You can't do it; you can never repeat a performance, and as soon as you say, "God, I want to do that again," you're finished. You will be strangled and impotent, and everything you do today will be spoiled. This is my attitude towards everything in life.

DUBAL: Then what is your feeling about the critics who are always thinking of performance in terms of a certain standard?

JANIS: Critics are amazing—only too often they are deaf. They don't hear what you're actually putting out because so often their mind is focused on what they expect from you. You may be playing something magnificently, but they will not hear it because they are looking for something else. Although I love Beethoven and feel him deeply, a critic will kill me for it since in his mind I'm just supposed to play Rachmaninoff, Chopin or Liszt. The critics are performers' natural enemies.

DUBAL: What is the best state of mind for practicing?

JANIS: You are at your best when you are in a state of *attention*. You are aware of everything, at the same time as you are focused on details. It's like looking at a painting—you see something in it that is very beautiful, and yet you see the whole painting too. Attentiveness means you've got the broadest vision. Only then are you able to listen to your own playing in the most meaningful way.

DUBAL: Do you feel that this is an age of performance rather than one of composition?

JANIS: Yes, but I think we need more new music, don't you?

DUBAL: Of course, but musicians often complain that some of the so-called avant-garde music is so convoluted that one could spend a lifetime deciphering a single score.

JANIS: That's true, yet I do see some of the young people performing it. I only wish it said more to me.

DUBAL: What do you think of the word "serious" when applied to classical music?

JANIS: That darn word "serious." First of all, music is not necessarily meant to be serious. It has a lot of humor in it. I'll tell you when I know an audience is bad: If I'm playing *Pictures at an Exhibition,* and they don't laugh after the "Ballet of the Chickens," then I know this is a bad audience. Because they think that everything is serious, even when it's hilarious. Music has every conceivable emotion in it. I think humor is too often lacking in the young pianist's approach. All the truly great pianists—Hofmann, Rachmaninoff, Horowitz, Rubinstein—all had tremendous fun. And their encores were pure magic, with no stress and strain. But today there is a tendency for everything to be deadly serious with everybody, including myself, frightened and deadpan up there.

DUBAL: Yes, so often performers look absolutely terrified because they *are* afraid. Their audience has come to a serious event expecting an immortal performance, and they might not measure up.

JANIS: Yes, it's like church; it's all so stiff and regimented. The art of music must be flexible and alive wherever it is played.

JACK MITCHELL

Johannesen was born July 30, 1921, in Salt Lake City, Utah, where his early training took place. At eighteen he studied with Robert Casadesus and later with Egon Petri. He also studied composition with Roger Sessions. In 1944 he made his New York debut. He won first prize in the Ostend (Belgium) International Piano Festival in 1949. In London he received the Harriet Cohen Medal. Johannesen has frequently toured the United States, South America, Russia and Australia. He is the founder of the Casadesus International Piano Competition and President of the Cleveland Institute of Music.

Grant Johannesen

Grant Johannesen

DUBAL: You are one of the rare pianists who realize that there is more to the piano literature than the usual hundred pieces.

JOHANNESEN: Yes, to me, the piano literature is an endless garden of delights. It's a shame that pianists don't seek out the music that suits them best, instead of playing what they think is expected of them. For example, if someone like Arthur Rubinstein had a successful program back in 1940, legions of pianists felt they had to be heard in the same program in order to be taken seriously.

DUBAL: The last time I heard you in concert, you played the Grieg Ballade in the form of variations on a Norwegian folk song, Op. 24.

JOHANNESEN: Yes, the Grieg Ballade was once as standard as the Mussorgsky *Pictures at an Exhibition* is today. It was played back in the early part of the century by many pianists.

DUBAL: Yes, Godowsky, Rachmaninoff, Hofmann and Grainger played it. Arthur Rubinstein told me that Godowsky told him to learn it, and so he did. But it is not an easy work to bring off in a hall.

JOHANNESEN: I think you are right about that, but I think it is a significant piece, because it represents a certain marvelous school which had a lot to do with the emergence of Impressionism in France.

DUBAL: Yes, the French were very taken with Grieg.

JOHANNESEN: That's right. They always credited him with being one of their inspirations.

DUBAL: It's a pity that this major set of variations by the most famous Norwegian composer of all time is ignored.

JOHANNESEN: It is sad. Grieg wrote it with his heart's blood. But it certainly isn't the only thing that is ignored. Think of the vast Schumann repertory that is ignored, and the Fauré repertoire, which was neglected for so many years.

DUBAL: There are those who have said that you are responsible for discovering him, at least in the U.S.

JOHANNESEN: That is probably because I recorded the whole literature of Fauré for the piano before anyone else did. Getting neglected work on disc is one of the reasons for recording, as I see it. But still he remains relatively unknown in comparison to his enormous worth. So much of the great French piano literature is sealed from us in America.

DUBAL: What do you think might be the explanation for this?

JOHANNESEN: Perhaps the music is just too sophisticated. Even in France there are many marvelous French works that are neglected. For instance, the Dukas Sonata and Variations on a Theme by Rameau or the Sonatine by Roussel, which is one of the most interesting of all French pieces, are rarely played. I can never interest students in this repertoire.

DUBAL: And once their studies are through, they may never have the chance to learn them again.

JOHANNESEN: Absolutely; too often they fall into the syndrome of playing what Virgil Thomson called the "wow" pieces: the Tchaikovsky First, Rachmaninoff Second and so forth.

DUBAL: And now, of course, the competition route, which places such a great premium on the "wow" pieces, makes it even more unlikely that they will learn Chabrier or Fauré or Sévérac.

JOHANNESEN: That is why the competition I'm involved with, the Casadesus Competition at the Cleveland Institute of Music, is attempting to get young artists to study important American *and* French masterpieces. Now, we ask the final group of participants for a work such as the *Concord Sonata* of Ives, the Elliott Carter Sonata or the Boulez First Sonata. Unfortunately, we also have had Ravel's *Gaspard de la Nuit* down in that same group. But we're taking out the *Gaspard* because we decided we really must stress the fact that young artists should learn unusual repertory. It's astonishing to think that the piano repertory today is in many ways more narrow than it was back when I was a student. So often you hear students say, "I want to play a modern piece, so I'll play the such-and-such by Bartók or Stravinsky." But this has nothing to do with modern music. These are really the *classic* composers of the twentieth century. Unless our young people study truly modern works, contemporary works, they won't have much to say about Chopin and Liszt in the long run.

DUBAL: Look how Balanchine as a choreographer could shed new light on older music as well as be an artist of his time.

JOHANNESEN: To me he is one of the miracles of this century. He has been the best example of how to take a classical form, the ballet, and make it vital and contemporary. His works are for today, even if he uses Tchaikovsky as his music. I remember when I went to Leningrad with the Cleveland Orchestra many years ago, one night we went to see the Kirov Ballet do *Sleeping Beauty*. And I sat there thinking, "Tchaikovsky must have seen this production." It was locked in time; it was as if it should be in a museum. But that's no compliment to a composer. If his music is going to live, it has to live according to what is being said today. I've had students whom I assign, say, the Copland Piano Variations. And they say, "I may be American, but I feel more comfortable playing Liszt." I can't quite understand that, being American and growing up here, they don't feel right with the kind of sounds that Copland felt and heard so successfully, why that should be stranger than Liszt to them.

DUBAL: How did you come to be president of the Cleveland Institute of Music?

JOHANNESEN: I first visited the school when I went to Cleveland many years ago. And I can remember being extremely taken with it. The first president was Ernest Bloch, and he created a school which was modeled on its great European counterparts. Most of the schools in our country, except for the Juilliard School, grew without much planning. Anyway, the presidency of the institute was offered to me at a time in my life when I very much wanted to share my ideas with others. And what better place to do it than a school that attracts a very high caliber of student—students who really are aiming for a performance career. Although you know how few of them become soloists in the end.

DUBAL: What do you do about these students who wish for a concert career but are not likely to become soloists?

JOHANNESEN: Since chamber music is becoming a great focal point of musical interest in this country, I often try to encourage students who are not likely to be the virtuosos of the future to really study chamber music. I also encourage them to study the lieder duos which are neglected in this country. It astonishes me that this whole beautiful repertoire goes unheard, simply because there aren't enough pianists who will take the extra time to learn it. The pianist must study languages, poetry, and he or she must also learn to coach singers while developing enormous sensitivities to sound. I feel passionately about the lieder repertoire because it is so beautiful and because I think it offers pianists a satisfying life. In Europe, every small town has a lieder series as well as a piano series.

DUBAL: I know that Robert Casadesus, who was the last great pianist born in the nineteenth century, was one of the great influences of your life.

JOHANNESEN: Yes, that's right. Robert was born in 1899. And yet he was, like Schnabel, a modern pianist. Both of them looked to Toscanini as their great influence. These were men of our time, men who didn't dress with flowing ties or long hair. They looked like businessmen; they wanted their appearances to be neutral.

DUBAL: Yes, Casadesus was cool and elegant. When you first listen to his records you think, "Oh, he plays with no rubato, this is such straight playing." But, days later his performance is still with you and his phrasing sounds so "right."

JOHANNESEN: Yes, the rubato was so subtle, and yet there was lots of rubato in his playing, but it never had much to do with excesses of personality; it was solely based on his feeling for the music.

DUBAL: Of course, in the big concerti, like the Saint-Saëns Fourth, he was Olympian. His recording of it is a treasure.

JOHANNESEN: And this was a work he never even played in performance.

DUBAL: Wasn't there something unusual about Casadesus's debut in this country?

JOHANNESEN: Yes, Madame Casadesus told me when he made his debut he played the Mozart *Coronation Concerto,* and it was unheard of at that time to make a debut with such a simple, unshowy piece. You were supposed to come with your big guns. But fortune had it that Toscanini was in the audience at the Philharmonic that night and he asked him to play with him the following season. He had addressed himself to the Mozart in that most beautiful, intimate way, as if he were caressing the music. I can see why he and George Szell got along so beautifully. They were both patrician.

DUBAL: What was he like as a teacher?

JOHANNESEN: He was a wonderful teacher for those who could grasp what he was getting at. He had an enormous ability to show you what the structure of music was, for instance, in large works, such as the B minor Sonata of Chopin, or the Schumann Fantasia, or the Liszt Sonata. He had a way of describing this music which took you from beginning to end in a flash. He guided you. It was this gift which always made his concerts seem so short. You always thought, "Is it possible, is the concert really over?" Ravel said of Robert that only a composer could play the piano that way.

DUBAL: And what a fine composer Casadesus was; of course you play his work.

JOHANNESEN: Robert took his composition very seriously but he didn't impose it on anyone. And although he was writing music on planes and trains, he had a large output, which included seven symphonies. In many ways his style of composition reflects his style of performance. He seems like a latter-day Scarlatti in his writing. It's not like Ravel or Debussy's music in any way. It is objective and astringent, and harmonically it's much like Roussel.

DUBAL: You, too, are a composer, isn't that right?

JOHANNESEN: I don't really think of myself as a composer, but I have written a lot of music in my time. Every pianist should compose. When I was sixteen I wrote a four-hand piano sonata and sent it to Hindemith at Yale, thinking, "Well, I'll take a chance at this." And miraculously, he wrote and accepted me as a pupil. But I was always much more wrapped up in the piano than in composition.

DUBAL: And wasn't Nadia Boulanger a teacher of yours, too?

JOHANNESEN: Yes, and she was a pupil of Fauré's.

DUBAL: Another neglected French composer you have played is Chabrier.

JOHANNESEN: I remember once sitting in a master class of Casadesus when his wife, Gaby, suddenly came into the room and said, "Do you know this is the seventieth anniversary of Chabrier's publication of the *Bourrée Fantasque?*" And of course, most of us thought, "Well, yes, isn't that interesting." But then Robert went on and said, "The reason we feel so strongly about this is that we think it was the first truly modern piece of French piano music." This sort of remark was typical Casadesus. He lived in music in such a special way, and of course, he very generously passed some of this on to me.

EDGAR OBMA

Born January 21, 1906, in Copenhagen, Denmark, Johansen studied there with Victor Schiøler. From 1924 to 1929 he toured Europe. In 1939 he joined the faculty of the University of Wisconsin in Madison as the first artist-in-residence in the U.S. An early exponent of the music of Busoni, he has recorded the complete solo piano works. Johansen has also committed to disc all of Bach's keyboard music, and for years he has been recording dozens of albums of the Liszt literature. Johansen is also a voluminous composer.

Gunnar Johansen

DUBAL: What were your musical roots?

JOHANSEN: By the time I was ten my urge to make music became irrepressible, but my father, who was a musician, didn't want me to become one. Fortunately, he was often away for weeks at a time, and each time he came home he heard real improvement, and his words became encouraging.

DUBAL: Encouragement can be the best teacher of all.

JOHANSEN: Oh, absolutely! Without it there is little hope. Teaching is such a tricky matter. My fellow Dane Victor Borge recently reminded me of our lessons with Frederic Lamond, one of the last great Liszt students, who must also have been one of the least-gifted teachers in the world. He was a fascinating person, the spitting image of Beethoven, and we all thought he behaved the way Beethoven must have behaved. At a lesson you would play for two or three bars and he would shout, "No, no, not like that!" and every two or three bars, he would stop you. When the lesson was over, you would remember nothing because you were so discombobulated by all the information and interruptions. This was the worst possible way of teaching.

DUBAL: I know of your great admiration for Ignaz Friedman, who was domiciled in Denmark during World War I.

JOHANSEN: The Danes took Friedman to their hearts. I remember one season when he gave twelve recitals, all sold-out, but somehow I got a stage seat. He played the Prelude, Aria and Finale of César Franck, and he was bathed in sweat. My teacher, Victor Schiøler, studied with Friedman and he told me that the Franck was learned only days before this concert. Friedman was a virtuoso with a staggering technique and an imagination to equal it. Just listen to his records.

DUBAL: Later you worked in Berlin with the eminent Busoni student and disciple Egon Petri.

JOHANSEN: That's right. I came to Berlin at fourteen and began studying with Petri when I was sixteen. It was he who made the deepest impression on me as a musician and pianist. It was Edwin Fischer who steered me to Petri. After a month with Petri I went to Fischer to play. At that time he was married to a very wonderful person, one of the Mendelssohns—Leonore, an actress. The Fischers were amazed at my playing of the Chopin G-flat etude, the *Butterfly,* as you call it in this country.

I remember their pleasure at the quickness with which I had absorbed the hand position of the Busoni school.

DUBAL: Was it Petri who inspired your passion for Liszt?

JOHANSEN: I always cared for Liszt, but my feeling for his breadth came chiefly through Petri, who kept me on my toes. My lessons with him were never ordinary. He would say to me, "Bring me some Liszt, *Transcendental Etudes*." So at the next lesson I brought in six out of the twelve, and at the next session the others. Of course my work could not have approached perfection but Petri never said, "Bring them back again." The lessons were one great forward motion. He was interested in showing me the flow of things. I was with him for two years and I cannot tell you how valuable his advice and counsel were to me.

DUBAL: Berlin was a great center of pianism at that time. Didn't Busoni himself come back there after World War I?

JOHANSEN: Busoni did come back in 1920, but by then he had sworn off piano teaching. Later I was told by Mrs. Busoni that all requests for lessons slid into the wastebasket. He guarded his time jealously. Perhaps he sensed that he didn't have much time left—he died at fifty-eight in 1924.

DUBAL: Did you ever hear Busoni play?

JOHANSEN: Indeed I did. I heard his first concert after his return to Berlin. I well remember how very excited I was while looking at the announcement of his programs outside of Wolf and Sachs, which was the foremost management at that time. Busoni was a monumental program-builder. The bill announced that he would perform the *Goldberg Variations* of Bach, the Weber A-flat Sonata, the first performance of his Toccata as well as the Sonatina on Themes of *Carmen* and Liszt's *Don Juan Fantasy*. Two nights later he was to play Beethoven's *Hammerklavier* Sonata and the twenty-four Preludes of Chopin. Just as I finished reading I noticed two fantastic-looking people approaching arm in arm. It was the great conductor Arthur Nikisch and Ferruccio Busoni. You can imagine my thrill at seeing both these giants together.

DUBAL: What was your opinion of Busoni the pianist?

JOHANSEN: He was the *colossus;* he outshone all others. In Germany we didn't speak of Mr. Busoni, we spoke of *Der* Busoni, as if he were a monument. His presence on stage was immense. He filled the hall. Petri used to say that the music became dematerialized, he brought it into another sphere. It had a mystical quality. . . . I met him only once, June

12, 1924, six weeks before he died. Face-to-face with him, I felt I was in the presence of genius.

DUBAL: Did you ever play for him?

JOHANSEN: He never heard me play, though I had the privilege of playing the first performance of his revised version of his Variations on a Theme of Chopin. Mrs. Busoni, however, did attend the recital.

DUBAL: May we now speak of Liszt, who looms large in your career, as he did in Busoni's and in Petri's?

JOHANSEN: Liszt wrote so much that it has taken a century just to estimate its value. As a pianist, Liszt must have played with a greater freedom and abandon than had ever before been known on any instrument. As a composer, I agree with Princess Wittgenstein, who said that "Liszt threw the spear of music farther into the future than anyone." It has taken a century to properly assess his voluminous output. . . . It has been one of my preoccupations to record Liszt's music. Actually, it has taken more than twenty years of very concentrated work just to record his "original" piano music. Now I am recording the transcriptions and opera paraphrases also, as well as things like the fifty-six Schubert-Liszt songs.

DUBAL: The Liszt recordings, like so many other of your projects, are monumental, and yet you have had time for many other things, including your interest in ecology and education. I believe in the 1960s you founded something called "The Leonardo Academy."

JOHANSEN: Leonardo da Vinci had hoped to start an academy, so he made an extraordinarily beautiful emblem for it which said, "Leonardo da Vinci Academia." Surrounding his name was a design which historians now call the knot design. It is a most intricate arabesque which represents the interconnectedness of knowledge.

DUBAL: But today we live in a highly specialized world.

JOHANSEN: Yes indeed, and this was one of my reasons for beginning the academy. Knowledge and learning had become so atomized, so fragmented, that I thought that Leonardo's concept of learning should be revived. This was in 1964, before there was any discussion of interdisciplinary learning. In the meantime, it has become almost an everyday term. Buckminster Fuller has been preaching "synergistic learning," very much like Arthur Koestler does in his book on creativity. You see, creativity is actually a matter of "*bisociation*"—one thing reinforces the other. For example, take a Beethoven sonata. It is far more difficult to learn the first sonata than it is to learn the second.

DUBAL: Speaking of learning, I remember when at the last hour you substituted for Peter Serkin when he was scheduled to play the Beethoven Sixth Piano Concerto (which is really the Violin Concerto in Beethoven's unknown piano version) with Ormandy and the Philadelphia. You had a spectacular success; it was even written up in *Time* magazine.

JOHANSEN: Yes, they called me in Wisconsin at two o'clock in the afternoon—I had never seen the work before. The rehearsal took place at four o'clock the following day; the performance took place that night. When I met Ormandy, he said to me, "Do you have the cadenza?" I said, "What cadenza?" I thought I was going to improvise a cadenza like in Beethoven's time, but Ormandy said, "Here's the cadenza," all eleven pages, which I had to sight-read at the rehearsal.

DUBAL: That must have been a harrowing experience.

JOHANSEN: It was. When Ormandy learned that I had never seen the score and that I learned it overnight, he told me he nearly had a heart attack!

CHRISTIAN STEINER

Ruth Laredo

Born November 20, 1937, in Detroit, Michigan, Laredo is a graduate of the Curtis Institute, where she studied with Rudolf Serkin. She made her New York orchestral debut in 1962 with Stokowski at Carnegie Hall, and her New York Philharmonic debut in the Ravel G major Concerto under Boulez. At Hunter College, she gave the first live performances in New York of all ten Scriabin sonatas. She was also the first pianist to record the complete solo piano works of Rachmaninoff. Laredo is currently in the process of preparing an edition of Rachmaninoff's piano music for C. F. Peters. She has received three Grammy Award nominations.

Ruth Laredo

DUBAL: Have you ever had a mentor in your career?

LAREDO: I sure could have used one at many points but basically I've been at it alone. I have never had a teacher, with the single exception of my first real teacher, who died when I was fourteen, who was interested in me as a person. His name was Edward Bredshall, and he was a wonderful guy. Thanks to him, I got very involved with music when I was about ten years old. My mother, who was my first teacher, took me to him. Thanks to him I had a hell of a good time playing the piano. He gave me Stravinsky and Bartók. He threw everything at me, and I learned them fast. I was fearless, and he encouraged that. He'd dare me by saying, "You can't play this." And I'd say, "Oh, yeah?" and I'd bring it in the following week. Bredshall was a complete musician and an intellectual; he was interested in everything. When I would go for my lessons I would listen to opera, and look at Chinese art. Edward Bredshall was probably the closest thing to a mentor I've ever had.

DUBAL: It sounds like you had quite a remarkable introduction to music. You must have been terribly sad when he died. And afterwards, as you say, you were on your own.

LAREDO: Yes, and I have been on my own all these years. I would have loved to have a teacher or conductor take an interest in me, someone who might have made the way easier for me, in music or in life, but sadly there has been no such person in my life.

DUBAL: Do you think that talent ultimately wins out?

LAREDO: No, I do not. I think that talent can be ignored, or even scoffed at. I think it's a matter of luck sometimes, whether a talented person finds his niche in life. And I don't really believe that the right things always happen. Perhaps with all the Russian music I play, I'm becoming a pessimist.

DUBAL: What does success mean for you as a musician?

LAREDO: When you're a musician, every time you play, you're starting from scratch. So, to my mind, success doesn't exist. It's an artificial concept.

DUBAL: Recently you played for the first time the mammoth Brahms B-flat Concerto, though Brahms, always whimsical about his own creations, called it "a tiny, tiny pianoforte concerto with a tiny, tiny wisp of a scherzo" in a letter to a friend. Tell me your history with the Brahms No. 2.

LAREDO: When I was a kid, I heard Rubinstein play the Brahms B-flat, and I was sure I had just heard the world's most beautiful piece. I wanted to play it more than anything. I was in high school at the time, so I sort of played through it after school for about a week. But I had other things to do that were more pressing, and my teacher at the time did not ask me to learn it. But I *loved* it. And of course having studied with Rudolf Serkin, and having heard him as well as many other great pianists play it through the years, I had become very familiar with it; though I had never actually had an occasion to learn and perform it, and I never knew whether or not I would, although I had played the Brahms First Piano Concerto in concert. But finally fate had it that I would play it with Joseph Silverstein conducting. So I began a grueling regimen of work because I had to learn it in practically no time at all. Well, I thought that I had played difficult music before, but this Brahms concerto is titanic. The architecture is like a cathedral with no top to it; it reaches up forever. The concerto is one of the most beautiful things in the world; you can hum it, you can sing it—but to play it is something else. It's not just stamina or fortitude that's required; there's an intellectual process that goes along with this music. How to sustain this kind of architecture is really what the performers must solve. It's a real *tour de force* to play this piece. I love Brahms and it is a real satisfaction knowing that I have played both of his piano concertos in my lifetime.

DUBAL: Arthur Rubinstein also loved Brahms with a passion. How did you feel about Rubinstein's playing?

LAREDO: It is only recently that I have come to appreciate Rubinstein's art. I don't know what took me so long. In the past few years I have been listening to his recordings more and more, especially his Chopin. It is so unique, and it speaks to the heart. He was such a great artist. He was always in love with life, and his joy is transmitted through his music. Too often musicians get into a rut, and they feel that the only thing that's important in life is music and musicians. But Rubinstein was a connoisseur of culture in the best and broadest sense of the word. He loved so much about life.

DUBAL: Why do you suppose there are so few women on the international concert circuit, while there are just as many women as men in the music schools? Is it that women are held back by motherhood?

LAREDO: That could be a partial explanation, but I doubt that that's the only reason. You know, Madame de Larrocha is a mother and so is Bella Davidovich.

DUBAL: And you have a daughter.

LAREDO: Yes, I do. It takes a lot of stamina and a lot of dedication to be both mother and pianist. I remember listening to Gina Bachauer on the radio a few years ago. She was describing the life of a woman on the road, and what it's like after the concert, going back to your hotel room, and being alone so much of the time. It can be a very lonely and difficult life.

DUBAL: And the physical demands of piano playing are very great, too, aren't they?

LAREDO: For me piano playing comes from the whole being. You know, when I play Rachmaninoff *Etudes Tableaux,* my legs hurt. Figure that out! It isn't just your hands that are busy and working hard. Playing the piano is a total physical involvement, it involves your entire body. Your hands are just an extension of your body when you play the piano, and you have to use your body in a special way for each different kind of music. People are always saying, "How can you play such big music? You're only five foot one." But, it has nothing to do with your height or weight, or how large your fingers are. It has to do with how you use your strength, how you manage to convey certain ideas—if you have ideas; how you express them. Your femininity and size are really just details.

DUBAL: Speaking of total involvement of the body, do you dance, or do you like to watch dancing?

LAREDO: It's funny, but when I was in music school, whenever I went out with fellow musicians, the worst dancers were usually the pianists. They had no rhythm at all, at least with their feet. I guess you either have a feeling for dance or you don't. I am crazy about watching dance: when I watch dancers, I learn about phrasing. There are some pianists who say they learn how to phrase musically by listening to opera singers. But I think dancers have so much more to tell me. This season I worked very closely with dancers because I played the world premiere of Peter Martins' work called *Waltzes,* which is based on Schubert dances. It was a great joy.

DUBAL: On the day of the concert, what do you find yourself hoping for?

LAREDO: Something which happens very infrequently: a feeling of ease, of relaxation, of being one with the music and the audience so that I can rise above myself and make music on a different level than I normally do. When that happens, I feel wonderful. It is not like any other feeling on earth. So often the piano is lousy, or the audience is coughing, or you are nervous, or your concentration is off—there are so many things that can go wrong in a concert situation. So when I have a concert like the one I just played in San Francisco, where the piano was fine and I was relaxed, and the audience seemed very attentive and right with me, I felt that I could do more than I was ever able to do before. I guess that's called inspiration. That's what I hope for. I don't expect it, but when it happens, it is really something.

DUBAL: What is the fundamental difference between playing for yourself and playing for an audience?

LAREDO: Basically, the dimension of the sound has to be very different. I find that every time I play in public I learn something I didn't know before. For instance, no matter how many times I've played the Liszt Concerto No. 1—and I've played this piece a lot, even as a child—there is something new to be discovered. Also, you have to play to suit the particular dimensions of the hall. You have to tailor your playing to different specifications every single time.

DUBAL: Is this done by instinct after a while?

LAREDO: Yes, by instinct, and your decisions must be instantaneous. I know where the last seat is, and I project to that person out there.

DUBAL: What about your pedaling? Is that worked out at home?

LAREDO: No. Pedaling is like breathing; you do it when you have to. It happens instinctively, unconsciously. I never write in a pedaling because you have to do it differently each time because the piano and the acoustical situation varies so much from place to place. You can't make any generalizations about pedaling, except to say that it changes all the time.

DUBAL: Isn't it terrible that a pianist cannot get to know his concert instrument? It's out in the world, so to speak; constantly changing. Isn't this frustrating?

LAREDO: Sometimes I wonder if it isn't better not to know the piano. Some of them I don't want to know; in fact I don't ever want to see them again.

DUBAL: How do you deal with bad instruments? Do they make you angry?

LAREDO: It's just something you learn to cope with. You learn to be philosophical about them. Actually, I think all the bad instruments have improved my playing, although I don't wish it on anybody to have to play a concert on a bad piano. It's easy to play with a beautiful sound if you've got a gorgeous piano. But what do you do when the piano isn't gorgeous and you still have that sound in your ear that tells you what you want? You learn to really listen and try for certain kinds of sounds, whether they're in the piano or not. It makes you aware of what you must create yourself, and that involves your legato, or your pedaling, or certain kinds of phrasing that you must be very strong on.

DUBAL: Do you worry much about the condition of your hands?

LAREDO: No, I don't walk around like Scriabin did, with my hands in gloves and things like that. I cook, and I do dishes. I try to live as normal a life as I can, because if you're too careful, that can be a problem in itself.

DUBAL: I have asked many pianists if they feel guilty about not playing more contemporary music, but that is not a question I can ask of you. You have played a great deal of contemporary music, especially in the early years of your career.

LAREDO: Yes, during the years that I was at Marlboro, there were real live composers around, and we did a lot of their music. It was fascinating. Leon Kirchner, who was a very close friend of mine during those years, would conduct works by Berg, Schoenberg, Webern and Bartók, and he got me interested in playing these things. So for years, I was very involved with this kind of music. It was like a world within a world, because at Marlboro at that time you also had Casals and his rather backward-looking musical tastes. As great as he was, he did not like music beyond the era of Brahms, and he was very definite about that. So when Leon Kirchner and his colleagues would come to Marlboro for a performance, Casals would stay home. Fortunately, I was able to benefit from both influences: Casals and the nineteenth century, and Leon Kirchner and other important composers of the twentieth century. We performed and learned new music week after week. I'll never forget the day they decided at Marlboro to record the Schoenberg Septet. I had played that piece so often, and I knew it so well that the day before the recording session, I didn't have to prepare anything because I had been playing it so much. It was so much a part of me, that I just walked in the next day and we sat down and recorded it. It astonishes me to think about it now; but that's how close I was to that kind of music then. Today, it would be like speaking Chinese. One must stay with a language for it to be spoken fluently.

DUBAL: You received a Grammy nomination for your all-Barber recording. Did you know Barber? I know he was very tough on performances of his own music.

LAREDO: I cannot say that I knew him, but I met him a number of times. My graduation from the Curtis Institute took place on his birthday; it was his fiftieth birthday. And there was a program of all-Barber music to celebrate it. It was just a coincidence, but I had prepared the Sonata to graduate with. So I was part of that celebration. There was a dazzling array of musicians in the audience, including Barber and Menotti. It was quite a task, to play that piece for Barber. But he came back to me after the concert and very warmly congratulated me, and he wrote on my copy of the Sonata: "*Brava, bravissima.*" Of course I treasure that autograph.

DUBAL: What is the role of logic in your interpretations?

LAREDO: I think that logic can only go a certain distance in music. I find that the most inspired performances are always those which are inexplicable from a logical point of view. If I try too hard to understand any piece of music intellectually, I find that it thwarts my musicality. There has to be a combination of intelligence and intuition. As a performer and as a listener, I find that you miss an awful lot of the music's feeling if it is completely filtered through your intellectual processes. For instance, with Rachmaninoff you must really let yourself go, and feel what he is expressing. It's a mistake to try and analyze Rachmaninoff too carefully, there's so much emotion connected with him.

DUBAL: Is that perhaps why he is so popular?

LAREDO: Yes, and getting more popular all the time.

DUBAL: You are now involved in editing Rachmaninoff's music. What is it like for you to edit music, some of which is very well known?

LAREDO: It's actually an extremely interesting process, one that I hadn't known anything about until I began working on this project. There's an opportunity to apply what I know of Rachmaninoff's personality to the work, and having played all of his music I feel that I have come to know his personality very well. There was something very austere about Rachmaninoff's personality as a pianist and as a composer. I knew immediately that the first editions that were furnished to me by the Peters Publishing Company had to have been edited by someone, as they were filled with all kinds of extraneous markings that were not characteristic of the man, and after I got some manuscript copies from the Library of Congress, I knew I was correct in my assumption. There was not an extra accent or line on any of his original manuscripts. Rachmaninoff is clear, logical and precise. Once I saw the originals, I felt strongly that the works that I had been given to edit had to be cleaned up. I took what I call the "*graffiti*" away. The piece that was altered beyond recognition was the C-sharp minor Prelude, Op. 3 No. 2, the most famous of any Rachmaninoff work. There are bad editions with four fortes marked, and all kinds of tempo markings and other fussy things he never would have written. What a difference between these corrupt editions and the autograph manuscript, where everything is so clean, plain and clear. Slowly we are beginning to understand the difference between what the composers wanted and what the editors decided they wanted. A bad editor can put his imprint on a piece of music just as a bad pianist can in performance.

DUBAL: Have your performances of Rachmaninoff taken on a different aspect as a result of the editing project?

LAREDO: Absolutely; I look at pieces I haven't played since the editing in an entirely different way. It's important to realize that recordings should not be the last word, no matter who they are by.

DUBAL: So is it frustrating for you to listen to your recordings now, ones that were influenced by those, as you say, "corrupt" editions? Do you wish to record these things again?

LAREDO: Of course. You are never happy with what you did last year; you want to do it again because you've always learned something new. But in the end, you have to be philosophical about any performance, either on a record or in a concert.

DUBAL: Do you remember any music as being particularly difficult from a technical point of view?

LAREDO: Sure, the Chopin etudes. Did they ever give me grief. But that's why we want to study them—to build our technique. Serkin gave me the Chopin etudes to study instead of exercises. And Mr. Bredshall gave me Prokofiev to play. I should tell you, I never studied technique in my life. I never worked on any of those finger-breaker exercises. They are so deadly and dull.

DUBAL: Did you learn your Ravel repertoire as a teenager?

LAREDO: I learned the Ravel repertoire mostly when I was young so that the extreme difficulties somehow didn't bother me. *Gaspard de la Nuit* came into my life at fifteen. I just didn't know how hard it was. There's not enough time in your life to learn everything, so there are some works you have to learn when you are that young. Also, they are oftentimes too difficult for an older person; it's like learning a language early.

DUBAL: And what about Scriabin?

LAREDO: Scriabin's music was a struggle. The left-hand parts are murderous, and it's so convoluted, I didn't learn any of it as a child. It is in no way children's stuff. It's so heated and unhealthy, one might say. Being shut up with Scriabin every day was not the easiest thing I've ever had to do. But I'm grateful that I did it because it opened up for me an entirely new aspect of piano playing. At Curtis, with Serkin, my life as a musician was far more circumscribed. The great Russian literature was played far less than the Germanic. If it wasn't for record companies, I might never have entered this glorious world.

DUBAL: Do you find that there is a lot of pressure to give the public something new every time you return to a city?

LAREDO: Yes, there is always the pressure of having to come up with a different program, especially in the United States. Perhaps it has something to do with our American penchant for obsolescence. We are obsessed with what is new, whether it is a toaster or a program. Some people will always feel cheated if they have heard you play the piece before. It's such a wonderful thing to play things that you've already played, and to not always have to grapple with new things. I'll never forget the three years I spent studying and recording all of Rachmaninoff, piece after piece; it was like climbing mountains forever. Only now do I get the full joy of playing some of it.

I've just played the *Appassionata* this year, and it's such a wonderful, new feeling for me because I had worked on it from the time I was sixteen or so. Having lived with it for so many years, it's like a new piece for me now, and yet it's an old piece, too. You have to have the chance to play things for years in order to have some kind of perspective on them.

DUBAL: Do you listen to many of your colleagues? And how do you usually respond to interpretations that are different from yours?

LAREDO: First, I love to listen to other pianists play. But I never superimpose my interpretation on someone else's playing. As well as being a performer, I'm a listener, and I need what music can do for me. Carrying my own ideas around too heavily could be very destructive.

NCN
CAL 104.3 FM NEW YORK

Born April 3, 1948, in White Plains, New York, Ohlsson began studies at the Westchester Conservatory. At thirteen, he became a student of Sasha Gorodnitzki and at eighteen he entered the Juilliard School. In 1966 he won the Busoni Competition, quickly followed by a victory at the Montreal International Piano Competition. In 1970 he became the first American to win the prestigious Chopin International Competition in Warsaw. Since that time he has played worldwide.

Garrick Ohlsson

DUBAL: Do you remember what your first musical experiences were?

OHLSSON: I remember that as a small child I used to sit for hours and listen to classical records. Nothing would make me happier. I was always drawn to music. When I was eight I began studying. My parents took me to a couple of local recitals, but they didn't really interest me too much. Then they took me to Brailowsky playing an all-Chopin recital at Carnegie Hall, which was very exciting for me. About three months later, I heard Rubinstein do an all-Chopin concert at Carnegie Hall and suddenly I realized *this was it.* I will never forget the opening of the F-sharp minor Polonaise, and I will never, as long as I live, forget the way the G minor Ballade sounded that night. I had never heard the piece, and I thought it was the most wonderful thing that had ever happened to me.

DUBAL: What was your early musical education like?

OHLSSON: I think I was long overdue when I began the piano at eight. I went through four years of the John Thompson method in three months. My first teacher, Tom Lishman, was a terrific teacher in many ways. We had a wonderful rapport and he never filled my head with nonsense, which I'm afraid can happen in the music-teaching profession. I'm not saying it happens a lot, but you hear some pretty strange theories now and then. Sometimes at children's recitals, you see kids who look like they still play with a coin on the back of their hand, or ones who look like they're swimming when they play. Some idiosyncrasies are encouraged too much. But Lishman didn't fill my head with any nonsense. He was very pragmatic, and he demystified the process of learning to play the piano, which I appreciated. By the time I was twelve, I was studying Chopin etudes. At that point he told me I could get much better technical work out of them than I could possibly get out of practicing scales. And that's the way I've been practicing technically ever since. I've always taken the technical work directly out of the materials I'm working on.

DUBAL: So at twelve you completely stopped playing scales and arpeggios?

OHLSSON: That's right. But you can't imagine how many piano teachers have gotten cross with me when I admitted that to them.

DUBAL: Why is that?

OHLSSON: Because it undermines their approach. Don't you remember being told, "You'll never be a pianist unless you practice your scales an hour or two a day" and that sort of thing?

DUBAL: Yes, perhaps such teachers breed compulsion. Even a Rachmaninoff couldn't get started until he did an hour or more of scale and arpeggio work. Do you really think Rachmaninoff needed to spend so much time warming up? Or was he a creature of habit, as so many pianists become?

OHLSSON: We are all creatures of habit to a point, but I can say without reservation that Rachmaninoff is one of the few pianists I really admire. Of course I never heard him "live," but the recordings are precious documents of a fabulous musical imagination.

DUBAL: Were there any other pianists you remember hearing in recital as a child who made a particular impression on you?

OHLSSON: The first pianist who ever made me listen to a slow movement was Richter, whom I heard when I was twelve. I had always wanted the slow movements to be over with. I was bored; it was like going to a sermon in church. The grown-ups always talked about how wonderful the slow movement was, but I just wanted to hear the fingers flying. Anyway, Richter played an all-Beethoven recital at Carnegie Hall in his first American tour. And when he got to the slow movement of Beethoven's Sonata Op. 2 No. 3 I thought, "Well, here we go." But I was mesmerized. And I remember seeing Rubinstein at that recital too, applauding very vigorously, and shouting "bravo" after it was all over. I'll never forget how thrilling it was to see one great pianist applauding another.

DUBAL: I'll bet you never imagined then that you would be the winner of the Chopin International Competition in Warsaw. Without that competition do you think you would be where you are today in your career?

OHLSSON: Probably not. Competitions are a way of really distinguishing yourself, and the other routes open to a young artist are few. For example, you might be lucky enough to have a teacher who knows a conductor well enough to arrange an audition for you. And if you're very good, the conductor might want to engage you. But then of course, he has to persuade his board of directors, and they're likely to say, "Well, why should we engage him when the public really wants to hear de Larrocha or Ashkenazy or somebody of that stature? Nobody will buy tickets!" But once in a great while this method will work. Or perhaps an unknown pianist might generate a local success, and if that happens, the conductor may write to a colleague or two of his, and word may spread slowly that way. Of course that doesn't happen very often and even when it does it's a very slow process. You have to have an awful lot of tenacity and a lot of persistence to make it in the music world. In other words, it's a lot more difficult to gain recognition without competitions.

DUBAL: Then what sort of advice would you give to the students you come in contact with who are gifted but who are not likely to win competitions?

OHLSSON: I don't really have a set piece of advice because I think, in the end, one's inner commitment to music is what is important. But that of course will not sustain the ambitious young potential Juilliard or Curtis student who is desperate for a career and wonders if he or she will make it.

DUBAL: If only we were taught to put the words "success" and "failure" in perspective.

OHLSSON: I agree completely. Do you think those second- and third-prize winners in competitions are really less gifted than the first-prize winners?

DUBAL: And then there are the people who do win competitions but don't stay afloat. How did you do it?

OHLSSON: I think timing is very important. For instance, I didn't enter the Chopin Competition until I was ready with a certain amount of recital and concerto repertoire, so that I wouldn't get stuck playing my winning piece or winning program over and over again. I also knew that even though I won the competition, I was still only at the beginning of my career. There's a glorious moment when you think you've arrived, but then all of a sudden you know you haven't. Two years and about 150 performances after I won the Chopin Competition (I'd just come back from my first tour of Japan, and I was feeling quite successful in a worldwide sense) I wound up in London and my manager asked me how it felt to be making my debut, and then she asked me if I was nervous! It is as if you are starting from scratch in every country, and the first impression you make anywhere is very important.

DUBAL: Do you ever have fantasies about being another kind of musician?

OHLSSON: No, not really, but I sometimes have nightmares about being a singer! I recently dreamt that I had landed a starring tenor role at one of the great opera houses even though I'm not a tenor at all. But as the curtain was about to go up opening night, I realized that I didn't even know the first notes of the role. This was obviously a dream filled with anxiety, and I should think this kind of dream would be familiar to most pianists. But more to the point, I sometimes imagine myself a conductor or a member of a string quartet. But I would really like to be a dancer. I am naturally something of an athletic pianist, and perhaps it all ties in.

DUBAL: Your hand looks very large to me.

OHLSSON: For a person who is six feet four, I have only an average-size hand, but in the world of piano playing I think it is considered enormous. I can squeeze out twelve notes in my left hand and eleven in my right.

DUBAL: Rachmaninoff had a similar stretch.

OHLSSON: Yes, something along that order.

DUBAL: And Rachmaninoff is a composer that fits your hand very well.

OHLSSON: Yes, I don't have the fear of Rachmaninoff that many pianists seem to have. To me, playing Rachmaninoff is not so different from playing Chopin. It's just for bigger hands, and there's more going on at one time. But I believe that if you can play Chopin, you can play Rachmaninoff. In general, I think the importance of the size of one's hands is a little bit exaggerated in piano playing. Having enormous hands can be a great advantage, but the average hand is plenty big enough for most tasks on the piano. Most pieces in the standard repertoire can be mastered by anyone with proper technical study and application. It's a matter of knowing how to move choreographically over the keyboard.

DUBAL: What is the most difficult piece you've ever played, if one can ask such a thing?

OHLSSON: Probably Rachmaninoff's transcription of the scherzo from Mendelssohn's *Midsummer Night's Dream*. Technically it's beastly. There are more notes running by per cubic square second of sound than you can imagine, and they have to be played very lightly and very discreetly. It really is the single most difficult thing that I can ever think of playing.

DUBAL: How is your memory?

OHLSSON: So far, I have very good retention. I am able to keep millions of notes in my head at a time. But I find that composers like Rachmaninoff and Scriabin, with their vast number of decorative notes, tend to slip out faster, unless one plays the pieces constantly. They stick in the hand better than the memory. Of course very modern works are also very difficult to keep in the fingers.

DUBAL: About modern works, which ones do you do?

OHLSSON: Not so many. About two years ago, I sort of took stock of my repertoire, and I noticed that there was an enormous hole from about 1912 to 1965. When I was at Juilliard I played quite a few premieres of new pieces and I was very familiar with what was going on in the avant-garde at that time. But since I've established my career, I have done only a very little, and unfortunately the public does not beat a path to your door to hear them again. This season I'll be playing for the first time the Wolpe Passacaglia.

DUBAL: I'm sure that is difficult, having heard some of Wolpe's other music.

OHLSSON: Tremendously difficult, and a tremendously effective piece. I think this is something that the public will catch on to, even though it is as modern and challenging as it is. Because it isn't abstruse. I'll also be playing some of the "classic" moderns, the Webern Variations, Op. 27, the Schoenberg Op. 23 pieces, and the Bartók Op. 18 Etudes, along with the Bartók concerti.

DUBAL: Those three Bartók etudes are stunning.

OHLSSON: They're absolutely extraordinary, and monstrously difficult. I find that after having learned them, even Bartók's mighty Second Concerto is not quite as formidable as it used to be.

DUBAL: What is your practicing procedure?

OHLSSON: I like to practice in the morning, to get up and wander around aimlessly for about an hour, and then marshal the forces together. Liszt said that we rediscover the basis of our technique and of our playing each day, which is very much the way it happens. It's not a mystical voyage of rediscovery, and yet I sit down and the world begins again. I do not have any set routine at all; my schedule depends on what I need to work on. When I'm on tour and forced to be a little more pragmatic, I outline what I need to accomplish. But when I'm sitting at home, I usually free-associate. I like to practice what appeals to me at the moment, but if I get nervous about things that aren't getting done I cram them in later.

DUBAL: What are your feelings when you're performing on stage in a major concert hall?

OHLSSON: There are times when it feels so wonderful that you can't imagine doing anything that stimulates you in a more positive way. You feel totally potent. You feel like you can do anything you want. Everybody loves you, and you are in love with them. But sometimes you're scared, and sometimes you're in-between, and sometimes you're both at once. I find my reactions to performance to be extraordinarily varied. Most of it comes from inside, though, how *I'm* feeling about the atmosphere.

DUBAL: Do you like playing in New York?

OHLSSON: I love playing here. It is my home town, really. But sometimes it can make me nervous because I've got so many friends here. When I play Los Angeles, or Chicago or London, the audience is anonymous in a way. But in New York I know all the personalities, the cross-currents. I know the political climate at places like Juilliard; I wonder whether so-and-so will like this or dislike that.

DUBAL: Where is the most far-flung place you've ever played?

OHLSSON: I suppose that would be a small town in New Zealand, which is the farthest place south on the globe with a concert hall. As I'm sure you know, a pianist must be willing to go to extremes.

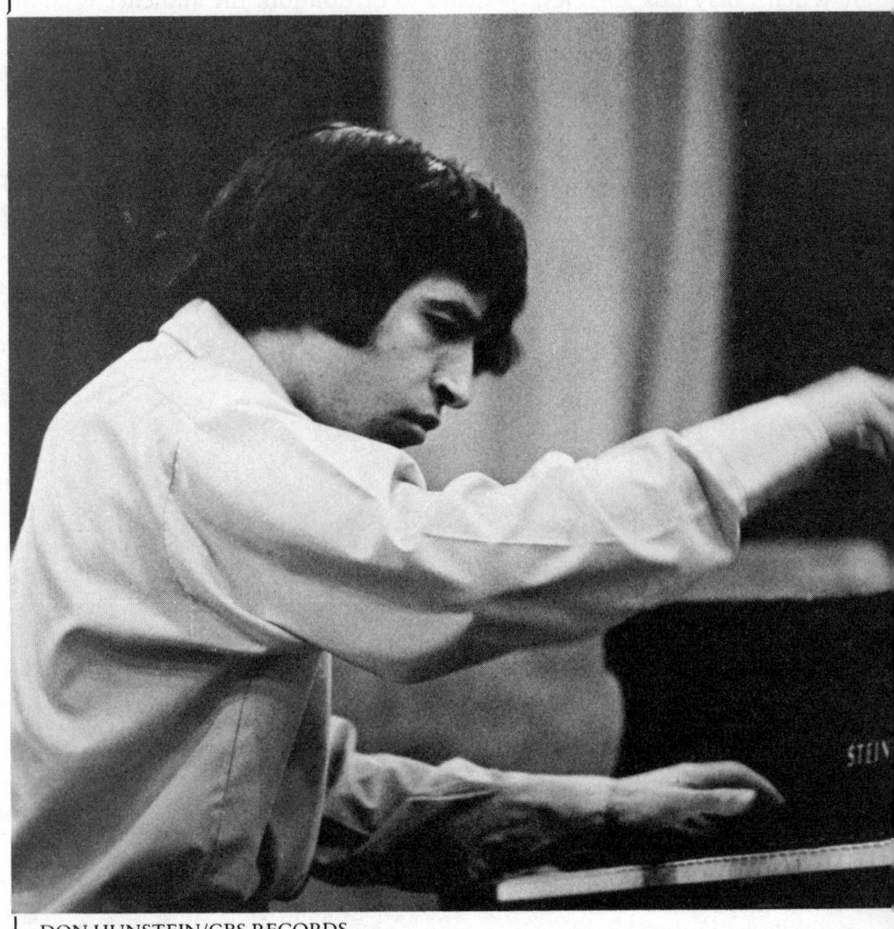

DON HUNSTEIN/CBS RECORDS

Born April 19, 1947, in New York City, Perahia was a piano student of Jeanette Haien and Mieczyslaw Horszowski and also studied conducting at the Mannes College of Music with Carl Bamberger. In 1972 he won the Leeds International Competition and in 1975 Perahia became the first recipient of the Avery Fisher Artist Award. He made his first tour of Japan in 1977. Perahia is one of the foremost pianists of his generation.

Murray Perahia

DUBAL: Schnabel once said that he only played music that was greater than any performance of it could be.

PERAHIA: Yes, I agree with that. Great music is always greater than it can be performed, which is why it is a constant challenge.

DUBAL: Would you consider an abstract work like a Schubert sonata to be of a higher order than a song, where the music characterizes the words?

PERAHIA: Each genre has its own expression and aspiration. But a song from Schubert's *Winterreise* cycle reveals a depth of emotion far beyond the meaning of the words. That's what's magical about the finest lieder.

DUBAL: I admire your Mozart concerto recordings in which you are also conducting. Tell me about your experience of conducting.

PERAHIA: I'm not really a conductor. I had my conducting debut with members of the Baltimore Symphony. I thought it went well; but on listening to the tape I had doubts about my ability. Later I worked with the English Chamber Orchestra, and I enjoyed that immensely. With them I programmed a symphony between two Mozart piano concertos which I conducted from the keyboard. However, I found that my performance of the symphony was drastically inferior to the concerti on the program.

DUBAL: Why was this?

PERAHIA: I don't have the technical expertise that a conductor really needs to shape an orchestra so that it can achieve a performance by just watching the stick. It's not a part-time job. So now my conducting only takes place in the Mozart concerti, where the concept of music-making is more like chamber music. Now I go into a rehearsal and say to the oboe player, "I've thought about this phrase a lot, but I don't feel natural with it yet." So he'll play it, and we'll talk about it. Eventually we'll create a performance among ourselves. My role then is not so much conducting as directing and focusing a performance. A real conductor needs the kind of technique that a pianist must possess.

DUBAL: Your playing has been likened to Dinu Lipatti's for its lyric and chaste qualities. Have you ever heard that before?

PERAHIA: Yes, I have heard it, but it embarrasses me because I admire Lipatti tremendously.

DUBAL: Like Lipatti, you are rather an intimate player. How do you feel about playing in such mammoth halls as Avery Fisher at Lincoln Center and the Royal Albert Hall in London?

PERAHIA: The big halls tend to intimidate me a little bit. Partly because a great deal of the repertoire was simply not intended for such big spaces. There's a kind of intimacy which can be achieved in small halls, where one feels one can reach the entire audience. Great artists like Horowitz, Arrau, Serkin and others have managed it but it is an art in itself. I remember hearing Rudolf Serkin perform the Schubert A major Sonata Op. posthumous. I was sitting in the last seat of Carnegie Hall, all the way on top, and every nuance was projected. I can't tell you what that performance meant to me. It may have changed my life. But for me, the big hall will always be daunting because it threatens the intimacy I try to create. Certainly Schumann, with his mosaic-like and fragmented thought, is not for the big hall. It's not like the Lisztian rhetoric, which is geared for big halls. In fact, I've just played the Liszt Sonata in B minor, which comes to life better in a large hall.

DUBAL: One might even say that Liszt invented "public music" for a large hall. What are your thoughts about the Liszt Sonata, which is so often called his greatest work?

PERAHIA: It is the Faust theme in music. It is diabolical, erotic, and it embodies what we now know of as "Lisztian." It is Liszt's autobiography in music. In the Liszt Sonata everything is exposed whereas in Schumann, for instance, there is much left to the imagination.

DUBAL: Schumann is certainly one of your great passions.

PERAHIA: Yes, for many years, I was obsessed with Schumann. He was the composer who touched me the most. Perhaps some of my enthusiasm has worn off, but just a little. I still feel that Schumann's emotional world is tremendously affecting and vulnerable.

DUBAL: Do you know the critical writings of Schumann?

PERAHIA: Oh, yes. I love reading them. Schumann was one of the great writers on music. His writings give you real insight into the way he thought about music, and they give you a strong sense of the musical standards of the time. He loathed the easy popularity of such piano virtuosi as Herz and Kalkbrenner, as well as the operatic pomposity of Meyerbeer.

DUBAL: Tell me about your collaboration with Sir Peter Pears on Schumann's *Dichterliebe,* Op. 48.

PERAHIA: That recording meant a lot to me. Of all my recordings it gives me the most pleasure to listen to it. It was while we were making that record that I met Benjamin Britten. I had the good fortune to play the *Dichterliebe* for him, as well as some solo pieces. He also loved Schumann. I particularly remember going through "*In der Nacht*" with him. It was a revelation to see how one great composer thought about another. It was fascinating to see how undogmatically Britten looked at a score.

DUBAL: Have singers such as Pears influenced you musically?

PERAHIA: Yes, Peter Pears was a very important influence. I have often had his voice in my mind. Janet Baker is another singer whose voice I love, and I admired Maria Callas enormously. In addition to singing, I am also influenced by orchestral color, and I try to imitate orchestral sonorities on the piano.

DUBAL: Do you study more than just the piano works of a great composer?

PERAHIA: Yes, I spend many hours studying their other works. For instance, with Schubert, I'll go through all the songs and the quartets. Last summer I went through a few of Schubert's unknown operas. Although they were disappointing musically, they still taught me a great deal about Schubert's style. For me, it is very important to have a complete picture of the composer.

DUBAL: Do you ever have your concerts taped so that you can listen to them later on?

PERAHIA: Yes, and it can be very instructive. When I hear it back, I think, "Did I really play it *that* fast?" Or, "Why didn't I give that section more poetry or feeling?" This never fails to amaze me, because after a concert I am never sure how it went.

DUBAL: When von Bülow conducted an orchestra not only did the musicians stand but they memorized their parts. Do you think memory has become a neglected aspect of musical training?

PERAHIA: I feel very strongly that musicians should know the piece that they're playing from memory, even if they're playing in a quartet, though that's difficult of course. Unless you can play without music, you really don't know the piece completely.

DUBAL: Nietzsche once said that life would be a mistake without music. Could you do without it?

PERAHIA: Frankly, for me, this is an inconceivable thought. Look at

Beethoven, Smetana and Fauré, who composed some of their finest works after they became deaf. Of course, these are extraordinary examples, but, in my case, I know that I would at least be able to hear the music I already know in my head.

DUBAL: Do you think there is any reality to the romantic notion of the long-suffering artist?

PERAHIA: I don't know whether there is or not. I do know that we all have problems living in a post-industrial age, with the threat of annihilation hanging over us. It may be that an artist who might live in a more emotional realm than others suffers more openly about it.

DUBAL: Is it the responsibility of a good teacher to discourage students who they think will not succeed from attempting to have a career?

PERAHIA: Yes, I think the teacher must take a stand if the student doesn't really have the capacity to fulfill himself in music. Just because a student loves music doesn't mean he or she should be encouraged blindly. And music schools should be very selective about their auditions. People sacrifice their lives to unrealistic expectations.

REINHART WOLF

Born October 20, 1958, in Belgrade, Yugoslavia, Pogorelich studied at the Central School of Music in Moscow and later with Yevgeny Malinin at the Moscow Conservatory. In 1978 he won the Casagrande Competition at Terni, Italy, and in 1980, first prize at the Montreal International Competition. Later that year, he lost the Chopin Competition in Warsaw, thereby arousing a controversy that brought him international attention. On May 19, 1981, he made a sensational New York debut at Carnegie Hall. He has since played throughout the world, and his schedule is booked for seasons to come.

Ivo Pogorelich

DUBAL: When did you know that you would devote your life to the piano?

POGORELICH: I don't remember exactly when I realized that the piano would be for me. But I knew relatively early that I wanted to bring alive the part of my personality that needs to give. I knew I would become an artist of some kind.

DUBAL: What was your childhood like?

POGORELICH: It was a difficult life. I was always committed to practicing the piano, yet it was a hardship because I saw all the other children enjoying themselves after school. A child who wants to be a pianist doesn't necessarily understand how much he will benefit from all the work that is done rather effortlessly in childhood.

DUBAL: When did you really get motivated about your piano playing?

POGORELICH: When I first discovered how difficult it was to be really good at it, and how much you had to work and fight for real mastery. This happened when I went to Moscow to study, at age eleven. I studied at a special school for five years before I studied at the Moscow Conservatory. I was with children who had excellent training and who played well.

DUBAL: Which composer attracted you most at that point?

POGORELICH: Right at the beginning I fell in love with Prokofiev's music. I was given two pieces from the *Romeo and Juliet* cycle that Prokofiev transcribed for piano. They were wonderful character pieces, and I made a successful performance with them.

DUBAL: Have you retained your admiration for Prokofiev?

POGORELICH: Yes, I have, and as you know I have recorded the great Sixth Sonata, which Richter played often, and which Prokofiev premiered. And eventually I want to play all the piano concerti. I think some of the most valuable music of this century is by Prokofiev, and I do not mean just the piano music. His range is outstanding. I put him above Stravinsky. But I worry that Prokofiev is getting lost. Too many pianists play his music without looking at its meaning. They are content with the superficial effects of percussive brilliance. Suppose you participate in a competition—the Seventh Sonata has become a war-horse at these events. If you can play it cleanly you can get good marks. But the tragic and ironic aspects of that work are ignored.

DUBAL: Speaking of competitions, although you have won some, your career really took off as a result of the Chopin Competition, which you lost, but which created a furor among the judges.

POGORELICH: Yes, in one minute I was a star, and in three minutes I hit superstardom. Some of what happened was nonsense, but the main thing is I am playing concerts, which is what I always intended to do. You can't have a big career unless you play the competitions, which then spawn management, concerts and recordings.

DUBAL: Not everyone has the stamina for competition life.

POGORELICH: To be an artist requires more than talent. You need to have a bit of the soldier in you, not just for the performance but for facing all those who smile at you, but who speak behind your back.

DUBAL: Your concerts are packed, your records are hits; have you encountered much jealousy?

POGORELICH: Very much so, from colleagues who are challenged by my ability and fear it. And I've had particular trouble because of my age, because I am artistically mature and some people think that what I do can't be accomplished by someone only twenty-five.

DUBAL: Has this made you suspicious of people?

POGORELICH: No. This is a reality. I don't pay any attention to my detractors. I have always followed my own rhythm in life, and I do so now. But I wonder if some very valuable people are not victims of small people because they may not be as much of a soldier as I am. For instance, Glenn Gould, who was one of the greatest talents of the century, was just too sensitive to take part in the brutal competitiveness of concert-giving. Although I was not fortunate enough to have ever talked to him, I suspect that Gould was not aware of his weakness. He was not a soldier, he was a very delicate personality.

DUBAL: I think he was very self-aware and that he truly hated concert-giving. . . . When did you get to know Gould's art?

POGORELICH: In Moscow, where he was considered the greatest of the great. Unfortunately, like all of my generation, I never got to hear him in concert. But his records had a purity and clarity that I could find only in his playing.

DUBAL: Was there a particular recording which had a great impact on you?

POGORELICH: I think the most stupendous interpretations are the Bach

Three-Part Inventions. There he achieves a piano sound previously unknown to pianists. Neither Horowitz nor any of the other famous pianists of this century were ever able to produce anything like it, at least in my opinion.

DUBAL: Did any other of his records make that kind of impact?

POGORELICH: Nothing quite like that. I am of the opinion that his last recordings show a great decline, especially his second recording of the *Goldberg Variations*.

DUBAL: I think it shows an advance over his earlier version, the one that made him an overnight success. The later one has an inwardness revealing new aspects of the score.

POGORELICH: I feel it is done with a lack of structure and without Gould's wonderful rhythmic sense. I just don't find the wisdom in his playing that I do in the later playing of Gilels. But still, Gould added more to the development of piano playing than almost any other pianist. In virtually any piece he plays you can discover more beauty than in the entire output of most other artists.

DUBAL: What do you consider the criteria of great interpretation?

POGORELICH: A great interpretation must sound inevitable. But to make that occur, you must be the creator of a whole set of musical circumstances, in which the actors are rhythm, timing, agogics, accentuation, phrasing, pedaling and so forth, as well as an understanding of the aesthetics of the score. The musical line, the essence must be inevitable. In a sense you have to become a creator of the composition. Everything must blend into a perfect form. Look at Picasso's *Guérnica,* where you have three noses and four eyes, or an ear where the nose is supposed to be, or the eye where the ear is supposed to be. You may think it possible to add another eye, mouth, or three more teeth without spoiling the composition of the painting. But no. It must be the way Picasso made it. It was all inevitable.

DUBAL: You have told me that your wife, Alice Kezeradze, with whom you studied, has been the great musical influence of your life.

POGORELICH: Oh, yes, my wife has been my biggest influence. We say she was related to Franz Liszt because her teacher was a student of Liszt's pupil Siloti.

DUBAL: How did you meet your wife?

POGORELICH: It was like a Hollywood movie. I was at a beautiful reception, in a lovely home filled with antiques and paintings. I noticed a

Steinway piano, but thought it was probably not ever used. I sat down and played and soon someone made a very simple remark to me about my playing. Yet I could tell that there was great knowledge behind that remark. It was Alice who made it. I immediately asked her if she would give me lessons. She said, "Why not?" In October I started with a Beethoven sonata. I well remember that the first bars took us three and a half hours. The world's treasures began opening for me at that lesson. This was especially important for me because at that moment I felt that I wasn't getting enough from my teachers at the Moscow Conservatory.

DUBAL: Wasn't that during the black period at the Moscow Conservatory when so many great teachers died?

POGORELICH: That's right. They started to die off there left and right. Each day we went to the Conservatory expecting to discover a new black poster telling us of the next funeral service. During that time there was a terrible atmosphere of loss at "the House," as we called it, and it began to lose its importance for me.

DUBAL: How do you practice and how much?

POGORELICH: I do five hours a day if possible, but it's getting more and more difficult with my engagements. For me the best practice is when I have a practical task to accomplish. If I manage to fulfill it, then I've had a good day's work. Of course there are many different levels of work. Sometimes there is that deceptive level when you think, "Oh, how easy this is going to be!" But sometimes it's the opposite. When I first looked at Ravel's "*Scarbo,*" from *Gaspard,* I could hardly read the text and I thought, "I have to have a third hand to accomplish this!"

DUBAL: I think your "*Scarbo*" is amazing piano playing.

POGORELICH: Thank you; I am pleased with the outcome of the recording. But what I went through to make it happen!

DUBAL: Have you ever terminated a relationship with a piece that you performed often?

POGORELICH: Yes, I'm not going to play the Schumann *Symphonic Etudes* any longer, although I've recorded it, and it was one of my best stage works. I just don't have anything to say about it anymore. It's dry for me. Maybe I will come back to it in some years.

DUBAL: What repertoire are you working on now?

POGORELICH: I am working on a Haydn sonata. For generations Haydn has been considered a lesser genius than Mozart. But I say no, not true.

Even in his piano sonatas, Haydn goes higher and deeper than Mozart does in his sonatas.

DUBAL: Are you asked to play a large repertoire each season?

POGORELICH: I choose to play very little in public. Usually no more than two concerti per season, much less than my colleagues, and only one and a half or two recital programs per season. I try to keep my concert programs separate from what I work on at home.

DUBAL: What is the most crucial aspect of playing on stage?

POGORELICH: For me it is always one thing, that it should be as effortless as possible. You must know everything about a work in order for it to go easily under whatever circumstances—bad hall, bad audience, bad digestion.

DUBAL: Have you ever felt so exhilarated on stage that you became careless, or lost control?

POGORELICH: No, the control must never be lost. You are not there to be personally exhilarated. You are up there only to create art. You must be king on stage and dominate it.

DUBAL: In your preparation, what do you concentrate on most?

POGORELICH: I research every sound. By that I mean being constantly attentive to what I am playing at the moment. This involves using the ears as much as the hands.

DUBAL: Speaking of hands, yours are huge.

POGORELICH: My hands are very large, but that is not essential. Hands really should not be big. The important thing is a compact, flexible hand, and it's best if they are not too bony, but with pads on the ends of the fingers.

DUBAL: Have you ever had any curious things happen to you on stage?

POGORELICH: Oh, plenty of things. For example, I was on stage playing the Schumann Toccata once when a fly landed on my hand and started walking on it through the most difficult tightrope passages—and it held on! Suddenly it flew away and I was relieved, but just as I started the octaves in the other hand it descended upon me again. Perhaps the fly loved Schumann.

DUBAL: Do you know the charming episode in Paderewski's memoirs about the spider that came down its web only when he played the

Chopin etude in thirds? As soon as he finished it the spider would climb back up. It happened this way for months. Do you know Paderewski's music?

POGORELICH: No, I don't, except for the Minuet in G, though I do know that he mesmerized audiences.

DUBAL: We have often heard of the demonic forces that possessed Paganini and Liszt when they performed. Goethe defined the demonic as "that which intelligence and reason cannot account for. It is something external to my nature, but to which I am subject."

POGORELICH: If the artist on stage has this quality he must let it escape. But this can be very draining, even dangerous, because the performer must release all of his personality and being, the way Horowitz could. He was white-hot—his passion and volcanic power, his ability to excite, the fire of his temperament dominated the piano-playing world. I only wish he had not gone to play in Japan, where I heard him. Someone wrote of this performance that "Horowitz appeared in Japan as a beautiful antique vase, unfortunately broken in many parts." Because he didn't play his best he killed his legend.

DUBAL: How difficult it must be for such powers, such force to succumb to age. The world thinks of you as a god, and you're only human.

POGORELICH: The frustration must be terrible. To know that you once scaled the heights, but that the bull will finally defeat you.

DUBAL: I know you love to play in Japan.

POGORELICH: Yes, I do. I've played several times in Hiroshima. There are no more beautiful or appreciative young people in the world than in that city that was destroyed in seven seconds.

DUBAL: When do you think one is most receptive to great music?

POGORELICH: You never know when you are ready to begin to love music. Many don't get the chance in childhood and then they must wait. It's like falling in love with someone. You only know you're ready when it happens.

Born May 5, 1927, in New York City, Rosen graduated from Princeton University in 1947 and later received a Ph.D. in French literature there. He made his New York debut in 1951. From 1953 to 1955 Rosen was an assistant professor of modern languages at the Massachusetts Institute of Technology. In 1972 he received the National Book Award for his volume The Classical Style: Haydn, Mozart, Beethoven. *Rosen held the Charles Eliot Norton Chair of Poetics at Harvard for the 1980–1981 academic year. His career as a pianist has taken him on continuous world tours.*

Charles Rosen

Charles Rosen

DUBAL: You studied with Moriz Rosenthal, one of the giants in the history of piano playing, and you've written that there was a "gentlemanliness" about the pianists of his day that can never be recaptured.

ROSEN: Yes, it was a very extraordinary style of playing, which I don't know whether one can really do today. I've heard people try to imitate it, and it comes out sounding false. I certainly don't play the way Rosenthal did.

DUBAL: How old were you when you started your lessons with him?

ROSEN: The great tragedy was that when I started studying with Rosenthal at eleven, he was already seventy-five. He died just seven years later.

DUBAL: What was it like to have a lesson with Rosenthal?

ROSEN: He was an extraordinarily courteous teacher and, actually, this was a quality which came out in his playing. He would never, for example, say that I was wrong about anything. Instead he would say, "I have a different idea for this piece," and he would go to the keyboard and play it for me. He was a truly extraordinary man.

DUBAL: The composer who is probably closest to you is Beethoven. Who are the Beethoven players who have really affected you?

ROSEN: I would have to say Schnabel, from his recordings, and Rudolph Serkin, from concerts I attended when I was a child. Oddly, I had also heard Schnabel in recital, but he never played Beethoven at those times. Anyway, the pianist I heard most when I was a child was Serkin. In fact, one of the most beautiful concerts I have ever heard in my life was when he played the *Waldstein,* the *Les Adieux* and the *Hammerklavier* at Hunter College. Actually, I heard him do that program twice, once at Hunter College and once at Carnegie Hall.

DUBAL: Let's talk for a moment about programming a recital. You recently gave two Beethoven recitals which I felt worked very well. In the first, you played the *Waldstein,* followed by the great Sonatas Opp. 109, 110 and 111. In the second concert, you played the *Hammerklavier Sonata* and the *Diabelli Variations.*

ROSEN: Yes, they're not bad programs. The Opp. 109, 110 and 111 come out to be a little over sixty, maybe sixty-five minutes, so you have to put something else on. But you don't want to begin with the 109, because it's such a concentrated piece. It's a little difficult to get into it. So I decided to play the *Waldstein,* which is a marvelous piece, first; and one that an audience accepts very easily. Now the program is a little too long instead of being a little too short.

DUBAL: Seventy years ago, pianists would play the last five sonatas without blinking. But that's a little long.

ROSEN: Yes, by that standard, I suppose I'm okay. But for today's audiences that second program, the *Hammerklavier* and the *Diabelli* together is also long. They're the longest works from the end of Beethoven's life. The *Hammerklavier* is four movements, three of which are very long, and it lasts over forty minutes. The *Diabelli* is long as well. It is really thirty-four little pieces—thirty-three variations and a theme. But I'm told that the difference between the variations makes this rather an easy program to listen to. The first time, I tried it in London and people seemed very pleased about it. And I've played it four or five times since. I also played the two programs on two consecutive Sundays at Carnegie Hall recently. I thought it would be nice for people to be able to hear all the last, great works of Beethoven. It's a sort of bird's-eye view, if you will, of third-period Beethoven.

DUBAL: From a pianistic point of view, is the *Hammerklavier* the most difficult work of Beethoven's that you have ever studied?

ROSEN: Oh, no, I think the *Appassionata* and the *Les Adieux* are more difficult. I think the *Hammerklavier* has that reputation because it has a difficult opening. If you play the opening measures as written, that jump with one hand can be frightening, particularly with stage fright added in. Czerny, who was a pupil of Beethoven's, once wrote him a note—he was completely deaf at this time—saying, "There's a lady in Vienna who has been practicing your B-flat Sonata, Op. 106, for three months, and she still can't play the beginning!" That is, of course, just the sort of story that helped the *Hammerklavier* gain its formidable reputation. The interesting thing about the *Hammerklavier,* however, is that it really is a professional's piece, whereas most sonatas up until then, as hard as they were, still left room for the amateur. But, you don't play the *Hammerklavier* if you're an amateur; its size and structural complexity are altogether overwhelming. But it really isn't technically more difficult than, say, the *Les Adieux,* which has some extraordinarily difficult passages also.

DUBAL: Musically speaking, then, do you think it offers particular challenges—in the slow movement, for example?

Rosen: The slow movement is an extraordinarily beautiful piece if it is played with the *cantabile* and *espressivo* that Beethoven wanted. The difficulty of the slow movement is in its great length; it is a landscape lying before you. It lasts, depending on your tempo, between fifteen and eighteen minutes. I tend to play it rather on the slow side. And the challenge is to hold an audience's attention. I heard a magnificent performance of the slow movement from a great pianist once where he sort of slackened off just for a second, and people's attention began to wander. There's a dangerous point in it towards the end—about four minutes from the end. You have to hold your audience's attention. It's one of the rare pieces where I really do think about the audience while playing. As for the fugue, it's an enormously brilliant and very effective piece. But it's a little hard to listen to because it's so complicated and dissonant. Audiences can still be shocked by it, even in the late twentieth century.

Dubal: Have you felt the urge to play on fortepianos, which have become so popular recently in recordings?

Rosen: No, I don't really find that attractive at all; basically because it seems to me that most composers' imaginations—Beethoven's in particular—always exceed the instruments of their time. In one respect a fortepiano is a kind of a fraud because one assumes that there was a kind of instrument in the eighteenth century called the fortepiano which had a certain sound. But in fact there were lots and lots of different types of fortepianos, each having different kinds of sounds. A Viennese piano was so different from an English piano of the time that you might just as well have given them different names. Certainly Beethoven expected his music to be played on a great variety of pianos and the music was intended to meet that requirement. Personally, I think it is a mistake to try to limit the composer's imagination to the instrument he had in his house while he was composing. For instance, there are many passages in Beethoven which are easier to play on an old piano, while other passages don't "come off" on the old piano at all. Beethoven must have known what would work and what wouldn't, but he still wanted to write them. In other words, there are advantages to both. On the whole, I think the balance is in favor of the modern piano, particularly since the old pianos only work in halls that seat less than 200 people, and you can't make a living playing to audiences of that kind anymore.

Dubal: That's right. When Mozart played a new concerto for one of his subscription concerts in Vienna the audience didn't exceed 250. But even though he had to hire the orchestra himself, he was still able to pay a full year's rent from the profits.

Rosen: To play for an audience of less than 500 today, with the spiraling costs of transportation and hotels, is very difficult. Look at Broadway plays. We all remember the time when if a play didn't get very good notices, the manager, if he had faith in it, would keep it open until it attracted an audience. That's what happened with *Tobacco Road,* for instance, which was, for a while, the longest-running play on Broadway. Nowadays, if it doesn't get an audience right away, it closes because of the enormous expense of turning on the lights. This is a problem all of us in the performing arts are fighting, and I think it is getting worse.

DUBAL: In 1830, Chopin could have played for two or three hundred people in the little Pleyel Hall, and if there was a Rothschild or any other wealthy patron in the audience, his financial troubles would be over. I think many students still have the romantic notion that someone is going to come to their concert, hear their genius and sweep them off into stardom.

ROSEN: But, of course, careers always take a number of years to build. They never come about because of one person or one anything. Careers are made out of a subtle combination of things.

DUBAL: Has Beethoven been the great test of your career?

ROSEN: I wouldn't really say so. Beethoven is the composer I like to practice more than any other, but I'm not sure he's a greater test than, say, Chopin or Bach.

DUBAL: Does Bach come after Beethoven as the composer whom you like to practice?

ROSEN: I think most people like to practice Bach, though Bach is more of a problem to play in public, particulary the "Forty-eight," the great *Well-Tempered Clavier*. They were really not meant for public performance. So I don't play Bach very often in public.

DUBAL: You have tremendous variety in your discography. How do you feel about Liszt among the composers that you play?

ROSEN: I've always thought him a very great composer, but I have, I must say, very odd taste in Liszt. The fashion nowadays is to like the very late pieces, the strange, experimental pieces. But I prefer the early pieces. I think that old war-horse the First Concerto is an absolute masterpiece. I also think the *Paganini Etudes* are very great. I think they're much better than the Paganini originals, although I hope no violinist will take exception. And the great Fantasy on Themes from *Don Giovanni* is extraordinary. Liszt is the first composer who really thought about music as pure sound. Nobody before Liszt had any idea of what could be done with sound alone, given any musical material. It's very modern in that sense.

DUBAL: Debussy is another composer you have recorded. Do you find that he is played in a colder, more objective way than when Gieseking played him?

ROSEN: Yes, there's been a reaction. When I started playing Debussy everybody wanted you to play it Impressionistically, the way Gieseking did. Gieseking put a beautiful wash on Debussy; he brought out the iridescent quality of his music. Yet there were an awful lot of extraordinary rhythmic nuances in Debussy that you could never hear when Gieseking played it. So a number of young pianists at that time began to play Debussy a bit differently. Also, we began to play the twelve etudes of 1915, which Gieseking almost never played. I beat Gieseking by a year in recording the etudes; I think mine was the first complete recording of the set.

DUBAL: Yes, even the etudes were played impressionistically by Gieseking.

ROSEN: Yes. They were. But he was a marvelous pianist.

DUBAL: At a recent all-Schumann recital you gave, you played the great Fantasy Op. 17 with an unfamiliar ending.

ROSEN: This was because the noted scholar Alan Walker had published an article pointing out that the original manuscript, which is in Budapest, contained a very different ending from the one that was published. A photograph of the last page of the manuscript accompanied his article, but the next-to-last page did not appear. So, I contacted somebody at the Library of Budapest, who was kind enough to send me a photograph of the entire score. It turns out that the end of the last movement as Schumann originally wrote it was entirely different from the published version. Schumann must have changed his mind just at the moment of printing, because the manuscript has all the printer's marks on it; you can see the printer's handwriting on the manuscript itself. But the last page has been crossed out, and two measures of arpeggios have been put in instead. Once you've seen the original ending, it's very hard to play what was printed. The original ending goes back to the first movement, with the quotation from Beethoven's song cycle *An die ferne Geliebte.* And not only does it repeat the ending of the first movement with a different harmony; it changes one of the notes of the melody. The change of melody is very beautiful, and creates an entirely different harmony. It brings you back to the first movement, in real cyclical Schumannesque form.

DUBAL: Schumann often had second thoughts, especially late in life, when he altered some of his early works.

ROSEN: Yes, and I suspect that the reason was that he realized he was becoming insane. I think he went through his old pieces and removed anything that could be interpreted as evidence of insanity—anything very original, eccentric or peculiar. He took out at least two of the greatest details in the *Kreisleriana*. And in the case of the *Davidsbündlertänze,* Schumann altered some of the greatest things in the piece. New editions of Schumann that are coming out are all based on the last text, and they should really be based on the first one.

DUBAL: In some ways Schumann is still unknown.

ROSEN: That's right. This may be because, although he was perhaps the most original composer of the 1830s and 1840s, he was less capable than Chopin. That is, his music is less perfect than Chopin's and more difficult to perform. There are not many pieces of Chopin which don't work in concert, with the exception of a few works like the *Allegro de Concert,* which nobody plays. But there are pieces of Schumann—very great works like the *Humoreske,* the F-sharp minor Sonata and the F minor Sonata—which don't really come off that well in concert, but which are very great and very original in context and form.

DUBAL: You've recently recorded the Elliott Carter Sonata. How does the public receive it when you perform it?

ROSEN: Always very well. The one piece I was frightened of was the Carter Piano Concerto; I was afraid it was going to be difficult because when I first heard it, I hadn't been impressed. But then the more I played it, the more I thought it was perhaps Elliott's greatest work. And I played it twice with the BBC Symphony two years apart, and both performances went over very well.

DUBAL: You rank Carter very high in the twentieth century.

ROSEN: Oh, yes, I think he's a great composer.

DUBAL: You have played a fairly large amount of contemporary music.

ROSEN: I've played some contemporary music; there are about five composers that I play. But Boulez and Carter are the only living ones.

DUBAL: Well, that may be more than most play these days.

ROSEN: If you look back, Gieseking used to play Schoenberg back in the 1920s, and Claudio Arrau played Schoenberg's *Drei Klavierstücke* Op. 11. And one forgets that Rubinstein made a reputation playing Stravinsky's *Petrouchka* arrangement, which was made for him and which he helped to write. Every pianist plays some of the music that was being written when he was twenty or thirty. But after that, it gets harder and harder to learn new music and to appreciate it, so you stick with the composers you started with.

DUBAL: Is anyone writing interesting piano music today?

ROSEN: That's the trouble; composers are not interested in the piano anymore. Take Elliott Carter for example. He wrote a piano sonata in 1946, and he wrote the *Night Fantasies* recently. That makes about thirty-four years between piano pieces, which is a very long time.

DUBAL: Is part of the problem that many contemporary composers don't play the piano very well? For instance, does Carter play well?

ROSEN: No, not terribly well; but your question makes me think of Bartók, who was really one of the greatest composers of this century, and of all time. But if most musicians who love Bartók were asked what his greatest works were, they would probably name the string quartets, the *Music for Strings, Percussion and Celeste* and the violin sonatas. Very few would name the piano music. Yet Bartók was one of the greatest pianists of all time. There's that recording of Bartók doing the *Kreutzer Sonata* with Szigeti, in a live performance in Washington, D.C., where the piano playing *alone* is one of the great experiences of Beethoven. And yet, the only works of Bartók for the piano which seem to be at the highest level are the three etudes, Op. 18, and *Improvisations,* Op. 20. But I think that's revealing: Bartók's greatest works for the piano combine other sounds. For example, his imagination was released when he had some percussion instruments or some other kind of sound besides the piano timbre to do something with. I don't think the composers of this century since Debussy have been inspired by the piano.

DUBAL: I'm inclined to agree with you. When did you first hear Bartók's work?

ROSEN: I first heard Bartók when I was about sixteen or seventeen and I had such a strong reaction to his music that I actually became physically ill—I was completely overwhelmed by it. But suddenly I understood what it was about, and I began looking at the piano pieces. The etudes and the *Improvisations* are quite remarkable. The Second Etude shows the influence of Debussy.

DUBAL: Yes, Debussy was truly the founding father of twentieth-century music.

ROSEN: I very much agree. The etude was written right after Bartók's first real contact with Debussy. And one of the *Improvisations,* which were composed not long before the etudes, was written for Debussy's death. Bartók's piano music was very heavily influenced by Debussy.

DUBAL: What do you think of Messiaen's piano music?

ROSEN: I find it very difficult to work on Messiaen. I prefer listening to somebody else play it. There are very great musicians, like Peter Serkin, who know how to bring his quality out in performance. Messiaen composes by blocks. He juxtaposes one block with another, instead of developing continuous ideas. And I feel that the musical material has to be a bit more refined than Messiaen's is for this type of composing to succeed. Boulez composes that way, too, because he studied with Messiaen, but Boulez pleases me very much, and working on his sonatas has been a very great pleasure. If anything, his musical material is overrefined.

DUBAL: In which hall do you enjoy playing the most?

ROSEN: I think I'm like most pianists, I prefer Carnegie Hall to most other places. But there are other beautiful halls. I like the Albert Hall in London, but it has problems. Did you know that it once had a double echo? Sir Thomas Beecham used to say that the only way a British composer could hear a second performance of his work was to get it performed in the Albert Hall. Of course it's been acoustically renovated and now it has a beautiful sound. The trouble is it's too big. They only get in about 3,500 people, but they could seat 5,000 if they tried. That's just too big for a great deal of music.

DUBAL: You have recently recorded several Beethoven sonatas which are beautifully recorded.

ROSEN: Yes. I recorded them in the Concertgebouw of Haarlem, Holland, not the one in Amsterdam. It's a very beautiful old hall seating about 1,200 people. All wood and plaster, the kind of sound that musicians like, and there was a beautiful piano. The only trouble was that the hall just happened to be located right next to the most beautiful church in all of Holland, which has very famous bells, four-hundred-year-old bells, and they ring every quarter of an hour. If you're playing, they're just faint enough so that you can drown them out. But if you happened to pause at the wrong moment, these bells would suddenly be your accompaniment. I wanted to leave them in, but I was overruled! If people only knew what we go through with each recording!

MICHEAL SANDOR

Born September 21, 1912, in Budapest, Hungary, Sandor was a student of Bartók at the Liszt Academy. He toured Europe and made his Carnegie Hall debut in 1939. Sandor was a winner of the Grand Prix du Disque in 1965 for his complete Bartók recordings. His book On Pianò Playing *was published in 1981. In 1982 he received the highest decoration given by the Hungarian government for artistic achievement. He has made many transcriptions for the piano. Sandor is a Juilliard School faculty member.*

Gyorgy Sandor

DUBAL: I've been reading your recent book *On Piano Playing,* which is full of technical suggestions. How did you come to write it?

SANDOR: It's really just the logical extension of my years of experience; and I thought it might be of value to students. These days, so many pianists are suffering from tendinitis and other hand problems, and I truly believe that the application of the principles of my book would eliminate many of these problems. It is tragic to think how many pianists have become incapacitated unnecessarily.

DUBAL: Why does this happen so frequently?

SANDOR: Bad work habits and a desperate lack of basic knowledge. I think most pianistic problems stem from the fact that the weak muscles are being strained to the limit, often damaging them.

DUBAL: We know that Schumann even used a mechanical device to strengthen his weak fourth finger. And the result was paralysis for life.

SANDOR: No device should ever be used on the hand. But even without such implements I've known many pianists who have damaged their hands, or have constant aches and pains as a result of faulty motions in their practicing. Instead of learning how to correct these motions, they practice until the muscles are completely desensitized.

DUBAL: So you think all of this is a result of improper movement?

SANDOR: Oh, absolutely! One must not develop finger strength, one must learn to utilize the stronger muscles. The technical part of my book explains how to activate these respective groups of muscles so that they never feel uncomfortable or tire while playing. There is never any reason to tire physically at the piano, even if you have to play three Rachmaninoff concertos in one sitting.

DUBAL: In your book you reduce technique to five fundamental motions and patterns. What are these motions?

SANDOR: They are 1) free fall, 2) the five fingers, 3) rotation, 4) staccato and 5) thrust. "Free fall" analyzes lifting, drop, landing and rebound processes. "The five fingers" concerns scale and arpeggio technique, focusing on adjusting motions, aligning the fingers with the respective forearm muscles, shifting and the proper use of the thumb. "Rotation" has to do with the different forms of rotational movement stemming from the forearm, in which you handle all the tremolos, trills and things of that nature. "Staccato" covers octaves, double-note playing and the like. The final principle, "thrust," involves the technique of chord-playing.

DUBAL: I was recently speaking to a former student of yours, a fine virtuoso, Barbara Nissman, who said that she owes everything to you. I asked her if she ever tired or had tightness or pain. She just laughed, saying, "Not a chance, I've studied with Sandor. . . ." Of course, it would be easier to grasp your method through demonstration than through the book.

SANDOR: Yes, when reading about technique, it is never as vivid as demonstration. And piano technique *must* be fused with the musical content; they must not be separated.

DUBAL: In your book you also discuss "the human performing mechanism," which involves an analysis of the muscles, flexors and extensors. Just as pianists generally don't know how pianos are made, they often know very little about their own anatomy.

SANDOR: Yes, basic mechanics are often ignored by teachers. I think this is because they believe that art and mechanics are mutually exclusive. Musicians live on traditions and rituals, and so we never learn from our teachers some very fundamental things.

DUBAL: Piano teachers all seem to have opinions on the subject of relaxation.

SANDOR: The trick is to mobilize the fingers in the most economical way by shifting the forearm slightly, according to the needs of your fingers. We must understand properly the functions of the large and small muscles, then there will be no tensing or strain. Too often the method of teaching is arbitrary.

DUBAL: So you have decided to be scientific about technique. Could you, for example, tell me what motion you would use for the Prokofiev Toccata?

SANDOR: Of course . . . number 4, "staccato technique," and if done properly, this piece, so often considered an exhausting work, will never tire you.

DUBAL: Surely this doesn't mean there are no technical difficulties.

SANDOR: Naturally there are difficulties, but there are no *problems*. If you want to play Liszt's *Feux-follets* pianissimo at maximum speed, with perfect evenness, sensibility and tonal imagination, I guarantee that this is a very difficult thing to achieve. However, there should be absolutely no *problem* in anybody's mind about how to practice it and what type of motion to use.

DUBAL: So, knowing the proper motion can save a lot of time.

SANDOR: One must avoid all kinds of unnecessary mechanical work. Time is important, especially for us pianists. You have an unlimited repertory to learn. Beethoven didn't write thirty-two sonatas for the English horn. . . . I'm very much against learning unnecessary etudes. If you want to study octaves, learn the Chopin "Octave Etude," don't learn Czerny's. Life is too short. Art is beautiful; don't deprive yourself.

DUBAL: Do you believe that your way is the only right way?

SANDOR: Please don't think for a moment that unless you play the piano exactly the way I say, you can't be a good pianist. There are some wonderful pianists who practice very differently from me.

DUBAL: I know that you studied with Bartók for four years. What was he like as a pianist, teacher and man?

SANDOR: It was an overwhelming experience. He was a wonderful person, reserved, very sensitive, extremely well-mannered. He was more than a great musician; he was a great human being. Not only was he extremely knowledgeable about the arts, but he seemed to know a great deal about everything. Surely he was one of the great geniuses in the history of composition; though, as you know, he never taught composition, just piano. As a pianist, he was colossal and he knew the literature intimately. I will never forget my first lesson with him. He sat down and simply played a scale. To my amazement, he played it unevenly. His scale was alive. It came from somewhere, and went somewhere. It wasn't stagnant, or bland. Such freedom was a revelation to me.

DUBAL: Was Bartók a great technician?

SANDOR: He was technically a virtuoso on the level of Prokofiev, Dohnányi, Rachmaninoff and Busoni. And as an interpreter, there are no words to describe the fusion of his world with that of the composers he played. Sequences of notes were turned into richly expressive melodies; harmonies and chords were bursting with tension or brought soothing relief. His rhythms danced with grace or angularity. His Scarlatti, Bach, Mozart, Beethoven and Debussy were highly personalized and filled with the spirit and pulsating life of the creative instinct.

DUBAL: Did you get the opportunity to study his own works with him?

SANDOR: I studied all of his major piano compositions with him, including the First and Second Concerti.

DUBAL: And didn't you give the world premiere of the Third Concerto?

SANDOR: That's right. . . . Bartók died in September 1945. I was with him frequently during the five years he was in the United States; I was with him at the last moments of his life and at the funeral too. Yet there was no mention of a third concerto. Like a miracle on December 3, 1945, the composer Tibor Serly called to tell me that Bartók had written a third piano concerto. He asked me if I wanted to present it. I then got in touch with Goddard Lieberson at Columbia Records, a great admirer of Bartók's, who got in touch with Eugene Ormandy. The first performance took place January 26, 1946.

DUBAL: And that was really the last piano concerto to truly enter the international repertoire.

SANDOR: That's true. I think it was popular from the very first.

DUBAL: I know that you studied composition with Kodály. Do you consider yourself a composer?

SANDOR: I am a transcriber and arranger of various works for the piano, but I am not a composer. I studied composition with Kodály so as to become a better musician. Kodály was an interesting teacher. He never told you what to do; he only told you what *not* to do. He was a subtle man, but also very direct. I last saw him in 1967, just a few months before his death. He had heard that it was my birthday and he wrote me a note saying "Many happy returns for your birthday. Live slowly so it lasts longer." He was a wonderful human being; very impressive, with a Christ-like face. And he remembered anything and everything he ever heard musically, including every note that any student of his ever wrote.

DUBAL: You have recorded the complete works of Bartók, Prokofiev, Kodály and so many others. But long ago you were regarded as a Liszt specialist.

SANDOR: Yes, because isn't every Hungarian supposed to be a Liszt player? I love his music, and of course I've recorded the *Mephisto,* the Sonata and other pieces, while the *Funérailles* has been very important in my repertoire.

DUBAL: There will always be the question of whether Liszt was the greatest pianist of all time.

SANDOR: Yes, the little mystery will go on forever, but I think it was Anton Rubinstein who said we are all corporals compared with Liszt, and this sentiment was repeated again and again by Tausig, Rosenthal and hundreds of others. Whether or not he was the greatest pianist of all time, one can judge from his compositions his unique knowledge of the piano.

DUBAL: I know you judge competitions. What are your feelings about these piano tournaments?

SANDOR: They are very unwholesome; a contagious disease which now covers the whole globe. In the good old days, we had maybe five or ten important competitions to launch performing careers, and that was bad enough. They can do tremendous damage to young artists. But they are good for the committees who participate, for the jury members and for building teachers' names. I myself very often judge international competitions. It's like playing God.

DUBAL: You mean to say you don't have any moral trepidation about playing God?

SANDOR: Yes, I do, but I try to play God the way I think God should play. I always look for that talent which has a quality of originality, instead of the uniformity which has become the status quo.

DUBAL: What is the first criterion of competition playing?

SANDOR: The first criterion is no wrong notes, and this also applies to recorded performance also. So in this respect as well as others, competition playing and recording have very real similarities. Both demand a degree of standardization. When recording a composition, an excessively individual rubato or phrasing may be enjoyed the first time, but by the tenth time the listener will be irritated with it. So there can be no very interesting rubatos or lingering pauses, which are so important in a live performance, where the visual and acoustic elements justify these nuances. Similarly, during concert performance one's touch can be unique and varied, but on records one's touch is homogenized by the electronic equipment. From the studio to the miking to the Dolby to the master-tape and the pressing—not to mention the editing—we are far from the live performance.

DUBAL: Are you saying then that live performance and recording are really two different worlds of playing?

SANDOR: Absolutely! One must cultivate two different kinds of interpretation. These two modes of performance have very little in common. We also have to overcome the myth that we can get the real truth from recording "live" performance. There's no mike that can take the extreme ranges without distortion of some kind. There's nothing I hate more than being given a tape of one of my live performances. It's inevitably awful.

DUBAL: Do you think that it is important to play the composer's whole output?

SANDOR: If I care about Bartók, I don't just play the *Allegro Barbaro*, I want to know the whole of his work, or as much of it as possible, even those works outside of the piano. It's like climbing a great mountain. When you can play the entire oeuvre, the view of that composer is even more wonderful than if you played only your favorite pieces.

Born December 21, 1953, in Budapest, Hungary, Schiff studied at the Franz Liszt Academy. He won prizes at the International Tchaikovsky Competition and the Leeds Competition, as well as Hungary's Liszt Prize. He subsequently gave many concerts throughout Europe and made his American debut in Carnegie Hall in 1978. Since then his career has taken him throughout the world with ever mounting success.

Andras Schiff

LAURA LYNN MINER

DUBAL: I've just heard your excellent recording of Bach's *Goldberg Variations*. Where does the Leipzig Master stand in your musical hierarchy?

SCHIFF: I will tell you very fervently that Bach is my favorite composer. He is my god, and he always will be. I always studied Bach, even from my first lessons. But at the age of fourteen I truly began to understand him. At that time I went to London to study with George Malcolm, the harpsichordist. He opened up a whole world for me.

DUBAL: When you were studying with Malcolm, did you play Bach on the harpsichord?

SCHIFF: No, because curiously enough, Malcolm hates the harpsichord. He prefers to play Baroque music on an instrument which is a hybrid harpsichord with about ten pedals on it so that he can then make all sorts of effects—including crescendos and diminuendos. Purists look down on this but Malcolm doesn't care. He is a fantastic musician and a wonderful pianist; and my feelings about the harpsichord are very much akin to his. For me it is like a sewing machine.

DUBAL: Perhaps this is because it is alien to the central European Romantic tradition which you spring from, where the harpsichord is hardly known.

SCHIFF: I think you are right. I'm not too keen on fortepianos either. But Malcolm did instill in me a sense of scholarship and a real understanding of Baroque procedures.

Bach gives practically no instructions at all. In a way he forces you to become the composer yourself. You must learn so many things, from tempi and dynamics to phrasing and articulation. The more knowledge you have of the Baroque style the better. One should know all of Bach's works, including the Passions and the cantatas. To play Bach in an arbitrary or rigid way is awful.

DUBAL: Did you hear the recordings of Glenn Gould when you were growing up in Hungary?

SCHIFF: Gould was one of my childhood idols. When I was about thirteen, I heard his famous recording of the *Goldberg Variations* and it was a revelation to me. The record came from Russia, where he is a hero, a legend. Then, just a couple of years ago, I actually got to meet him. I was playing the *Goldberg Variations* in Toronto, and Glenn heard it on radio. Imagine my excitement when he invited me and the violinist Gidon Kremer over to his studio. He died nine months later.

DUBAL: What was Gould's studio like?

SCHIFF: The studio was packed with machines—tape-recorders, video players, all sorts of mechanical things. But there was no piano. He showed us films that he had made, and he talked about my performance of the *Goldberg Variations* in detail. We talked until six in the morning, but Gould remained fresh. He had extraordinary energy and extraordinary charm. I felt that I was in the presence of a very happy and fulfilled person. He lived absolutely the way he wanted to and I think he accomplished what he had set out to in his fifty years. For me, nobody could play polyphony like Gould. He could control five voices more intelligently than most others can control two.

DUBAL: I know from hearing your records and concerts that, in addition to Bach, Mozart is another one of your favorites. You once said that he comes to you naturally. What about Schubert, who also looms large in your repertoire?

SCHIFF: Schubert is also natural for me. Beethoven, however, is not. I am working on him all the time; there is no piece of Beethoven's that I am completely satisfied with. But Schubert is a melodist, more in line with Mozart, and I love melody. For me, Schubert is a great painting of nature. I always hear water in his music. There is never a flashy passage in Schubert; it's all integrated. His chordal writing and voicing is so beautifully transparent. Schubert is a master of balance. In my opinion, he is the most sensitive composer. I sit for hours balancing chords in Schubert and getting the voicing I want. The opening of the B-flat or G major Sonata cannot be beautiful enough. It is something you work at all your life.

DUBAL: It never ceases to amaze me that Schubert lived to be only thirty-one, and Mozart to thirty-six.

SCHIFF: I know what you mean, particularly in the case of Mozart. Schubert was a genius but he was also a human being. There are works he grappled with that are unfinished—the sonata form was not as natural for him as lieder. Any piece of poetry, bad or good, and he was ready to set it. But Mozart's completeness, his constant perfection, it cannot be judged by normal standards. He was superhuman.

DUBAL: Of twentieth-century composers, I know you love Bartók.

SCHIFF: My teacher in Hungary, Pál Kadosa, knew Bartók well. They were friends, though it wasn't easy to be Bartók's friend. He was a very lonely and introverted man. Anyway, Kadosa, who studied many of Bartók's works with him, taught me not to play Bartók percussively. Bartók is always thumped so brutally that all of the tonal beauty in his music is lost.

DUBAL: It was Stravinsky who initiated the idea of the piano as a percussive box. In fact, around 1910, there was quite a trend away from Romantic music and the singing tone.

SCHIFF: I know. For me, Stravinsky's ideas are often cynical, and at times I question his sincerity. He was always so clever. But Bartók never joked. Everything was composed with passion.

DUBAL: Do you miss Hungary?

SCHIFF: No, I lived there for twenty-five years, that's long enough. I don't feel Hungarian at all. I am not patriotic. Being a Hungarian Jew, I feel more cosmopolitan, European. I think we should all get rid of any ideas of nationalism. Though, there is a difference between this and forgetting your roots. Look at Japan, where I love to play. They are getting Americanized in a frightful way. They are losing their culture. I've met Japanese musicians who don't even know how to sing a Japanese folk song.

DUBAL: How were the audiences in eastern Europe?

SCHIFF: I must say the audiences there are sensitive. I really miss them. The Russians are wonderful. I think they are among the best audiences in the world. The Russians have wonderful antennae to new things. That's why they were wild about Gould when he came there. They understood instantly that he had found a new dimension in interpretation.

DUBAL: Do you have any plans to go back to the Eastern Bloc countries?

SCHIFF: No, because I am afraid I could not get out again. I have too much to risk, I don't trust them.

DUBAL: In general, how do you view the audience?

SCHIFF: Whether I am playing in Carnegie Hall or a small town, I play to the most sensitive, music-loving people there. I never simplify for an audience.

DUBAL: You have occasionally been criticized for a lack of drama in your playing. How do you explain this?

SCHIFF: I think some critics confuse subtlety and understatement with lack of drama. I prefer to suggest things to my audience, not to force things down their throats. I give my audience credit for fantasy and imagination. I'm not interested in raping the music or the audience, and I get very angry when I listen to exhibitionistic performers. Instead of assaulting my audience I like to indicate the drama through sonority and the timing.

DUBAL: I understand completely. There is altogether too much noise in the society for us to go to a concert to be bombarded with sound.

SCHIFF: Yes, all the noise around us hurts me—traffic noise, street noise, amplified rock-and-roll. People come to a concert and can't hear pianissimo passages anymore. Their ears have been destroyed. I'm sure that in Handel and Bach's time, people had better hearing.

DUBAL: The world has to have been quieter then.

SCHIFF: But I find that most people today don't want silence, they want noise all the time, and that includes that ridiculous thing called Pachelbel's Canon. That's now the most well-known piece of Baroque music. It's on TV, in the movies, on the radio. You cannot escape Pachelbel's Canon.

DUBAL: I think it's preferable to the beer jingles and the Doublemint commercial. As Aldous Huxley wrote, "Orpheus has entered into an alliance with Pavlov."

SCHIFF: Yes, this is the Brave New World! And it expresses itself in the piano-playing world in the emphasis of technique at the expense of music. The hand muscles bulge, but ears are not trained and taste is never developed. The teachers should help, but they themselves practice mindlessly. For me the quality of sound is everything. In these large concert halls today, pianists work hard to get a big sound. Many pianists get stuck in a *mezzo forte* area and above, but with little coloring going on below.

DUBAL: Of the pianists of the early part of the twentieth century, who do you like most?

SCHIFF: I used to listen to Rachmaninoff quite a bit; he was wonderful. And I listen to Schnabel, though less now than once; for me it's not as deep as Edwin Fischer. I also love to listen to Cortot.

DUBAL: Then tremendous virtuosi like Horowitz and Hofmann are not usually for you?

SCHIFF: Naturally, I admire what they can do instrumentally. They have tremendous ideas, and they produce such pianistic color and effects as to make one's hair stand up like a punk-rocker's. But I believe that I am not in that line. They are great instrumentalists but they are not great musicians, because the composer is secondary. The public says it is going to hear Horowitz and the composer is in his shadow. When I go to a concert it is to hear a performance of a Mozart concerto, or a Chopin sonata. A pianist I adore is Mr. Arrau; I have the utmost respect for his art. He never loses sight of the composer.

DUBAL: What is your opinion of the conductors of today?

SCHIFF: I think this is a difficult time for conductors. There are no longer giants around like Furtwängler, Fritz Busch or Klemperer. And there are very few like Mr. Kubelik, who takes time, who cares, who really knows the music. Today we have the jet conductors who fly from one orchestra to another. And do you know that most of them hate concertos? It's the thing they concentrate least on. Think of it: I work on a concerto for years, and the conductor looks at it for five minutes before the rehearsal, if ever. It's really scandalous.

DUBAL: Which concertos do you enjoy playing the most?

SCHIFF: I find the Mozart concerti the pearls of the concerto literature. To be able to give a great performance of one is the greatest joy. But it happens rarely. A Mozart concerto must be carefully worked out, and then rehearsed over and over. But there is no time.

DUBAL: How do you usually feel after a concert?

SCHIFF: If nobody comes backstage, I feel terrible. Then again, sometimes I can feel terrible even if they do, because I'm still involved with the performance. I try to be nice to everybody; I'm glad to see them. But often I'm a little out of it.

DUBAL: Do you worry about memory during concerts?

SCHIFF: I consider myself lucky because I don't have any fear of memory problems. Of course this is an attitude that I cultivate, because if you think you will have a memory slip, it will come within two seconds. I concentrate on form and on where I am, and I don't even think of the memory.

DUBAL: Do you do your best playing at home or in concert?

SCHIFF: I always play better on stage than I do at home. On stage I can let go. In the studio I am quite analytical and very, very critical.

DUBAL: Are critics necessary?

SCHIFF: No, they are not, and they do a great deal of harm, not so much to the musicians as to the public and managers who take them seriously.

Who is this critic to tell everybody, especially the people who were not at the concert, what kind of an artist I am? The quality of the majority of music criticism is atrocious, and I'd be delighted if it all ceased.

DUBAL: I know you love to play chamber music.

SCHIFF: Yes, I love playing music with others. There is a warmth in it that one cannot duplicate in anything else. In Budapest when I was growing up, there was a great circle of doctors, lawyers, engineers and intellectuals who would get together twice a week to play. But today, home chamber-playing is dying out, which is a pity because I think amateur musicians are essential to the future of music.

DUBAL: Do you think classical music should be part of the school curriculum of young children?

SCHIFF: I do not think classical music should be forced on anyone. Children and adults should come to it on their own. Forcing anyone to love Beethoven will backfire. Listen to this horrible story. I recently had to play a concerto in Florence, Italy, and there was a general rehearsal which the schoolchildren of the town were forced to attend. It was awful. I felt they just hated Beethoven. I started to play the *Emperor Concerto,* and the noise was devastating. One of the children threw something at my eye. It felt like a stone; fortunately I was okay. But I'll never forget it.

DUBAL: What do you feel is essential to good listening?

SCHIFF: A lack of prejudice. You have to be open. I have found that many musicians become very analytical, very technical, and very close-minded when they listen to music. The result is they just can't enjoy it. I know people who are not musicians who are excellent listeners. I see it in their faces. They just light up.

Born July 24, 1947, in New York City, the son of Rudolf Serkin, he began studying at the Curtis Institute at the age of eleven. There he studied with his father and Mieczyslaw Horszowski, as well as Lee Luvisi. He appeared publicly and toured the United States during his teen years, making his New York debut in 1959. Serkin has recorded the standard literature and is a leading exponent of contemporary music. His recordings of Schoenberg and Messiaen have been widely praised, as have his performances of the standard repertoire.

Peter Serkin

DUBAL: Peter, did you always want to be a musician?

SERKIN: Yes, not necessarily a pianist, but something! I used to compose quite a bit. On some level I always felt that my family background was a kind of inspiration. My father is a pianist, my grandfather, Adolf Busch, was a violinist and a composer, his brother Fritz was a conductor, his other brother was a cellist. And it all goes back several generations. I knew the Busches, and I had the opportunity to hear many of their and my parents' friends: Toscanini, Horszowski, Casals, Marcel Moyse, all such wonderful musicians. From a very early age, the sounds of their music-making came through. I think I was inspired to love music by them. I remember being gripped by certain things. The Fifth *Brandenburg Concerto* was unforgettable. What an experience that was! I was about ten, and turning pages for my dad.

DUBAL: Were you pushed into becoming a musician?

SERKIN: No, just the opposite, which may have been one of the things that helped me. My parents actually tried to discourage me from becoming a musician. And that may have pushed me to try hard to learn something about music and piano playing.

DUBAL: Is there a right way of educating a child musically?

SERKIN: No, I don't think so. But there are certain key elements like analysis, counterpoint and harmony that seem to be neglected these days. Most often they're studied only because they're required, and then by rote. In order to get their degree, students will put up with them. Theory is no longer taught in the way it was in Bach, Mozart or Chopin's day. Back then the first things one learned were the principles of voice leading, counterpoint and harmony. I think there's great value in studying all the basics of music as well as solfège and dictation.

DUBAL: Is this because we are fixated on performance?

SERKIN: Yes, the focus seems to be on the playing rather than on learning anything about what one's playing.

DUBAL: So you recommend good schooling for musicians?

SERKIN: Yes, I'm very traditional-minded in that sense. I really believe in a thorough musical education. Also I think that one should be very careful in picking one's teachers. I feel very fortunate to have had such great musicians as Horszowski, Karl Ulrich Schnabel, as well as others, as teachers.

DUBAL: Do you find there is a kind of sameness about performance today?

SERKIN: Generally speaking, yes. There isn't enough risk-taking among performers today. Maybe that has to do with the fear of offending anyone and the great desire to be accepted. But if you're motivated by that, then you're caught in a real bind, because anything that's really bold or audacious about the original conception of these composers—and the great ones were very audacious—will be lost. There was a great integrity to each one of those composers and a certain ruthlessness that went along with it.

DUBAL: And you think this is too often missing today?

SERKIN: Yes, I often think our pyrotechnical ability adds up to very little. Maybe art has become too easy, too comfortable. Maybe we need to understand the role of pain in art. Art isn't meant to be just a nesting place, a comfortable place to retreat to. If everything is rounded off, and distilled, and made pleasant, then it becomes meaningless. It devalues the entire expression.

DUBAL: Do you have any interest in non-western music?

SERKIN: Oh, yes. I love all kinds of music—Indian, Tibetan, native American and Japanese. And of course the Japanese love western classical music. They are very receptive to other people's cultures. In fact, much of what we think of as Japanese is based on old Korean or Chinese court music or dance, and was really assimilated by them, as they're now doing with western music. I appreciate the way they're relating to western music. For instance, their record buying seems to reflect an appreciation of real quality and soulfulness in terms of the performers they choose. They buy a lot of the old records that are now out of print in America and Europe by some of the great old European artists. They seem to really thrive on the records of Schnabel's, or Szigeti's, or Adolf Busch's—artists I happen to appreciate very much. The Japanese are extremely sensitive esthetically. For instance, they pick up on Beethoven's greatness with fresh ears. They're not as jaded as some of us are.

DUBAL: Yes, in the west, particularly in Europe, the sense of awe at great western music has been lost.

SERKIN: Yes, that's too bad. But I don't think that's any reflection on Beethoven. Because to my mind, Beethoven doesn't reflect the status quo at all. His music was revolutionary, and it retains that characteristic as far as I'm concerned. And as interpreters, we need to rediscover this. This doesn't mean we have to invent contrived, quirky ways of playing his music. We don't have to inject the music with a bold, revolutionary character; we just have to find it.

DUBAL: Do you think that the best players of Beethoven are German, Debussy French, Chopin Polish, and so forth?

SERKIN: No, I don't attribute that much to an accident of birth. In fact I think it's silly to think in those terms. The Germans were the worst of all when it came to this. And it's ironic that many of the musicians they call their own were really of mixed descent. Beethoven was van Beethoven—of Flemish descent; Haydn was a Croat; Mozart and Schubert were Austrian; and you can go down the line like that.

DUBAL: May we talk about methods of practice?

SERKIN: Yes, this is a subject which has always interested me. And, oddly, it's not something that we pianists talk about together very often. It's generally a private matter. Though in teaching, of course, one has to discuss this with the student.

DUBAL: Are there practicing methods that you use? Of course the word "method" is a difficult one.

SERKIN: Yes it is; dangerous, even, because it often implies a very rigid application of rules.

DUBAL: Have you ever read Eugen Herrigel's *Zen in the Art of Archery,* which is really a book about non-method? And do you suppose that thinking in terms of Zen might be useful for piano students?

SERKIN: I have read the book, and I think there is much to be said for its notions about relaxed concentration and appreciation of the whole process of whatever one's doing instead of focusing only on goals. I think an introduction to Zen could be very useful to the student who pushes and struggles with music, especially with the goal in mind of impressing others. The study of music should really be the appreciation of a piece of music as it unfolds in the process of performing or practicing.

DUBAL: Do you practice every day?

SERKIN: Not necessarily, especially when I'm on the road. I don't tend to practice all that much then.

DUBAL: So you're not compulsive about it.

SERKIN: No, not at all. In fact I'm quite the opposite. Even though I tend to practice every day, it's more a function of daily choice, a self-renewing kind of process rather than a guilt-ridden approach where if I don't practice I'll feel bad about it.

DUBAL: Did you experience such guilt in connection with the piano? So many of us grow up with that feeling.

SERKIN: Oh, sure. I've had it. And it creeps in there easily, too. Especially when one is feeling anxious about performances that are coming up.

DUBAL: Yes, you can't just *will* the music to be learned when you're playing a Messiaen work. There are a lot of notes there and there is no way around the work. You have to keep at it.

SERKIN: Yes, I often thought in the past that pianists, like ballet dancers, need to do a certain amount of daily work in order to keep in shape. In fact, I had a whole set of formal exercises that I did every day. Lately, however, I find that I am rejecting formulas more and more.

DUBAL: But did you feel better when you did these exercises?

SERKIN: I thought I did, yes. I thought it was helpful, but now it's over with. I develop these methods or styles of practice for a while, but they tend to last maybe six months at a time at most. I'm always looking for a new approach.

DUBAL: So scales and arpeggios play no role at all in your practicing?

SERKIN: They did for a while, but I was always trying to make music with the scales. I began with the basic scales and arpeggios and trills, but I would try and inflect them and maintain interest and concentration in what I was doing, as if I were playing a piece by Bach. I focused on tone instead of automatic playing, on just being able to rip off the scales. The scale is the very basis of diatonic music, and too often we forget this. When playing scales, it's important to think about the tones and what interval we're on, the connections between them. From the scales I went to very simple etudes, by Cramer, or Clementi, and of course the Bach *Inventions* and preludes and fugues. And finally on to the Chopin etudes.

DUBAL: You did this every day?

SERKIN: Yes, and of course, it is all great music.

DUBAL: Even a Cramer etude can be great; though students today don't seem to play them very much anymore.

SERKIN: Yes, they are great; I think so too. I love the Cramer etudes and in a way I prefer them to the Clementi etudes. So I really enjoyed the whole process. And it would take an hour or two hours before I'd even get to practice the pieces I was going to perform. For a while I didn't even practice other pieces. And, oh, yes, I also did the Brahms exercises for a while too. These are not well-known either. They're more in the style of exercises—they are not real pieces. But they are very interesting and very challenging. In fact, they're so difficult that it can be quite dangerous to play them. One can really hurt one's hands, so it requires a certain suppleness of approach. In other words, I'd sometimes realize how much I was stiffening up in the process of working on them, and I felt that that was some kind of warning signal.

DUBAL: In general, do you find Brahms's piano music to be awkward?

SERKIN: It's not so much that the writing is awkward as that it requires a certain looseness, a certain suppleness, physically, to play it well.

DUBAL: I suppose that's why people who haven't thought enough about how they practice get tendinitis and cramps in the hand.

SERKIN: Yes, very easily. Not only is inattentive practice counterproductive, but it actually can be dangerous.

DUBAL: You were talking a moment ago about the diatonic scale, and hearing each interval. But as a musician who has played a great deal of contemporary music, have you ever regretted, as Busoni did at times, that the piano is divided into half steps only? Have you wished that you had an instrument that had quarter tones and even smaller divisions of sound?

SERKIN: Very much so, yes. Not only quarter tones, and such, but for classical music, I would love to be able to bend the intonational notes, to emphasize the half steps, leading tones and to relate everything to where the harmony is going, to what the home key is, and what the dominant is. Which is, in fact, the way people used to tune pianos. It would be wonderful if people would develop that approach again, to tune according to what the piece of music is. If it's a piece in B-flat major, the A will be quite different from a piece that's in A major.

DUBAL: Yes, I understand. So you've had some frustration with the well-tempered system of tuning.

SERKIN: I don't feel it as a frustration as much as just another element. I wish I were a string player sometimes, so I could do these things. But at the same time, it's very interesting to play the piano and try to bring out the illusion of altering the intonations. It's dangerous to talk about this, because it sounds completely hocus-pocus. But in fact, one can do things, just by the attack, just by thinking something very strongly. By thinking of a C sharp as being high, one can affect the way one plays that particular C sharp. It'll sound like it leads to the D, and so forth.

DUBAL: So one can dream a sound the way one wants to hear it, and then produce it as a result.

SERKIN: Yes, it's a deep discipline. That's why I found it refreshing to start with something very simple, as simple as a scale, and then very simple pieces that couldn't distract me with their structural complexity. I try to do simple things well first.

DUBAL: You seem to be as interested in the creative aspects of practicing as in the finished work.

SERKIN: Yes, I have always been very enthusiastic about the process. What carries me through to the public performance is my personal relationship with the music. That's why I go on all kinds of trips, so to speak, where I'll concentrate on a single composer for a year or more. I like to develop a strong personal relationship with a certain kind of music, or a certain composer's music, and the only way that this can be done is to give it my full attention. In the process of studying the music, you might as well play it for other people, too. But the starting point is very personal. I often study music that I do not play in concert.

DUBAL: Don't you have thoughts like "Oh, I should have played this in public, because I've spent all these hours on it, and I must not waste the effort"?

SERKIN: No, because I don't consider the time I spend with music an investment. I really do appreciate the entire process. When I practice, it's because I want to. I think one's attitude has a lot to do with how much one gets out of practice, even if it's just scales for an hour and a half. I think if one is really focusing one's mind on what one's doing, that can be very worthwhile. Practice is a very peaceful way to spend a day, I think. But as soon as it becomes an annoyance, or if I feel like my mind is straying from the music, and the process is becoming semi-automatic, then I'll stop. That's part of the discipline, to know when to stop.

DUBAL: Do you practice with a metronome?

SERKIN: Yes, once in a while, but my thinking about the metronome has changed. I used to think that one's sense of rhythm is something so internal, organic and biological that it had nothing to do with the mechanical regularity of the metronome. But now I have a very different point of view. So I sometimes practice with a metronome if only to discover my idiosyncrasies; the presence of a metronome will reveal any odd things I might be doing. Then you can ask yourself if it is really a good idea to hold back that much at the end of that measure. The metronome can help you become aware of what you're doing, and it gives you the opportunity to question it. You might decide to deviate from the metronome, but at least you will have a greater knowledge of what you're doing, and the degree to which you're doing it. Of course this does not mean that I would ever subscribe to a metronomic style of playing. The idea of playing classical music to a click is anathema to me. Then again, music shouldn't really be the free-for-all you hear these days, particularly "romantic" music. People forget that to steal for rubato one has to give back, and that's the meaning of the word. It's not just a matter of doing whatever you feel at the moment—to go double-tempo for two beats and then push ahead for three. Also the question of bar lines arises. I used to think that bar lines were irrelevant in classical music. In Mozart or Beethoven's music, for instance, I felt that they were quite unimportant. But again I have revised my thinking here. I now feel that the first beat, or the first measure of a phrase, is vital to the sense of the whole phrase. There must be a strong feeling of impulse in the first beat—which gives a metric meaning to the rhythm and structure of the music.

DUBAL: Is this particularly so in the Classical works of Mozart, Haydn and Beethoven?

SERKIN: It applies to them as well as to Chopin, Brahms, contemporary music. All great music, really. Rhythm is the key to real musicality. No matter how fluid, elegant or nice a phrase may be, without that quality of strong rhythm and meter, it's somehow failed.

DUBAL: Do you make use of the tape recorder in your practice?

SERKIN: Yes, and I've always used it. Ever since I was a kid. Sometimes I would read through a score, record the orchestral part, play it back and play the piano solo part along with it. I was about ten or eleven years old at the time and it was a lot of fun.

DUBAL: Did you ever use it just to compose, improvise and analyze what you're doing?

SERKIN: I've taped improvisations with friends, and I've really enjoyed that. But I haven't used a tape recorder to compose. I generally compose either away from the piano, or at the piano.

DUBAL: Do you find that you are inhibited in the recording studio?

SERKIN: Yes, I've had trouble letting go in recording sessions.

DUBAL: But no problem on the stage?

SERKIN: On the stage, and also at home, I feel much freer. But I think my recording is getting better now. Basically, the real dialogue is between oneself and the music, and just having mikes and a producer there shouldn't necessarily be inhibiting.

CHRISTIAN STEINER

Born December 14, 1914, in Chicago, Illinois, Tureck made her Carnegie Hall debut at twenty-one in the Brahms B-flat Concerto. Besides her involvement with Bach, Tureck has premiered many modern works. She holds four honorary doctoral degrees, including one from Oxford, and has been a visiting professor at numerous universities, including Columbia University and London University. Tureck is the author of the three-volume work An Introduction to the Performance of Bach *and founder of the Tureck Bach Institute. Her papers and manuscripts are housed in the Mugar Memorial Library of Boston University, and complete recordings of her public recitals, lectures and master classes are available for study and research in the Tureck Archive at the Library for the Performing Arts at Lincoln Center.*

Rosalyn Tureck

DUBAL: So many young students are unlucky in their early training. How do you remember yours?

TURECK: I was very lucky with my teachers, though altogether I studied with them for only ten years. I made my debut at the age of nine. My first teacher, Sophia Brilliant-Liven, was a Russian and she was a student of Anton Rubinstein himself.

DUBAL: So you were immediately inculcated in the Russian tradition?

TURECK: Yes, the really great Russian tradition. In a way, I was raised with Anton Rubinstein. Brilliant's teaching was very severe and strict, with an emphasis on good technique, fine piano tone, legato and a disciplined musicianship.

DUBAL: Who was your next teacher?

TURECK: He was Jan Chiapusso, a Dutch Italian, who had studied with the great Leschetizky. He was an excellent pianist, as was my previous teacher. Here again, I was enormously fortunate. Chiapusso had a very broad education. He opened my eyes to Greek sculpture, to philosophy, even to Javanese music. At fifteen I knew all about the gamelan orchestra. He opened a whole world for me.

DUBAL: Was it Chiapusso who introduced you to Bach?

TURECK: No, I had played Bach since I was a baby, but he discovered my facility for Bach. My previous teacher never let me know that I was unusual, nor did she tell me that Bach was any more difficult than Mendelssohn. My awareness burst forth through this enlightened teacher.

DUBAL: What did he give you at your very first lesson?

TURECK: He gave me a Bach prelude and fugue, and some other works. Three or four days later—I had two lessons a week—I handed him the music to the Bach and he said, "What's this? You have it memorized? All right, play it!" Afterwards, he said nothing to me about my performance, but he assigned another prelude and fugue. I then went on to the other piece for the rest of the lesson. The same thing happened three days later, and after I had memorized another prelude and fugue he couldn't contain himself. He said, "My God, girl, if you can do this, you should specialize in Bach!" So even as a teenager I was giving all-Bach concerts in Chicago, while playing all kinds of other music as well.

DUBAL: When you auditioned for Juilliard, what was your program for the jury?

TURECK: I played the Beethoven D minor Sonata, Op. 31 No. 2; Chopin's G minor Ballade; Liszt's "*La Campanella*"; the Bach-Busoni Chaconne and lots of Bach preludes and fugues from *The Well-Tempered Clavier.* I was only sixteen years old, but I'd had wonderful training. The Juilliard faculty were all famous—Siloti, Friedberg, Friskin, Josef Lhevinne, Samaroff . . . .

DUBAL: I was once told that at the audition you came prepared with all forty-eight preludes and fugues and you simply asked the jury, "Which one would you like to hear?"

TURECK: Not quite true; I presented many of them for my audition, but I had not learned all forty-eight. However, it was my first ambition to learn all forty-eight once I began studying with the celebrated Olga Samaroff.

DUBAL: Wasn't it just at this time that you had a revelation about Bach?

TURECK: Yes, within two and a half months, a dramatic incident occurred. I had been learning the preludes and fugues and other music of Bach furiously. I must say that I was a very fast learner—I could consume the score. I remember that my lessons were on Fridays, and Madame Samaroff already had an idea of how quickly I learned. Anyway, on Wednesday afternoon, I started on the A minor Prelude and Fugue from Book I of *The Well-Tempered Clavier.* You know how extraordinarily complex that fugue is. Well, I looked at it, and this may sound funny, but I lost consciousness. I didn't faint, nor did I fall off the chair, but I completely lost consciousness.

DUBAL: Did such a thing ever happen to you before?

TURECK: Yes, in fact it was not too unusual for me. It had happened rather frequently at other people's concerts, at moments of excruciating beauty.

DUBAL: How long was this episode?

TURECK: I just don't know how long it lasted; it may have been five minutes, it may have been half an hour. But the fact is that when I came to, I had an insight into the structure of Bach's music. And I knew at once that, to realize this new insight into Bach's world, I needed to create a whole new technique of playing the piano. Suddenly, I knew how my fingering apparatus needed to be changed to make Bach's music live properly on the piano, to tear it away from nineteenth-century pianistic practices.

DUBAL: Were you frightened when this happened?

TURECK: Not one bit. This experience was a privilege, and it came through the subconscious. After all, Chiapusso had given me real musicological training. I was already investigating other keyboard instruments.

DUBAL: What happened at your next lesson?

TURECK: As I said, this took place on Wednesday, and my lessons with Samaroff were on Friday. From Wednesday on, I dropped everything, and for two full days I learned only four lines. Ordinarily, I would have learned three concertos. Well, I came in for my lesson and told Samaroff that I had only prepared four lines for her. She said, "Heaven, have you been ill?" I said, "No," and explained to her what had happened to me; then I played the four lines for her. "Well," she said, "It's absolutely superlative, but it's impossible! How can you build a whole way of playing like this? Perhaps a few bars here and there, but what you are doing is physically and intellectually impossible to sustain." But the fact was that I'd gone through a door into a whole new world, and now I could not go back—even though it would have been much easier and safer to continue as I had all along, because I had already had a great deal of approval and success. But from this point on, for my artistic growth, there was no way but to build and find everything for myself from scratch; to create every inch of the way.

DUBAL: What a fascinating story! And I can't help but wonder if it would have happened without the influence of a mentor like Chiapusso. Is it enough for a child growing up in this complex society to have excellent schooling, or is the mentor, the person who takes a personal interest, the crucial element?

TURECK: That's an interesting question, especially with all the problems —social, economic and political—confronting us, and especially the young, today. By twenty I had graduated from Juilliard, and I was launched into a career from the start. I was lucky, of course, to have had wonderful teachers who came out of a wonderful pianistic tradition.

But, in my opinion, more important than anything else is the principle of the inner creativity of the individual. Because everything I have done has developed out of myself. Thought and study and constant travail filled my years of Bach study and, in the end, this has come out of myself only. I've always believed in people—there's hardly a person in the world who isn't born with some wonderful talents. The tragedy is the lack of development of the personality and/or the talent in our society. The most important thing is the development of the inner person. As that develops, the personality becomes increasingly creative.

DUBAL: Let's speak a bit about the performance of Bach. You often perform Bach in very large halls. Is Bach conducive to large spaces?

TURECK: We must remember that Bach was originally played in very large churches. I know this because I have made an extensive tour in what is now East Germany of all the towns in which Bach lived and worked; and I have been in many of the churches in which he actually played. In fact, I have played a number of organs from Bach's time, although it is not known for sure whether Bach played any of these himself. But these are very bright and brilliant instruments. So there's no question about it, Bach knew big sound.

DUBAL: I have always admired your performance of Bach's *Chromatic Fantasy and Fugue*.

TURECK: Thank you. You know, it's a stupendous canvas and it is very difficult in many ways. I took twelve years before I allowed myself to play that work in public because I felt there were so many things to be solved.

DUBAL: Which editions did you consult?

TURECK: In this work I studied the twenty-two extant manuscripts that circulated in the eighteenth century, as well as sixty editions. But in the end, both in the text and interpretation, the editions I play from are my own.

DUBAL: That brings me to the thorny subject of modern scholarship, especially in Baroque performing-practice.

TURECK: Yes, one must not think that my work in Bach is confined to J. S. Bach alone. It wouldn't have any validity. One has to know the roots of this almighty genius before one can even begin to understand what he could do. One must work from the very foundations of the music. One must understand the instruments, the music of previous times—the Renaissance, medieval times and so forth.

DUBAL: What you are describing is the very essence of scholarship.

TURECK: Yes, and this has become my mission at the Tureck Bach Institute. I teach everyone—pianists, harpsichord players, clavichord players, lute players, the oboists and recorder players—in this way. I've also conducted cantatas and motets, and, of course, I have worked with singers.

DUBAL: How do you approach your task?

TURECK: In my teaching, I always uncover for the student the sources of manuscripts, the first printings, the historical performance practices, discussing with them the possibilities of using other instruments. So the scholarship is always interwoven with the artistic, the practical, the technical—the fingering, the phrasing, the loud-soft, and so on. It is all of a piece and nothing must be separated. So, you see, my performance has always been the tip of the iceberg.

DUBAL: Do you prefer Bach on the piano or harpsichord? Your recitals of the *Goldberg Variations* on piano and then harpsichord are a real programming innovation, and it seems to be an extension of the kind of scholarship or inquiry that we have been discussing.

TURECK: Yes, when I do the double performance of the *Goldberg Variations,* each instrument has equal musical validity. I'm not playing one in preference to the other or showing that this is better than another. They all belong. There is too much competitive interest in instruments these days. Contemporary music, with its breadth of texture, sonority and style, also teaches us not to be taken in by a single kind of sonority.

DUBAL: Yes, there always seems to be a debate about which instrument Bach is to be played on.

TURECK: Indeed! We have become over-concerned with sonority and texture at the expense of the music. It is important to remember that Bach was not in the least pedantic by nature or practice. Then again, our emphasis on instruments has resulted in the field of musicology, which has been enormously important to our musical thinking. On the other hand, in the excitement of discovery, one sometimes goes overboard and falls in and drowns. I grew up with the harpsichord, clavichord and organ, and the differences are part of my blood and bones. I accept and love them all.

DUBAL: The *Goldberg Variations* has been part of your life since you were a teenager, isn't that so?

TURECK: Yes, I began to study it when I was around eighteen, in my second year at Juilliard. I learned it in five weeks. I remember that the night before I was to play it I put it under my pillow, to be sure that somehow the notes would stay in my memory.

DUBAL: They are very difficult on the piano, aren't they? They are easier on the double-manual harpsichord.

TURECK: The work has a reputation for great technical difficulty, and it deserves that reputation. But if you play it pianistically, as a virtuoso piece, which is what to avoid, it is easier. The day after my performance of the variations at Juilliard, which went very well, Ernest Hutcheson, who was then president of the school, met me in the corridor and told me how sorry he was to have missed the performance. He said that Harold Bauer had once told him the work was impossible on the piano. I looked up at him innocently and said, "Oh, I didn't know it was impossible." And in fact I'd learned this work never thinking for a moment that it was difficult on the piano.

DUBAL: Obviously you were thinking of the greatness of the score.

TURECK: Yes, the *Goldberg Variations* is a work about which there is a tremendous amount to say and, at the same time, it is a work for which there are no words. It is an infinite work of art. After the opening aria, the thirty variations traverse the whole experience of man. And the return to the beginning aria at the end is one of the most sublime moments in all art.

DUBAL: When you play your two performances of the *Goldberg* with all the repeats, you give your audience quite a bit of credit for its attention span. Do you ever think about the limitations of your audience?

TURECK: You've hit on a very interesting point. You know, I'd rather play to people who know all or nothing than to those who know a little. I must confess, however, that I pay no attention whatever to my audience. I have no interest in what they think, yet I have an infinite sense of connection with them, an unending faith. To my mind, a performance is the test of what you have gone through with a work in order to end up with something near your goal.

DUBAL: You are known to have said, "I do what Bach tells me, I never tell the music what to do." When pondering over an unsolved problem in your Bach playing, do you often find yourself wishing for a conversation with him?

TURECK: I remember in my early years, the gigue from the E minor Partita worried me very much. As you know, it's a most unusual gigue with a very strong character. At the time I was studying with Arnold Schoenberg and I asked him what he thought about it, its characterization and tempo. He looked at it and sang the opening phrase, and I instantly knew I had it. Since I couldn't ask Bach, I asked Schoenberg; and I've always managed this way.

DUBAL: I am sure that on your wall you must have a portrait of Bach.

TURECK: Oh, yes.

DUBAL: Do you ever think of the image of the man, his physiognomy, before you?

TURECK: Oh, yes, oh, yes. I have studied the face, I can't say how many times. One studies the face; one thinks about the man, about the character.

DUBAL: He had a limited cultural background.

TURECK: There's no question but that he came from a limited cultural background—at most a middle-bourgeoisie attitude and surroundings. He had no pretenses socially.

DUBAL: Was he a great man, do you think?

TURECK: It depends on what you call a great man. He was a big mind and a big spirit. He was an enormously passionate, emotional kind of person, with a profound insight into form and structure. He had an uncanny knowledge of how to put things together. Everything is so complex and yet so simple in the end. This is one of the greatest miracles of Bach, coupled with the fact that the quality of emotion is so remarkably varied. This is what I aim for in my playing. This is one of the great enchantments of Bach, the versatility; and the miracles that you see and hear going on every moment in virtually everything he's ever written.

DUBAL: If you had a chance to hear Bach himself play his own music for a half hour, would you choose to hear him on the organ or the harpsichord?

TURECK: I would have to choose the organ. Bach was a very great performer on the organ. Of course, he knew the harpsichord, and he played string instruments—he played everything. But I would want to hear him on the organ. And I would settle for five minutes; I would not demand a half hour.

Born April 11, 1933, in Debrecen, Hungary, Vásáry made his debut at the age of eight in a Mozart concerto, and a year later gave his first piano recital. He went to Budapest to the Franz Liszt Academy, where he studied piano with József Gát and composition with Kodály. During this time he won the Franz Liszt Prize. He taught at the academy until he left Hungary in 1956. In 1959 he made his first appearance with the Berlin Philharmonic and in 1961 his first appearance at the Royal Festival Hall, London. He has made many tours of the United States. Recently he conducted performances at the Budapest Opera.

Tamás Vásáry

SUSESCH BAYAT

DUBAL: You are a great believer in nutrition and the importance of good physical condition for the pianist.

VÁSÁRY: I am convinced that our general condition is greatly influenced by what we eat. And I am very excited today because I was reading an article on a new kind of vitamin therapy that sounds like it could be very useful for pianists. It was written by a doctor who has made tests on Olympic champions to find out which vitamins they lacked. You know pianists are athletes, too. They need to be in excellent shape. I have to record the *Brahms-Paganini Variations* soon, and if there is the slightest pain in any finger, I won't be able to do all I can. So I'd like to go see this doctor.

DUBAL: When did you become aware of nutrition?

VÁSÁRY: About six years ago. It was just around the time I was scheduled to do the first session of my complete Rachmaninoff concerto recordings. I got food poisoning and I became very ill. I literally stopped eating. It was two weeks before the recording, and I was afraid that I wouldn't survive the ordeal of six hours of non-stop playing that would be required of me because I was so weak. But when I went to the piano to practice a bit, I found that for the first time in ten years or more, I was completely free of a kind of rusty feeling in my joints. At first I attributed this to an injection which the doctor had given me. But later I realized that this was because I had inadvertently stopped eating meat. All my life I had been a heavy meat-eater; and ever since I stopped eating it my hands have felt better. Also, I've experimented with vitamins and I have found that on days of high stress, especially when I am giving concerts, I take four times as many vitamin C tablets as usual.

DUBAL: You obviously have tremendous stamina, because you have made many recordings as both pianist and conductor lately, including Mozart concerti, in which you are playing with and conducting the Berlin Philharmonic. Do you enjoy the dual role?

VÁSÁRY: Yes, it's very satisfying. I've wanted to do this all my life, and now I'm finally having the opportunity.

DUBAL: How does an orchestra react when you are both soloist and conductor?

VÁSÁRY: There is often a dissonance between the conductor at the podium and the orchestra because it is the conductor's job to control, but the orchestra unconsciously rebels. But when I am playing as well as conducting, the orchestra feels less resistance because I am also playing an instrument. We are equals, like chamber musicians. Then the thing I cherish most can happen. The members of the orchestra no longer use just their eyes, but their ears, too. We are all listening to each other, and this is the finest kind of music-making.

DUBAL: So how does it feel to play a Mozart concerto with another conductor?

VÁSÁRY: There is a problem, definitely. Once you have conducted them yourself, you start to miss the cohesiveness of a performance.

DUBAL: Is conducting a new interest of yours or did you always yearn to head up an orchestra?

VÁSÁRY: "Yearn" is a very good word because it suggests my frustration at having to wait years before I got my first chance to conduct. At five, I was constantly conducting an invisible orchestra. I would ask my sister or my mother to play a recording of a symphony, and then I would conduct with my mother's knitting needle. I would have such a good time. I'd stop the recording to correct the second oboe and the first bassoon, and tell them how I wanted everything to sound.

DUBAL: Did you study conducting in addition to the piano when you were growing up?

VÁSÁRY: Not nearly as much as I wanted, because I was also composing, so there was never enough time. Also, I had to choose among them because I had to make a living. Life in Hungary was very difficult at that time and the piano was my best chance of achieving success.

DUBAL: So what happened to your dream of conducting?

VÁSÁRY: It was buried, until finally I was given a chance to conduct at the Budapest Opera. But as fate would have it, the next year was 1956, the Hungarian Revolution, and I had to leave Hungary. I was uprooted, and life was very difficult. The conducting was again put aside, for years, but after I got married and moved to London, around 1970, the possibility of conducting re-emerged. Now I am conducting even in Budapest. It is all destiny; if I had stayed in Hungary I would have been only in the pit of the opera house conducting, and I would not have traveled the world playing the piano.

DUBAL: So you believe in destiny.

VÁSÁRY: Yes, you sometimes feel for years that your dreams are being withheld from you; but later you find out that those years were very well spent. After I left Hungary I had nothing—no concerts came for a long time, I felt destiny was against me. Yet when I look back, it was during those first very bleak years that I established the main body of my repertoire as a pianist.

DUBAL: Do you think the conducting has had any particular influence on your piano playing?

VÁSÁRY: Since I have been actively conducting, I feel more freedom musically; in greater control of my listening powers. Sometimes listening back to one of my piano recordings, I say to myself, "Ah, I just missed in that phrase what I really wanted." I didn't yet have my conductor's ear to control myself.

DUBAL: Who is the musician who has most influenced your playing?

VÁSÁRY: Annie Fischer. One of the great musical experiences of my life has been hearing and knowing the great Hungarian pianist Annie Fischer. It is a spiritual experience to hear her Mozart and Beethoven.

DUBAL: Annie Fischer studied with Dohnányi. Did you ever play for him as a youngster in Hungary?

VÁSÁRY: Yes, I did and it was a great honor to play for him. I was eight years old when he heard me. He listened carefully and he was kind. I remember his humanity. He told my father I should study with him, and that we should move to Budapest. But we could not do this because my father had to work in another town. I did go to play for him occasionally, but then the war broke out and everything fell apart. Dohnányi, the director of the Franz Liszt Academy, left Hungary. I never saw him again, but I have the memory of a great human being.

DUBAL: What did you play for him? And what did he say to you?

VÁSÁRY: I played one of my own little compositions, and he said, "Why are you staying in the key of F minor so long? You must modulate to another key!" I also played Haydn's G major Sonata. Later I learned from my father that Dohnányi had said that my playing was overburdened by learning. It lacked the naturalness of a child. I remember also playing the melancholy C-sharp minor Waltz of Chopin, Op. 64 No. 2, and he said, "Tamás, it's too sad." I said "Why? It's a sad piece." "Yes," he said, "but it's too sad coming from an eight-year-old." At the time I was hurt, it *was* a sad piece, and I felt him very unjust. Today I understand what he meant. He was trying to let me know that I was not having a proper childhood. He would say, "How many hours do you practice a day?" and I would reply, "I practice four hours." "That's too much," he would say, "Go out and play games."

DUBAL: It's admirable that Dohnányi understood so much about a child.

VÁSÁRY: And yet he also treated me seriously; I am very sorry that circumstances prevented me from continuing my relationship with him. He might have spared me a lot of problems, because he understood that I was losing my spontaneity, and, in fact, I did lose it through my teen years. The child doesn't quite understand that he is often being over-praised and petted not because of himself, but because of a talent, an abnormality really, a secretion like a pearl in an oyster. It is awful to be loved for one's gifts or achievements instead of oneself. It was only through a great deal of suffering that I regained my spontaneous and natural feelings about music and life.

DUBAL: With the hectic schedule you keep, how do you manage to stay in touch with your feelings?

VÁSÁRY: I remember my dreams, which are miracles of communication. I love to analyze them. They keep me in touch with myself.

DUBAL: How did you get involved in dream analysis?

VÁSÁRY: I became interested in the work of the great psychiatrist C. G. Jung. You must read Jung's autobiography *Memories, Dreams, and Reflections*.

DUBAL: Do you have recurring dreams?

VÁSÁRY: Yes, I often dream of horses, and when I do, it is a reflection of my energy state. If a horse loses a race, I know that I am in bad shape, I am abusing myself, I am overworked. If I don't listen to this message, I become run-down or I get the flu. On the other hand, when I dream of healthy horses running freely in the fields, I know that I am in good shape and that I am ready for new challenges.

DUBAL: Do you have other animal dreams?

VÁSÁRY: Oh, yes, there is the recurring dog dream. This occurs before important concerts. The dog takes my hands in his mouth and I am terrified that he will bite them . . . but he doesn't.

DUBAL: What do you suppose is the significance of this dream?

VÁSÁRY: I think it goes back to my very first concert as a child. I was given some money for playing and my parents thought I should have a souvenir of the event. So we went to buy a piece of china, a sculpture. The choice was between a black-and-white china dog and a colored bird. I wanted the bird, but my mother said, "*No,* take the dog." I asked her why. She said the bird symbolizes flight and that my success would fly away if I took it; but that the dog would be faithful. And so it has been to this day, the dog rests on my piano. For me it represents the pianistic profession, the career, the outside world. And though it is a faithful dog, it is also frightening. He keeps my hand in his mouth.

DUBAL: And today, if you could choose between the bird and the dog?

VÁSÁRY: Ah, that is the question. You see, the bird is freedom, the symbol of spirituality, of the non-competitive world. And the bird is also naturally musical, its song soars to lyrical flights. Today, if I had the choice, I would choose the bird.

DUBAL: Let's discuss the composer whom you are most closely associated with in the public's mind—Chopin.

VÁSÁRY: Chopin's music has a dreamlike quality, even a hallucinatory one. Yet in his art everything is distilled to perfection. His playing must have possessed a technical finesse and nuance of the finest gradation. In his music there was always the love for an idealized Poland, a country he wept for and danced for. And in the waltzes and mazurkas he has enshrined youth. He had a natural grace as a dance composer that is unrivaled. And there is the nostalgic element of his music which is often painful, for through him we look for ourselves.

DUBAL: Yes, all of these elements and more are in his music, which makes him so vulnerable to distortion and sentimentality.

VÁSÁRY: Yes, no composer is handled so insensitively. The purity is destroyed.

DUBAL: The writer Vladimir Nabokov said we must make a distinction between "sentimental" and "sensitive," "sentimentality meaning the non-artistic exaggeration of familiar emotions."

VÁSÁRY: Yes, that's so true, and in the case of Chopin, one can tell much about the person who languishes in it to provoke "feeling." Look how the nocturnes have become nightmares instead of night-pieces.

DUBAL: The etudes are an obsession with most pianists because, without them, piano music written after 1830 is a closed door from a technical point of view. But how difficult are the Chopin etudes in your opinion?

VÁSÁRY: I think that they are the most difficult piano pieces ever written. Each one presents a relentless muscular challenge, there is never a moment to relax. And yet it is all in the context of the most transparent music. The textures are almost Mozartian.

DUBAL: Yes, Chopin and Mozart are difficult to play because of this transparent quality.

VÁSÁRY: Indeed, as a performer you must pay very dearly for this. Such music reveals every mistake, everything can be heard, every pedal smudge can be heard. I grew up with them and I have always been astonished by Backhaus's technical know-how on the recordings he made in the 1920s.

DUBAL: Are there other artists whose Chopin you admire?

VÁSÁRY: Lipatti certainly; Clara Haskil, who was not necessarily known for her Chopin, was very poetic. And, oh, yes, Fou T'song is a wonderful mazurka-player.

DUBAL: What intrigues you most about live performance?

VÁSÁRY: I love the improvisatory element of performance which interacts with my conception of the score. On stage it is life or death, and some very essential parts of you may surface which go beyond the logical, cerebral functions. Only on stage, during high tension, can one find his own truth if one knows how to listen for it.

DUBAL: This reminds me of the Schlegel lines which Schumann appended to the opening of his Fantasia Op. 17: "Through all the varied sounds which fill the world's many-colored dreams, one gentle tone may be barely heard for those who listen in secret."

VÁSÁRY: Yes, how many pianists have brooded over that motto, as they begin that tremendous canvas.

DUBAL: You are an idealistic person. How do you reconcile the great contradictions inherent in career-building with being an artist?

VÁSÁRY: Daily life is so much in contradiction with the real needs of an artist. More than anything, we need peace, quiet and time for meditation. One often wants to get away from society and live in the forest.

DUBAL: Is it fame that makes you wish for the forest?

VÁSÁRY: You know, the more famous you are, the more recognized you become, the more you are thrown off the path of the life you feel you should lead.

DUBAL: Do you have a philosophy of art?

VÁSÁRY: To my mind, art reveals our spiritual qualities as human beings, and we are now at an intense moment in history, when it is more important than ever to attend to our spiritual selves.

DUBAL: So, great music is a manifestation of our spiritual consciousness.

VÁSÁRY: Yes. Through the keyhole of art we can see ourselves clearly. We all have everything in ourselves: the good, the exalted, the evil. There is an ancient saying that what is above is under, and in the small there is the whole universe. In one sound there is the whole universe, too.

Born June 20, 1946, in Nuremberg, Germany, Watts studied in Philadelphia, and at the age of ten he played a Haydn concerto at a Philadelphia Orchestra children's concert. In 1963 he made an overnight sensation playing the Liszt E-flat Concerto with Leonard Bernstein on national television. A recording debut followed. Watts made his London debut with the London Symphony in 1966. In the fall of 1967 he made his first world tour for the U.S. State Department. He played in Russia in 1973. At age twenty-six he became the youngest person ever to receive an honorary doctorate from Yale University.

André Watts

© 1979 PETER SCHAAF

DUBAL: How would you characterize the tension you feel in performance?

WATTS: There's both positive and negative tension. The positive is normal nervousness, which can be stimulating. The negative can be a terrible burden. It's a loss of confidence that can undermine your performance. When you say to yourself, "Don't mess that passage up, like you did yesterday in Des Moines," and this haunts your performance, it can be very self-destructive. You have to guard against it very carefully, it's always trying to creep in.

DUBAL: If there is a piano in a room are you capable of being indifferent to it?

WATTS: It's very hard for me to walk past a piano without touching it. And I don't mean the keyboard necessarily. If I'm in a room with a piano I have to get close to it; though sometimes this embarrasses me, I have to at least walk by and brush against it.

DUBAL: Could you ever feel this way about another instrument?

WATTS: No, though I've always felt a certain envy for violinists and cellists who have been living with the same instrument for years, at home and in concert. So, believe me, I get very impatient when I hear a violinist telling me his instrument "isn't responding." And I think, "Hey, buddy, you're complaining about your own instrument when I've never even laid eyes on this monster in front of me!"

DUBAL: So how do you come to terms with each new "monster" you are given to play?

WATTS: Here is my method, and when it works, it works like a charm. When I arrive at the hall I calmly gaze at it for a long moment. This is my way of saying "hello" to it. I never touch it right away. But then I sit down to play and the piano reveals its qualities to me. Very quickly I find out if the bass is muddy or the treble is weak, and here begins my psychological adjustment to the instrument. I now have to make a choice. Will I be friends with the instrument or will I spoil a whole evening fighting with it? In order to make friends, I must accept the weaknesses of the instrument. This is the state the piano is in. It's not trying to get you. It's not trying to do you out of your success with your concert. Of course this state of mind isn't always easy to achieve—it involves a very critical kind of adjustment. It's heartbreaking to realize that so many of the effects you have worked your guts out for will be lost. But there will inevitably be someplace in the piece you're playing where a pianissimo will be aided by the weak treble; or where a blurry resonance will create a wonderful wash of sound. So you must allow yourself to feel that somehow the piano will help you.

DUBAL: Because you had a kind of overnight success after you played the Liszt E-flat Concerto with Bernstein on national television, you were spared the torture of competitive life.

WATTS: Yes, my luck was incredible. My career was handed to me on a silver plate. I never had to scratch or scramble. So instead of agonizing over career building, I've had the luxury of ruminating all these years, about what the music means. I've had the freedom to examine where my playing was going. My musical development was all I had to worry about.

DUBAL: When did you come to study with Leon Fleisher?

WATTS: About four or five years into my professional career. Despite the early success, I realized that I needed to play for someone on a regular basis. And Fleisher was my choice, something I've never regretted, because we worked splendidly together. Leon was never into any ego power nonsense. We were there to make music. I remember him saying, "I'm not here to make little Fleishers. I'm here to listen to you, and present out of my experience possibilities you may not have thought of." Not that he never got annoyed with me. I remember the time I brought him the MacDowell Concerto in the two-piano score which has the orchestral part reduced for a second piano. He picked up my music and slapped it back down on the piano and said, "What's this? Don't you have the complete orchestral score? You can't know a concerto without knowing the full score!"

DUBAL: What were some of the things he emphasized during lessons?

WATTS: Leon seldom let up on the subject of tone production; that didn't mean he wanted me to produce any specific kind of sound. It was just that he wanted me to constantly be in touch with the sound that I wanted—to figure it out ahead of time. That's part of music-making—to decide ahead of time that in that next passage I'm going to want a little more point. He also spent a lot of time talking to me about relaxation. In general, Fleisher was good for me psychologically. He made me understand when I was practicing out of guilt instead of real need. His point to me was that there's nothing wrong with guilt-practicing, just as long as you know what it is. He made me realize that too many compulsive needs can spell grief for the touring artist. Anyway, I'm not so sure that practicing ten hours a day has anything to do with perfection. It has more to do with being virtuous. Because truly careful practicing cannot be sustained for that kind of a stretch. It becomes rote—it's like doing calisthenics. And at a certain point in your life all those extra hours are not going to improve your technique.

DUBAL: I know you have played with the conductor Sergiu Celibidache, who refuses to record.

WATTS: Oh, yes, there is much to learn from him. He is a very difficult, brilliant and complex man. Once in Israel we had a marathon schedule, the Brahms B-flat Concerto twelve or thirteen times in fifteen days. I remember how obsessed he was about a certain note in the second movement of the concerto. He said to me, "There's only one place in the cosmos where this note belongs, and it is up to you to find it." So every night after the performance he would come up to me and say, "Close, but not quite—not yet." And he was right.

DUBAL: An audience is not always aware of the ways in which a performance might fall short of the musician's aspirations.

WATTS: Nor are they aware, sometimes, of the extent to which we must bare our souls on stage. In my personal life, I am rather private. But when I'm on stage I don't hide anything. If you are holding back in any way, believe me, you will damage the music. The opposite side of the coin is knowing never to play to impress. That's an act of hostility. If your performance communicates "I'll show you," then everything goes haywire. That was one of the joys of hearing a Rubinstein recital—he was always playing in the spirit of giving and there was no intimidation. The older I got, the more I admired his non-neurotic, open style of playing—he took amazing chances out there—and I became a wild admirer of his.

DUBAL: Did you ever meet Glenn Gould?

WATTS: Yes, I did. I met him a few times. He was a fantastic person—very brilliant and certainly not crazy by any means. Different, yes; but not crazy. I remember he once said to me, "André, you wouldn't really play a piece like *La Campanella* if there were no such thing as the live concert." And I said, "Yes, I would, Glenn. I like the piece very much." And I think he was genuinely disappointed. To him, *La Campanella* meant playing to the gallery—it's a show piece and nothing more. But I don't play to the gallery, I play for the people; and anyway, even if there were no such thing as live concerts, I'd still want to play *Campanella* for myself because it's such fun. But Gould had the most wonderful sense of humor. Just listen to his transcription of Ravel's *La Valse*, which is on a videotape. He's unbelievable—Glenn has a giant on the dance floor. He starts at triple forte instead of the usual atmospheric beginning.

DUBAL: Do you have any of Gould's fascination with technology?

WATTS: I'm not really very technology-oriented. In fact, one of my recordings, the *Live from Tokyo,* is on compact disc, and I have the copy, but I don't have the machine. I don't even worry that much about surface noise. I can manage to scramble through the undergrowth. I love some of the old Schnabel and Backhaus recordings with that wonderful haze on the tone. It's a patina that's very nostalgic. I'm still awestruck every time I hear Schnabel's recording of the slow movement from Schubert's big D major Sonata. Technology or no, each time the melody returns it's in an absolutely different color.

DUBAL: Speaking of those large Schubert sonatas, how do you get an audience to hold its applause after the long first movement? I once asked Rubinstein this question, and he said he didn't even mind the premature applause in this case.

WATTS: Fleisher used to say if they applaud between movements and you don't want them to, it's your own fault. He didn't mean you should hold up a sign that says "Don't Applaud"; he meant that an audience will understand what you want if you establish a powerful connection between the movements. Of course there's always the crazy in the audience who flips out at every tonic chord. I'll never forget when Heifetz came backstage after I had played the Schubert G major Sonata. It was actually a case where the audience did applaud after the first movement, and I actually put up my hand to stop them. Heifetz was very complimentary about my performance, but he said something that has always stayed with me. He said, "Young man, never shush your public!"

Born July 26, 1929, in Sofia, Bulgaria, Weissenberg played his first concert at age eight. He studied piano and composition with Pantcho Vladigerov. Weissenberg graduated from the Juilliard School in 1946, and in 1947 he won the Leventritt Award and made his American debut with Szell and the New York Philharmonic. He then toured the world continuously until 1956. Then, after a ten-year hiatus, he resumed his concert career to great international acclaim. His repertoire ranges from Bach to Bartók and Stravinsky. Weissenberg has also written a musical, La Fugue, *which opened in Paris.*

Alexis Weissenberg

DUBAL: Do you remember when you first discovered music?

WEISSENBERG: I don't think there was a specific day when I suddenly discovered music. I have been connected with it ever since I can remember; just as I was connected with the piano from the beginning—I was predestined for it, I was born for the piano. Any visions, images or dreams I had were immediately transformed into sounds, either imagined or heard; and those connections between sounds, images and particular places which may have impressed me when I was a child remain in my memory forever.

DUBAL: Were you a child prodigy?

WEISSENBERG: No, I was not. But I occasionally played in public when I was a child, though I was never exploited. You are only a child prodigy if your parents exploit you as such.

DUBAL: Did you have difficult times in Bulgaria with the war encroaching?

WEISSENBERG: I didn't really suffer that much from the war. My family was not killed and I didn't lose any close friends. But the fact that I was uprooted from Bulgaria did have a negative effect.

DUBAL: Where did you go when you left Bulgaria?

WEISSENBERG: In 1944 we went to Israel, which was then Palestine. Soon after, I went to America to study with Olga Samaroff.

DUBAL: She taught many big talents, including William Kapell. Did you know him?

WEISSENBERG: Yes, I was very close to Willy at the time, and had the occasion to hear him very often at his home as well as in concert. He remains one of the most impressive pianists I have heard.

DUBAL: Tell me about Samaroff.

WEISSENBERG: She was a brilliant woman who taught me in a marvelous way. She was one of the few teachers I have ever met whose pupils all played differently, and that you cannot say about many famous teachers. Individuality was something she respected. She had great insight into the personality of each of her students, and she let people develop their own way.

DUBAL: Before coming to Samaroff, did you have good training?

WEISSENBERG: I arrived at Samaroff's having been very well prepared by my first teacher in Bulgaria—Vladigerov, who was a very great teacher, indeed. But because of his love for me as a child, he sometimes let me be too free and go too far in my own way. When you are a gifted child and adolescent, you go through periods of performing the way you want, and often this involves a certain misunderstanding of the score. Samaroff was like penicillin for all this. You know, a bad teacher at the beginning of life can spoil a talent forever. Nothing can be worse. I've always been grateful that this never happened to me.

DUBAL: Were you given a lot of repertoire to learn as a child?

WEISSENBERG: I am also fortunate in that respect because both teachers gave me a tremendous amount of repertoire to learn very early. Only as a youngster can you learn easily and definitively. There is no doubt about it—I now learn far more slowly than when I was sixteen. So I learned many difficult concerti—both Brahms, the Rachmaninoff Third—early enough so as to never consider them difficult. These complex works are absolutely engraved in my memory.

DUBAL: What is the most formidable technical and musical task for a pianist to achieve?

WEISSENBERG: To play a Beethoven, Mozart or Schubert slow movement well. I wish more people would understand this. So many still think of technique as the Liszt rhapsodies. But to play the slow movements with perfect nervous and sound control is the sign of a great musician and technician.

DUBAL: Who are the most pianistic composers?

WEISSENBERG: Bach, Mozart, Scarlatti, Chopin, Liszt, Bartók, Scriabin, Prokofiev, Rachmaninoff and even Stravinsky, who had a fantastic knowledge of the piano. Even the piano version of *Petrouchka,* however difficult, is so logically fitted to the instrument that if you have the means to study it properly, it will eventually become a relatively easy piece to play. These composers had the physical ability with the instrument that enabled them to write for it well.

DUBAL: And the non-pianistic composers, who are they?

WEISSENBERG: Despite the popularity of the Tchaikovsky Piano Concerto No. 1, it is not difficult because of its famous octaves but because it is uncomfortably and illogically composed for the instrument. Even such great masters as Beethoven, Brahms and Schumann were not always at ease with the instrument. Very often they wrote symphonically instead of pianistically. They lacked an absolute and immediate sense of coordination between the two hands.

DUBAL: Why do some people succeed pianistically and others not?

WEISSENBERG: Some people are born with rich potential to invent a method that applies perfectly to the instrument. No teacher can provide this. Ultimately one must create a very personal system of organization and learn to compensate for any deficiencies.

DUBAL: Do you ever practice away from the piano?

WEISSENBERG: Very often. By now I know the instrument well, and my brain knows exactly how my hands would function on the piano. Of course there are some technical problems that one cannot overcome unless one tries them out at the instrument. But even so, I sometimes wake up in the middle of the night with a fingering that I never thought of while working at the piano.

DUBAL: I know that you are a Steinway artist, but what are the particular qualities you look for in a piano?

WEISSENBERG: Often when I go to choose a piano for a concert someone says, "Mr. Weissenberg, since you are playing Prokofiev tonight I am sure you will want this piano because it is very good for Prokofiev." This is sheer nonsense, because an excellent piano must be capable of everything. It must have a complete range. Then it's up to me to know how to control the piano sufficiently—to make the sound that suits Prokofiev or Mozart or whomever I'm playing.

DUBAL: Is performing a necessity for you?

WEISSENBERG: Yes, I don't think anybody is a performer simply because he likes to perform—I think he needs it. He needs it spiritually and psychologically—it's like breathing. Very early on, the natural performer knows he needs to communicate with people through his playing. And once he begins to succeed, the need becomes almost pathological.

DUBAL: It sounds like the audience is a very powerful stimulant for you.

WEISSENBERG: The audience is elemental. When that stage door flies open, I am immersed in the audience's excitement of expectation. I respond to it passionately. It is very different from walking to a piano in an empty hall.

DUBAL: Like Rachmaninoff before you, you have never been known to smile on stage.

WEISSENBERG: Playing the piano is very serious to me. I'm not there to smile but to bring the program to life—and I do that with all my might, and I play as well as I can.

DUBAL: What does it mean to play as well as you can?

WEISSENBERG: To play in the simplest, most personal way possible. I must cut away any extraneous effects which interfere with the broad lines and structure of the piece. This kind of logic is essential to the emotional impact of the music. If I don't accomplish this I fall into despair. Even if this is only because I failed to produce a certain pianissimo. That is sufficient to plague me, even if the audience was enraptured. You hate yourself because it was a lack of concentration that provoked the failure.

DUBAL: You seem to be very hard on yourself.

WEISSENBERG: Yes, emphatically yes; because I am frustrated by the constraints of time. To accomplish what I hope to, I would need three hundred years.

DUBAL: Even with these limitations of time, you've managed to play over a hundred concerts a year in every corner of the world, and in New York several times a season. Is New York still as necessary for a career as it once was?

Weissenberg: Absolutely. New York, Berlin, London and Paris are the four major cities in which an artist should perform each season, if possible. Performing in New York is something that has a unique effect on an artist.

Dubal: I know you love performing in Carnegie Hall.

Weissenberg: Ever since Tchaikovsky inaugurated the hall in 1891, its importance in American musical life has been pre-eminent. A great concert hall is not only brick and stone. One can say that it is like an old church where people have prayed. For me there is no difference between performing and praying or listening and praying. Both require the same kind of concentrated energy within. In Carnegie Hall the electricity of previous performances is literally imprinted on the walls. When I walk on stage, I absolutely know that Rachmaninoff, Paderewski, Hofmann, Horowitz and Rubinstein were there before me.

Dubal: I know that your playing was much admired by Rubinstein.

Weissenberg: I take that as the greatest compliment. He had the simplest, most precise connection with the music; and his playing was always personal and spontaneous. It was that of a very modern twentieth-century pianist, not of somebody who reminded you of the past or of old-fashioned piano playing.

Dubal: What is old-fashioned piano playing? Does it have to do with the liberties that were taken by Paderewski, de Pachmann or Rachmaninoff?

Weissenberg: What makes something old-fashioned for me is the imitation of what has been done in the past. You may play even more freely than de Pachmann or Rachmaninoff and still be a modern artist because your approach and conception is entirely your own.

Dubal: Although you are admired by many, you are a musician who is known to torment some listeners because your playing is not always "pretty" enough for them.

Weissenberg: Of course I know this. But one does not play in order to please people or to be liked by them. The only thing that matters is the music and our connection with it. It doesn't matter what people feel about me personally. I respect those who like me as much as I do those who don't. The public's reaction to what I do is as spontaneous as my own connection with the music. For me there can be nothing more personal than to make music. Like love-making, it is the strongest expression of one's innermost self.

JULIAN H. KREEGER

Born November 26, 1915, in Pittsburgh, Pennsylvania, Wild studied with Egon Petri. In 1939 he became the first pianist to give a recital on American television. Wild has played at the White House for six Presidents of the United States. He is also a composer of numerous works, including an oratorio called Revelations, *commissioned by the American Broadcasting Company. Wild has premiered many new works, such as the Paul Creston Concerto. His concert activity takes him all over the United States, Europe and South America, yet he has had an unusually large discography, including thirty concerti and over 160 solo works. He is on the faculty of the Juilliard School.*

Earl Wild

DUBAL: Was it important for a pianist to have a European reputation to succeed in America when you were launching your career in the 1930s?

WILD: It certainly helped if you came from Europe—it still helps. But little by little, we are producing our own excellent pianists, and we're getting over the European mystique. It's interesting, however, that when I tour South America, where the name Wild is unusual, the public is more receptive to me than in the United States. Names have always been mysterious things. Once it was fashionable to be a Polish pianist; now a Russian name dazzles us.

DUBAL: What was it like to be making your way as a pianist at the height of the Depression?

WILD: We had to be more practical in the Thirties. I had to play anything I could to make a living. My first job involved making orchestrations. During the Depression, the public only had money for the established stars; so the possibility of building a career seemed very remote. Fortunately, I landed a job as staff pianist at NBC in New York, which took me through the better part of the Depression.

DUBAL: It was at NBC that Toscanini picked you to be soloist in his own first performance of Gershwin's *Rhapsody in Blue.*

WILD: Yes! When Toscanini invited me to be soloist in the *Rhapsody in Blue,* I was amazed, for neither of us had ever performed the work. Needless to say, I learned the piece and played it on that November evening in 1942. The day after the concert, I was hailed as an authority on the music of Gershwin. Soon after, I learned the Concerto in F, and much later I transcribed some of his songs for the piano.

DUBAL: You often play transcriptions, don't you?

WILD: Yes, they tend to have wonderful period charm. I love the transcription literature, including the many lovely pieces which are neglected because they have fallen out of fashion. For instance, I often play Eduard Schütt's transcription of *Die Fledermaus,* for its pure joy and charm. Certainly it's fragmentary, but I'm not totally concerned with the so-called masterpieces. By being overly intellectual in their choice of programs, musicians often close their minds to some charming, and, in many ways, successful music.

DUBAL: Wouldn't many students do well to investigate this literature to help develop their technique instead of playing the usual exercises?

WILD: Absolutely. Transcriptions are marvelous for this purpose. They were composed as display pieces, so they are much easier on the ear than the standard exercises, and they pose endless pianistic problems. They also educate the student in style, orchestral sonorities and the legato sound of the voice. Transcriptions make splendid encores, as well. When Mr. Horowitz plays his *Carmen Variations* or another one of his wicked transcriptions at a recital, it's the talk of the town for the next month. If he doesn't, everybody leaves the hall feeling deprived!

DUBAL: One of the truly wonderful pieces you play is Carl Tausig's dressed-up version of the *Invitation to the Dance* by Carl Maria von Weber.

WILD: It was fashionable to embellish the music like that in the nineteenth century. Leopold Godowsky also made a transcription of it!

DUBAL: Yes, everyone attempted the *Invitation to the Dance* during the nineteenth century. It was considered an accomplishment. Later, Nijinsky made his famous leap in *Le Spectre de la Rose,* the ballet made from it.

I know you like to play Godowsky transcriptions.

WILD: How could I resist them? Many of Godowsky's transcriptions are so difficult and complex that they may easily become an obsession. They plague you! I've played quite a few and have always admired his spectacular pianistic conceptions. Because of their great physical demands, I find that I never have the total abandon that I wish for. They are even harder than they sound, what with their endless contrapuntal devices.

DUBAL: Naturally you play the standard literature, and Chopin appears frequently on your programs. Can you tell me your thoughts about the four ballades, which are among the greatest of Chopin's compositions?

WILD: The ballades are very mysterious pieces, and even though I've lived with them all of my life, I am constantly searching for a better way to project them. You can't be complacent about the ballades. After the tedious, minute technical work has been achieved, it is the most important and difficult task to create an improvisational atmosphere.

DUBAL: Is the coda in the F minor Ballade as treacherous as many have said?

WILD: No, not quite as horrid as rumor has it. The extreme difficulties contained in this coda may cause great anxieties throughout the entire piece. It must be allowed to begin rather calmly and to move forward gracefully but with momentum. It's important not to start with an agitated feeling. As you know, the opening of that coda has a marvelous low F—a bell tone. If you can properly place that in your ear, it will solidify the tempo.

DUBAL: In addition to Chopin, you've also played a large Liszt repertoire, which is known for its orchestral sound.

WILD: When I was very young, I played in many orchestras—the cello, the bass and later the flute. I must admit I played them all very badly; however, the experience left me with a wonderful feeling for the orchestra. Now when I play Liszt, I feel the latent orchestral palette in his piano writing. He thought orchestrally and placed the orchestra in the piano with unimagined ingenuity. Only in some of the glittery earlier works did he use the piano for its own sake. But in his mature works, the piano becomes an orchestra. It's that which has always attracted me to Liszt. In every aspect of the musical field, he was one of the greatest of geniuses. Liszt was the quintessential romantic, always searching; and he was so very human along with his great genius.

DUBAL: Yes, after Wagner wrote his autobiography, Liszt's friends wanted to know when he would write *his* autobiography. His answer was just wonderful: "It is enough to have lived it," he replied.

In some of your Liszt playing I detect little touch-ups in the texture. For instance, in *Les Jeux d'eau à la Villa d'Este,* you take out some of his tremolo-writing.

WILD: Yes, I do. Sometimes I think Liszt was carried away with his orchestral thinking. When there are too many tremolos, I am offended.

DUBAL: Are they too vulgar for you?

WILD: They're not vulgar, but you have to have just the right piano on which to play them. Sometimes the piano can be perfectly wonderful, but it can't accept the tremolos. So, I redo those passages. I usually turn them into arpeggios, or some pianistic device that is less offensive to me.

DUBAL: Your little changes would have been sanctioned by many Romantics. But you wouldn't do this to some composers, say Mozart, would you?

WILD: Actually, I love to make variants in Mozart. I think most Mozart playing today is very dreary because few performers take advantage of the opportunities Mozart suggested. But one has to be very creative to alter the text properly.

DUBAL: Yes, they would say that "Earl Wild is tampering with the text!" and they would want to tar and feather you.

WILD: I don't care—what is the page without the sound?

DUBAL: Who are or were the greatest pianists, in your opinion?

WILD: My favorite pianists are of the past—Rachmaninoff, Hofmann and Petri. Of course there were other wonderful performances by artists like Moiseiwitsch, but when it came to really big piano playing, only these three artists achieved the ultimate.

DUBAL: Rachmaninoff seems to be on everyone's list. What were his chief attributes?

WILD: It was his sense of rhythm and his sound. And yet, since he was always associated with Romantic music, he would feel rather strange when he played Beethoven. During one of his rare performances of the Beethoven First Concerto, he turned to the orchestra and said, "Gentlemen, since I am not a Beethoven expert, let's play this piece in tempo!"

DUBAL: Do you find that rhythm is one of the chief problems students have?

WILD: Oh, yes, when you're young, your nervous system is hyperactive. The music is so intense that students have a tendency to move forward too much, or in the serious places to overdo it by holding back. These days, young pianists seem to think that if you merely go very, very slowly, you are being profound.

DUBAL: Do you make any use of the tape recorder and metronome in your practicing?

WILD: I can't practice and get a natural rhythm with a metronome. If I feel unnerved when I'm playing something and the rhythm isn't good, I turn on the tape machine and discover where my nervous system is overtaking me. Of course I can hear it very easily when I teach pupils. I'm constantly chiding them about poor rhythm-control.

DUBAL: How do you get that fabulous sheen to the sound that I associate with you—especially in the upper registers? How is such a sound accomplished?

WILD: I only lift my hands off the keyboard to relax the muscles of the arms. I never lose contact with the keys. By keeping your hands right on top of them, you have better contact and more tonal control.

DUBAL: How do you deal with distractions from the audience when you are on stage—the coughing and that sort of thing?

WILD: Sometimes it's very difficult, because sounds always seem louder while you're concentrating intensely. And this applies to everything from coughing in the audience to the sound of air conditioners. Oftentimes when I hear someone blatantly coughing without using their handkerchief to dampen the sound, I feel as though I'm playing to a group of trained seals who are demanding to be fed! I try to focus completely on what I am doing at all times, but extraneous sounds can be so disturbing that my nervous system can suffer greatly.

DUBAL: What goes through your mind when you are listening to one of your own recordings?

WILD: That depends on so many things. It depends upon the occasion, my mood, the set on which the recording is being played, the room, and whether it's cold or hot outside.

DUBAL: Recording has come a long way since Edison. What is your opinion on the newest advances?

WILD: Sound is very much like clothing. One year something is chic, the next year it's out! First we had monaural, then we had stereo, then it was quadraphonic and wall-to-wall sound, and now we have computer sound—digital recordings and compact discs. Each has its own chic for the electronics people. One has to admire the great advances that have been made in the world of electronics, even though many valueless devices are being marketed for pure profit. I still like to listen to recordings from the Thirties, which to me are often fresher and more satisfying than many of the recent releases.

BIOGRAPHICAL NOTES

HUGH AITKEN (b. 1924). American teacher and composer. His *Piano Fantasy* is played by Gary Kirkpatrick on CRI SD 365.

ISAAC ALBÉNIZ (1860–1909). The eminent Spanish composer. He wrote the twelve works that make up *Iberia* from 1906 to 1909.

EUGENE D'ALBERT (1864–1932). German pianist-composer, born in Glasgow; one of the great pianists of his time. He studied with Liszt.

CONRAD ANSORGE (1862–1930). German pianist; a late pupil of Liszt. He toured widely including America. His compositions include a piano concerto and three sonatas. His playing was described as "metaphysical."

GEORGE ANTHEIL (1900–1959). An intriguing American composer and pianist. His autobiography *Bad Boy of Music* was published in 1945.

ENRIQUE FERNÁNDEZ ARBÓS (1863–1939). Spanish violinist and conductor. He transcribed several selections of Albéniz's piano suite *Iberia* for orchestra.

LEOPOLD AUER (1845–1930). Hungarian-born violinist and teacher who spent many years at the St. Petersburg Conservatory. He taught Heifetz, Misha Elman and Efrem Zimbalist.

JOHANN SEBASTIAN BACH (1685–1750). His keyboard music is the mainspring of a pianist's education. When his friend the instrument builder Gottfried Silbermann showed him his first pianos, Bach disliked them. Many years later, after the instrument had been improved, Bach played at the palace of Frederick the Great and gave his blessing to the new instrument.

GINA BACHAUER (1913–1976). Greek pianist who played with tremendous bravura.

WILHELM BACKHAUS (1884–1969). Leipzig-born Backhaus was a towering pianist. He recorded the thirty-two sonatas of Beethoven twice.

DAME JANET BAKER (b. 1933). English mezzo-soprano. One of the foremost lieder singers of our time.

MILY BALAKIREV (1837–1910). Russian composer. His piano music is unduly neglected. He was an excellent pianist, though incapable of playing his own treacherous *Islamey*.

GEORGE BALANCHINE (1904–1982). Russian-born choreographer, dancer and teacher. Director of the New York City Ballet. His work is of incalculable importance in the history of dance.

Samuel Barber (1910–1981). One of the most performed of American composers. He wrote his Piano Sonata for Horowitz. The composer loved the performance, which is on RCA ARMI-2952.

Simon Barère (1896–1951). Russian-born virtuoso. Glazunov said that he was an Anton Rubinstein in his left hand and a Liszt in his right hand. He studied with Blumenfeld and Annette Essipov (1851–1914). Barère's disc of Liszt's *Spanish Rhapsody*, the *Don Juan Fantasy* and Balakirev's *Islamey* are legendary.

Daniel Barenboim (b. 1942). Israeli pianist and conductor. He has recorded a large repertoire.

Béla Bartók (1882–1945). This great Hungarian composer's own piano playing has been issued by Hungaraton: Volume I, Bartók at the Piano 1920–1945 LPX 12326-33; Volume II, Bartók Plays and Talks 1912–1944 LPX 12334-38.

Mattia Battistini (1856–1928). Italian baritone, made his debut in *La Favorita* of Donizetti.

Harold Bauer (1873–1951). English-born pianist whose main instrument was the violin until he was twenty-one. His Schumann editions for Schirmer were once widely used. He can be heard in smaller pieces as well as his famous performance of the Brahms F minor Sonata on IPA/Desmar 112.

Sir Thomas Beecham (1879–1961). One of the most colorful figures in English music. His conducting repertoire was very large. He championed Delius and wrote a biography of him, while his autobiography, *A Mingled Chime,* appeared in 1943.

Ludwig van Beethoven (1770–1827). Earlier in his career he was called "the giant among pianoforte players." Beethoven's thirty-two sonatas, his variations and his five concerti are the core of the pianist's repertoire. Von Bülow called the sonatas "the pianist's New Testament"—the Old Testament being Bach's *Well-Tempered Clavier.* Busoni said, "Bach is the foundation of piano playing, Liszt the summit. The two make Beethoven possible."

Richard Rodney Bennett (b. 1936). English composer and fine pianist.

Alban Berg (1885–1935). Austrian composer. His only piano work is the often-performed Sonata Op. 1 (1908).

Ludwig Berger (1777–1839). German pianist and estimable composer. His twenty-seven etudes were once played but his music is now forgotten. His greatest student was Mendelssohn.

Hector Berlioz (1803–1869). Great French Romantic composer and writer on music. His *Memoires* are the most vivid autobiography written by any composer. He wrote no piano music.

Leonard Bernstein (b. 1918). Brilliant American conductor, composer and pianist. He studied piano with Isabelle Vengerova and Heinrich Gebhard.

HANS BISCHOFF (1852–1889). German pianist and editor.

ERNEST BLOCH (1880–1959). Swiss-born composer. His small amount of piano music is highlighted by an important sonata, 1935.

FELIX BLUMENFELD (1863–1931). Russian pianist, conductor and composer. He composed marvelously written piano music, the best of which is a set of Twenty-four Preludes Op. 17.

VICTOR BORGE (b. 1909). Danish pianist-comedian.

ALEXANDER BORODIN (1834–1887). Great Russian composer who wrote several pleasing piano pieces. The best is a Scherzo in A-flat, which Rachmaninoff recorded.

NADIA BOULANGER (1887–1979). Renowned French composition teacher. Aaron Copland, Virgil Thomson and Philip Glass are just a few of her famous American students.

PIERRE BOULEZ (b. 1925). French conductor and important composer. Maurizio Pollini's recording of the Boulez Sonata No. 2 (DG 2530803) is extraordinary.

JOHANNES BRAHMS (1833–1897). German master. Everything Brahms wrote for the instrument is of intrinsic interest to pianists. His Variations on a Theme of Paganini are among the great technical tests of the literature.

ALEXANDER BRAILOWSKY (1896–1976). Born in Kiev, a student of Leschetizky and later of Sauer. He was one of the first pianists to perform the complete cycle of Chopin works, which he did in seven recitals. In 1928 he became the first to record the Chopin E minor Concerto. Possibly his best playing on LP is the nineteen Chopin Nocturnes, RCA 16050-3.

BENJAMIN BRITTEN (1913–1976). Great English composer, the first to be raised to the British peerage. As a pianist, he can be heard on disc in his own songs.

BROADWOOD PIANO. The house of Broadwood & Sons incorporated the making of pianofortes into its keyboard-instrument business in 1773. This was also the year that Clementi published several of his sonatas, which have been regarded as the earliest works showing a full grasp of the piano. In 1783, Broadwood introduced the damper pedal. In 1794, it extended the compass of the grand piano to six octaves and was the first to experiment with iron bars in the previously all-wood instrument.

HANS VON BÜLOW (1830–1894). German pianist and conductor, one of the supreme musicians of the nineteenth century and a great influence on the course of interpretation. He studied with Clara Schumann's father, Friedrich Wieck, and later became a pupil of Liszt. Von Bülow was considered a profound and intellectual player; his playing was often contrasted with the tempestuous style of Anton Rubinstein's. He played the premiere of the Liszt Sonata in 1856, and conducted the first performances of *Tristan and Isolde* in 1865 and *Die Meistersinger* in 1868. His American tours were sponsored by the Chickering piano firm.

ADOLF BUSCH (1891–1952). German-born violinist.

FRITZ BUSCH (1890–1951). Famed German-born conductor. His autobiography, *Pages from a Musician's Life,* appeared in English in 1953.

FERRUCCIO BUSONI (1866–1924). Monumental Italian-born pianist-composer. Arthur Rubinstein wrote: "With his handsome, pale, Christ-like face and his diabolical technical prowess, Busoni was by far the most interesting pianist alive." His only disc recordings have been issued on the International Piano Archive label 104, and they give an indication of his technical and creative powers. Busoni's own music is rather cerebral, but it exerts a fascination on many musicians, though the public has never formed an attachment to it.

MARIA CALLAS (1923–1977). World-renowned American soprano of exceptional acting gifts. Many pianists have studied her bel canto singing as a model of phrasing and plasticity.

TERESA CARREÑO (1853–1917). The greatest Venezuelan pianist and a tremendous musical personality, she was called "the Valkyrie of the piano." As a child she played for Louis Moreau Gottschalk. Edward MacDowell later studied with her, and she frequently played his music. Unfortunately, she only made a few piano rolls.

ELLIOTT CARTER (b. 1908). Notable American composer. *Night Fantasies,* his latest piano work, has been given two splendid interpretations by Charles Rosen and by Paul Jacobs (1930–1983).

ROBERT CASADESUS (1899–1972). French pianist. His discs of Ravel and Debussy are beautiful examples of French piano playing. He was often heard in the two-piano literature with his wife, Gaby (b. 1900). Their son Jean (1927–1972) was also an expert pianist.

PABLO CASALS (1876–1973). Born in Spain, Casals was the most famous cellist who ever lived.

SERGIU CELIBIDACHE (b. 1912). Gifted Rumanian conductor and composer.

EMMANUEL CHABRIER (1841–1894). Colorful French composer. His *Bourrée Fantasque* was composed in 1891.

FEODOR CHALIAPIN (1873–1938). Russian basso, one of the greatest singing actors of all time.

SCHUYLER CHAPIN (b. 1923). Former manager of the Metropolitan Opera and musical administrator.

ABRAM CHASINS (b. 1903). American pianist, composer and writer. His book *Speaking of Pianists* (1958) is widely read. The eminent pianist Constance Keene studied with him.

CARLOS CHÁVEZ (1899–1978). Valuable Mexican composer. The American pianist Eugene List played the world premiere of the Chávez Piano Concerto in 1942.

JAN CHIAPUSSO (1890–1969). Dutch-American pianist and teacher.

FRÉDÉRIC CHOPIN (1810–1849). The greatest of all Polish composers. His music, virtually all of which is in the permanent repertoire, has a universal allure. Arthur Rubinstein once said, "It is extraordinary to observe how the most diverse audiences are conquered by the music of Chopin. . . . Chopin has a hold on the hearts of men everywhere. . . . I have always been struck by this fact when I played mazurkas in China, polonaises in Japan and ballades in Australia or South Africa."

MUZIO CLEMENTI (1752–1832). Born in Rome. He was the teacher of Johann Babtist Cramer, John Field, Alexander Klengel and Ludwig Berger. He played an important part in the history of piano-building as the manufacturer of the Clementi pianoforte. His *Gradus ad Parnassum* is a classic of the early literature.

VAN CLIBURN (b. 1934). American pianist, winner of the 1958 Tchaikovsky Competition. He returned to the United States to a hero's welcome.

ALBERT COATES (1882–1953). English conductor born in St. Petersburg. A proponent of Wagner and Scriabin. The Rachmaninoff concerto that Horowitz recorded with Coates and the London Symphony was reissued on Seraphim 60063.

HARRIET COHEN (1895–1967). English pianist, student of Tobias Matthay (1858–1945), Myra Hess's teacher. She brought to the public a variety of contemporary music, especially that of Sir Arnold Bax (1883–1953).

AARON COPLAND (b. 1900). Famous American composer whose Piano Variations, Sonata and Fantasy, dedicated to the memory of William Kapell, as well as a Piano Concerto, are his main contributions to the piano literature. Copland was often soloist in his concerto.

JOHN CORIGLIANO (b. 1938). American composer, a student of Otto Luening and Vittorio Giannini. His *Etude Fantasy,* premiered by James Tocco, is highly effective, as is the difficult Piano Concerto, which is recorded on Mercury 75118 by Hilde Somer. The composer told me that Horowitz sight-read the concerto for him.

PETER CORNELIUS (1824–1874). Composer and writer on music. His best-known work is the opera *The Barber of Bagdad*.

ALFRED CORTOT (1877–1962). One of the great French musicians, and a pianist and teacher of far-reaching influence. Many important pianists, such as Magda Tagliaferro, Vlado Perlemuter and Dinu Lipatti, worked with him. His Chopin playing is world-famous, and he was the author of the book *In Search of Chopin*. His many recordings display a unique freedom and flexibility in phrasing.

Johann Babtist Cramer (1771–1858). Important pianist and teacher. His set of one hundred etudes maintain their value.

Paul Creston (b. 1906). Noted American composer.

Carl Czerny (1791–1857). Austrian pianist-composer and one of history's eminent teachers. Studied piano with Beethoven. Czerny composed hundreds of etudes which have become the scholastic bread and butter of generations of students. His pupils Liszt and Leschetizky became the most potent teachers of the nineteenth century. Liszt modestly said that he owed Czerny "everything."

Halina Czerny-Stefánska (b. 1922). Polish pianist, especially admired for her interpretations of Chopin mazurkas.

Sir Colin Davis (b. 1927). Remarkable English conductor.

Claude Debussy (1862–1918). French master, one of the great innovators of music. His contribution to the piano literature cannot be overestimated. Debussy's complete edition of Chopin's music is published by Durand-Paris.

Norman Dello Joio (b. 1913). American composer. His Piano Sonata No. 3, 1947, is published by Fischer.

Emmy Destinn (1878–1930). Czech-born dramatic soprano whose repertory included eighty roles.

Ernst von Dohnányi (1877–1960). Hungarian pianist, composer, teacher. He can be heard on Angel S-35538 in his Second Concerto and the well-known Variations on a Nursery Song for Piano and Orchestra.

Felix Draeseke (1835–1913). Prolific German composer. Composed an interesting Sonata quasi Fantasia, Op. 6.

Paul Dukas (1865–1935). Eminent French composer. His Piano Sonata takes nearly an hour in performance.

Jan Ladislav Dussek (1760–1812). Outstanding pianist and composer. One of the first pianists to tour extensively, to turn his profile to the audience and to put pedal-markings in his music. His singing touch was famous, and his large output is filled with remarkable pages.

Erard piano. Celebrated French piano firm founded by Sébastien Erard (1752–1831). In 1821, Erard patented his double escapement mechanism, a finer "repetition action." This action prepared the instrument for the turbulence of the Romantics, and was soon adopted by all other piano manufacturers.

Gabriel Fauré (1845–1924). Great French composer. Grace, exquisite melody and harmonic ingenuity are found throughout his large contribution to the piano literature.

ANNIE FISCHER (b. 1914). Noted Hungarian-born pianist.

EDWIN FISCHER (1886–1960). Swiss pianist of enormous influence. Like Arrau, he studied with Martin Krause in Berlin. He published books on Bach and on Beethoven's piano sonatas. Fischer combined magnificent intellectual attributes with a white-hot temperament.

DIETRICH FISCHER-DIESKAU (b. 1925). Fine German baritone.

YAKOV FLIERE (1912–1977). Russian pianist, who studied with Igumnov. His performances are good examples of earlier, Imperial Russian training merged with a more modern and scrupulous view of the text.

MARGOT FONTEYN (b. 1919). English dancer; one of the most celebrated of her generation.

FOU T'SONG (b. 1934). Born in China. Studied with the well-known Polish teacher Zbigniew Drzewiecki. His Chopin playing is particularly admired.

ZINO FRANCESCATTI (b. 1902). French violinist. Played the Beethoven Violin Concerto in public at age ten. His career has been international.

CLAUDE FRANK (b. 1925). American pianist, born in Germany. He has recorded all of the Beethoven sonatas for RCA VICS 9000.

CARL FRIEDBERG (1872–1955). German pianist; studied with Clara Schumann. One of the leading teachers of his time. He taught such eminent artists as Bruce Hungerford and Malcolm Frager.

IGNAZ FRIEDMAN (1882–1948). Polish pianist and student of Leschetizky who played over 3,000 concerts worldwide with an invincible technique and richly poetic powers. His conceptions are often very original. His recordings of Chopin mazurkas are treasures. They have been reissued on Encore 303. He composed over one hundred piano pieces.

JAMES FRISKIN (1886–1967). Scottish-born pianist who was often identified with the music of Bach.

WILHELM FURTWÄNGLER (1886–1954). Renowned German conductor. Among his compositions is a Piano Concerto.

GEORGE GERSHWIN (1898–1937). American composer. He himself played the piano part in the premiere of *Rhapsody in Blue* in 1924, which has become the most-performed American concert work.

WALTER GIESEKING (1895–1956). German pianist. Recorded all of Mozart's piano music, as well as a great quantity of other German repertoire. His name, however, has become synonymous with the music of Debussy and Ravel, in which Gieseking showed himself to be one of the supreme colorists of the piano. His exploits as a sight-reader were legendary.

EMIL GILELS (b. 1916). Great Soviet pianist, born in Odessa, who studied at the Moscow Conservatory with Heinrich Neuhaus. Won the 1938 International Competition in Brussels. Made his first American tour in 1955.

ALBERTO GINASTERA (1916–1983). Argentine composer who incorporated the rhythms of his nation into traditional forms. For the piano there are twelve American Preludes, three piano sonatas—No. 1 has become a favorite contemporary sonata—and two concerti, both played by Hilde Somer (1930–1980).

GRIGORY GINZBURG (1904–1961). Student of Alexander Goldenweiser, an elegant pianist, played the first Russian performances of Gershwin's Preludes. His disc of Liszt's *Rigoletto Paraphrase* and *Faust Waltz* shows him at his best (Melodiya D 7663).

ALEXANDER GLAZUNOV (1865–1936). Eminent Russian composer and teacher. His music is influenced by Tchaikovsky. He wrote excellent piano music, including two sonatas and two concertos. His best-known work is his Theme and Variations in D minor, Op. 72.

CHRISTOPH WILLIBALD VON GLUCK (1714–1787). German opera composer.

LEOPOLD GODOWSKY (1870–1938). Polish virtuoso, one of the technical wizards of the piano. His compositions and transcriptions show a miraculous understanding of the instrument's potential.

SASHA GORODNITZKI (b. 1905). Born in Kiev. Pianist and teacher at the Juilliard School.

PERCY GRAINGER (1882–1961). Famous Australian-born pianist-composer, folklorist.

ENRIQUE GRANADOS (1867–1916). Spanish composer and pianist. The six works that make up his 1911 *Goyescas* suite, inspired by the painter Goya, constitute his masterpiece.

EDVARD GRIEG (1843–1907). The Norwegian composer was a good pianist but was dumbfounded when Liszt sight-read, in manuscript, Grieg's own Piano Concerto in A minor.

MARIA GRINBERG (1908–1979). Born in Odessa, a student of Blumenfeld and later of Igumnov. She taught at the Moscow Conservatory. Her Beethoven was earthy and she had a fine sense of form. Her Bach F minor Concerto, Franck *Symphonic Variations* and Shostakovich Concerto No. 1 can be heard on Westminster 8325.

SIR CHARLES HALLÉ (1819–1895). Born in Westphalia. Studied in Paris with Kalkbrenner. After 1850 he became a fixture of English musical life, founding the Hallé Orchestra in Manchester in 1857. As a pianist, Hallé appeared in London in the Emperor Concerto as early as 1848.

Charles Louis Hanon (1819–1900). French teacher, the creator of the group of five-finger exercises for the equalization of fingers.

Howard Hanson (1896–1981). Distinguished American composer and conductor.

Clara Haskil (1895–1960). Rumanian pianist, studied with Dohnányi and Cortot. Her playing was exquisitely polished.

Jascha Heifetz (b. 1901). Great Russian violinist.

Sir George Henschel (1850–1934). English singer, conductor, composer, born in Breslau, Germany.

Adolf von Henselt (1814–1889). German pianist-composer. His influence was deeply felt in Russia, where he lived for years. His two sets of etudes, Op. 2 and Op. 5, reveal a wonderful pianistic mind. His F minor Concerto was once in the repertoire. It is admirably played by the American pianist Raymond Lewenthal, Columbia MG-35183.

Henri Herz (1803–1888). Austrian-born pianist of fashionable variations and character pieces; among the most played of nineteenth-century composers.

Myra Hess (1890–1965). British pianist of the first rank. She was made Dame Myra Hess because of her extraordinary musical programming at the National Gallery Concerts in London during World War II. In her performance of the Beethoven Sonata Op. 109 on Seraphim 6045, she is at her finest.

Ferdinand Hiller (1811–1885). German pianist-composer of distinction. A student of Hummel. He was the first to play the *Emperor Concerto* in Paris. He composed many piano works, including the once-popular F-sharp minor Piano Concerto.

Paul Hindemith (1895–1963). Influential German composer. His *Ludus Tonalis* for piano fascinates many musicians.

E.T.A. Hoffmann (1776–1822). German novelist. He had a profound impact on German Romanticism. Hoffmann was also an important music critic who took the pen-name "Kapellmeister Johannes Kreisler." He wrote four piano sonatas of a very conventional character.

Josef Hofmann (1876–1957). Polish-born pianist, student of Anton Rubinstein and one of the commanding figures in the history of the piano. Hofmann was one of the most celebrated of all prodigies. The history of piano-recording begins with the cylinders he made for Thomas Edison in the late 1880s. Every collector should own his Golden Jubilee concert on 2 IPA/Desmar 5001. Harold Schonberg called him "perfection plus."

Mieczyslaw Horszowski (b. 1892). Born in Poland, he studied with Leschetizky as a "wonder child." He has taught many students at the Curtis Institute. He continues to play with undiminished skills.

Sol Hurok (1888–1974). Russian-born impresario. Exclusive manager of Arthur Rubinstein and many others.

Ernest Hutcheson (1871–1951). Australian-born pianist. He wrote the book *The Literature of the Piano.*

Konstantin Igumnov (1873–1948). Like Rachmaninoff, Josef Lhevinne, Scriabin and Goldenweiser, Igumnov studied with Nikolai Zverev, and later with Alexander Siloti and Paul Pabst. He was professor at the Moscow Conservatory and one of the most respected teachers, with a long list of distinguished pupils. Melodiya issued a four-record set (C 10-05519-26) commemorating his art as a pianist.

José Iturbi (1899–1980). Famous Spanish pianist. In the 1940s he appeared in Hollywood films.

Charles Ives (1874–1954). American composer. His two massive piano sonatas are great achievements. No. 1 can be heard by William Masselos on Odyssey 32160059, and No. 2, subtitled "*Concord, Mass.,*" by John Kirkpatrick on CBS MS-7192.

Leoš Janáček (1854–1928). Czech composer. His piano music represents only a small part of his output.

Pál Kadosa (1903–1983). Hungarian composer-pianist and teacher of many important younger Hungarian pianists such as Dezsö Ranki and Zoltán Kocsis.

Friedrich Kalkbrenner (1785–1849). German-born pianist of great technical finish. His large output for the piano is now ignored.

William Kapell (1922–1953). Fiery American pianist. His Khachaturian Concerto, RCA LM 2588, is captivating, and the Chopin Third Sonata on RCA SB 7643 is Chopin-playing of the highest importance.

Herbert von Karajan (b. 1908). Born in Salzburg. He has had one of the most spectacular careers in twentieth-century conducting.

Julius Katchen (1926–1969). Distinguished American pianist. Recorded a wide range of repertoire.

Wilhelm Kempff (b. 1895). Great German pianist; one of the finest musicians of the century.

Leon Kirchner (b. 1919). American composer and pedagogue.

Ralph Kirkpatrick (1911–1984). American harpsichordist. His biography of Domenico Scarlatti is highly regarded and his editions of Scarlatti sonatas are widely used.

Otto Klemperer (1885–1973). German-born. One of the finest conductors of the century. He held numerous posts throughout the world. As a composer he left six symphonies, nine string quartets and nearly one hundred lieder.

Karl Klindworth (1830–1916). German pianist and teacher. Studied with Liszt. Produced an interesting edition of Chopin's music, and also made important piano scores of Wagner's *Der Ring des Nibelungen*.

ZOLTÁN KODÁLY (1882–1967). Hungarian composer of strong personality. He composed little for the piano.

ERICH WOLFGANG KORNGOLD (1897–1957). Versatile Austrian-born composer. Artur Schnabel premiered his First Piano Sonata, which was composed when Korngold was eleven.

SERGE KOUSSEVITZKY (1874–1951). Russian-born conductor. Early in his career he became known as a double-bass virtuoso. A great champion of contemporary music, he encouraged and commissioned many American composers. He was permanent conductor of the Boston Symphony from 1924 to 1949.

MARTIN KRAUSE (1853–1918). German pianist and teacher. Studied with Reinecke at the Leipzig Conservatory. He was in close contact with Liszt from 1883. Later he taught at the famous Stern Conservatory in Berlin.

FRITZ KREISLER (1875–1962). Austrian-born, Kreisler is perhaps the most beloved violinist of the century. His collaborations with Rachmaninoff can be found in Vol. 4 of Rachmaninoff's complete recordings, RCA ARM3-0295.

GIDON KREMER (b. 1947). Virtuoso violinist born in Riga, Latvia, in the Soviet Union.

RAFAEL KUBELIK (b. 1914). Czech conductor, son of the famous violinist Jan Kubelik. He has also composed a great deal.

VILÉM KURZ (1872–1945). Respected Czech piano pedagogue.

FREDERIC LAMOND (1868–1948). With da Motta, the Scottish pianist Lamond was Liszt's last surviving pupil.

JOHN LAMONTAINE (b. 1920). American composer, studied with Bernard Wagenaar and Nadia Boulanger. The Piano Concerto Op. 9 is published by Galaxy.

KARL LEIMER (1858–1944). German pedagogue and Gieseking's only teacher. His two short books on piano playing were reissued by Dover in one volume in 1972.

WILHELM VON LENZ (1809–1883). Russian-born writer on music and a pianist. He wrote his personal recollections of Liszt, Chopin, Tausig and Henselt in a volume called *Great Piano Virtuosos of Our Time*.

THEODOR LESCHETIZKY (1830–1915). Polish-born pianist and a teacher of genius. Many of the world's aspiring pianists passed through his studio in Vienna. A tremendous inspirational force, he was the teacher of such important pianists as Annette Essipov, Fanny Bloomfield-Zeisler, Paderewski, Ossip Gabrilowitsch, Ignaz Friedman and Artur Schnabel. He was the apostle of beautiful tone and high virtuosity.

JOSEF LHEVINNE (1874–1944). Russian-born virtuoso pianist and teacher at the Juilliard School. His art can be heard on RCA VIC-1544. His performances of the Strauss-Schulz-Evler "*Blue Danube*" and the Schumann-Liszt "*Frühlingsnacht*" are unparalleled.

ROSINA LHEVINNE (1880–1976). Pianist and teacher of a legion of pupils at the Juilliard School. Her performance of the Mozart Concerto No. 21 (CBS MP38752) shows her great skill at the age of eighty.

LIBERACE (b. 1919). Popular piano entertainer born in Wisconsin.

GODDARD LIEBERSON (1911–1977). American record executive at Columbia, also a composer. Lieberson did much to promote the long-playing record in its first years.

DINU LIPATTI (1917–1950). Great Rumanian pianist. His recordings are all available. His recordings of the Chopin Barcarolle and B minor Sonata and the Schumann Concerto are incandescent interpretations.

FRANZ LISZT (1811–1886). Born in Hungary, he possessed the greatest pianistic mind in history. Liszt's biographer Alan Walker calls him "the Euclid of the piano." Busoni wrote, "we are all descended from him radically . . . are all branches of his tree."

ARTHUR LOESSER (1894–1969). Born in New York. For years he was the head of the piano department at the Cleveland Institute of Music. His Bach *Well-Tempered Clavier* can be heard on 5 Telarc 5029-5. His book *Men, Women and Pianos* has become a classic.

MARGUERITE LONG (1874–1966). French pianist and teacher. A student of Marmontel, Debussy's teacher. She was a favorite interpreter of many French composers. With the violinist Jacques Thibaud she established the Long-Thibaud Competition. She published two interesting books, *At the Piano With Debussy* and *At the Piano With Fauré*. Ravel dedicated his G major Piano Concerto to her and conducted, with Long as soloist, in a 1932 recording of the concerto, which can be found on Seraphim IC-6043.

YO-YO MA (b. 1955). Born in Paris of Chinese parents, he is the preeminent cellist of his generation.

LORIN MAAZEL (b. 1930). Born in France, he has had a career as a conductor since the age of nine.

GUSTAV MAHLER (1860–1911). The last in the line of Viennese symphonists. The solo piano had no place in his output.

GEORGE MALCOLM (b. 1917). English harpsichordist, pianist, conductor.

YEVGENY MALININ (b. 1930). Russian pianist and teacher. Student of Neuhaus.

ADELE MARCUS (b. 1906). Born in Kansas City, a prominent piano teacher at Juilliard. Student of Josef Lhevinne. Outstanding pianists such as Agustin Anievas, Horacio Gutierrez and Tedd Joselson have studied with her.

Frank Marshall (1883–1959). Spanish-born pianist; Granados's finest student.

Bohuslav Martinů (1890–1959). Czech composer whose best-known piano works are the Sixteen Etudes and Polkas, 1945.

Peter Martins (b. 1946). Danish-born dancer and choreographer, Balanchine's successor as the director of the New York City Ballet.

Josef Marx (1882–1964). Austrian composer. His works are richly colored and thickly scored.

Nikolai Medtner (1880–1951). Russian-born composer-pianist who studied with Vassily Safonov. He composed a large body of piano music, including three piano concerti. Gilels is the most important exponent of his art.

Zubin Mehta (b. 1936). Brilliant Indian conductor. Former music director of the Montreal and Los Angeles Philharmonics, presently of the New York and Israel Philharmonics.

Felix Mendelssohn (1809–1847). After Mozart he was the most astounding prodigy in music history. An important pianist, Mendelssohn concentrated on the literature of Bach, Mozart, Beethoven and Weber—one of his specialties being the Beethoven Fourth Concerto. In his own G minor Concerto he was unsurpassed.

Gian Carlo Menotti (b. 1911). Italian-born composer. Menotti has given pianists a concerto, recorded by Earl Wild. His operas are widely acclaimed.

Olivier Messiaen (b. 1908). French composer, teacher, leader of the French avant-garde. His *Vingt Regards sur l'Enfant Jésus* (1944) is his most celebrated piano work, lasting two hours in performance.

Nikolai Miaskovsky (1881–1950). Russian composer who wrote over thirty symphonies and dozens of piano works.

Dimitri Mitropoulos (1896–1960). Greek conductor and music director of the New York Philharmonic from 1950 to 1958. He was an eloquent pianist, a speciality of his being the Prokofiev Concerto No. 3.

Pierre Monteux (1875–1964). French conductor. Head of the Boston Symphony, the San Francisco Symphony, the London Symphony. Monteux conducted the world premieres of Stravinsky's *Petrouchka* and *Le Sacre du Printemps*.

Benno Moiseiwitsch (1890–1963). Russian pianist of international stature, student of Leschetizky. He possessed a warm, romantic temperament and a dazzling technique. His discs are treasures of the art of piano playing.

Ignaz Moscheles (1784–1870). Born in Prague, he was one of the finest pianists of his time. His output is large and contains excellent music. His G minor Concerto is a fine pre-Romantic work.

Marcel Moyse (1889–1984). Illustrious French flutist.

Wolfgang Amadeus Mozart (1756–1791). The immortal Austrian composer who was without doubt the greatest musical prodigy of all time. Mozart gradually switched to the piano from the harpsichord in the mid-1770s. He was one of the first to earn at least part of his livelihood from piano playing. His twenty-seven concerti were composed as vehicles for that purpose. They constitute the greatest of all contributions to the concerto form.

Mieczyslaw Münz (1900–1976). Polish pianist, student of Busoni, was on the faculty of the Juilliard School.

Modest Mussorgsky (1839–1881). Great Russian composer. His *Pictures at an Exhibition* is the most enduring piano work of the Russian national school.

Heinrich Neuhaus (1888–1964). One of the greatest piano teachers of the twentieth century and a pianist of delicate beauty. His legacy of pupils includes Zak, Richter, Gilels, Igor Zhukov and Radu Lupu; many others were inspired by him. His son Stanislav (1927–1980) was a colorful virtuoso. Neuhaus's book *The Art of Piano Playing* is published by Praeger.

Vaslav Nijinsky (1889–1950). Russian dancer and choreographer. One of the greatest artists in the history of the dance.

Arthur Nikisch (1855–1922). Born in Hungary, he was the first of the Romantic virtuoso conductors. His magnetism was unparalleled.

Leonid Nikolayev (1878–1942). A student of Vassily Safonov. He was an illustrious teacher at the St. Petersburg Conservatory.

Guiomar Novaes (1895–1979). Esteemed Brazilian pianist. In Paris she was the prize pupil of the distinguished teacher Isidore Philipp (1863–1958). She made a sensational New York debut in 1915. Novaes was an intimate player who excelled in Chopin and Schumann.

Rudolf Nureyev (b. 1938). Russian-born dancer of electrifying charisma.

Lev Oborin (1907–1974). Russian pianist and teacher. A student of Igumnov and the winner of the first International Chopin Competition in 1927.

John Ogdon (b. 1937). English virtuoso pianist. He recorded Busoni's mammoth Piano Concerto on Angel S-3719.

Johann Pachelbel (1653–1706). German baroque organist and composer.

VLADIMIR DE PACHMANN (1848–1933). Born in Odessa, he was one of the best-known pianists at the turn of the century.

IGNACY JAN PADEREWSKI (1860–1941). Polish pianist, composer and patriot. In 1919 he became president of Poland. He had the most fabulous pianistic career of his generation. He was buried at Arlington National Cemetery by order of President Franklin Roosevelt.

FERDINANDO PAER (1771–1839). Italian opera composer.

NICCOLÒ PAGANINI (1782–1840). Born in Italy, he was the most famous violinist of all time. His technique was diabolical; mystery and superstition surrounded him throughout his life. When Liszt first heard him it was his goal to become the Paganini of the piano.

LEE PATTISON (1890–1966). American pianist, a student of Schnabel's.

SIR PETER PEARS (b. 1910). Distinguished English tenor.

EGON PETRI (1881–1962). Born in Germany. He studied with Teresa Carreño and became a student of Busoni. His playing was sonorous and large-scaled.

FRANCIS PLANTÉ (1839–1934). One of the most important French pianists.

PLEYEL PIANO. Important French firm of piano builders. Founded in 1807 by the composer Ignaz Pleyel (1757–1831), a pupil of Haydn. His piano was lighter in action than the English piano, and was preferred by Chopin to all others. Pleyel was the twenty-fourth of his father's thirty-eight children.

JEAN-BERNARD POMMIER (b. 1944). Acclaimed French pianist.

FRANCIS POULENC (1899–1963). Widely performed French composer. His piano music is fresh, lyrical and often capricious.

SERGE PROKOFIEV (1891–1953). This Russian composer's piano music is entrenched in the repertoire. He studied with Annette Essipov. One may hear him in his own popular Third Concerto on Angel 34. He was a stunning pianist.

SERGEI RACHMANINOFF (1873–1943). Russian composer, pianist and conductor. Arthur Rubinstein said he was "the most fascinating pianist of them all since Busoni . . . in my strong opinion he was a greater pianist than a composer." Still, Rachmaninoff's piano music, especially the Concertos Nos. 2 and 3, have become the war-horses of the repertoire. All of his RCA recordings were reissued in five volumes in 1973.

JOACHIM RAFF (1822–1882). Swiss-born composer. Raff was frequently performed during his lifetime, but his 230 works have been all but ignored since.

MAURICE RAVEL (1875–1937). Great French composer who added immeasurably to the piano literature. Each of his pieces is gloriously conceived for the keyboard.

Carl Reinecke (1824–1910). German composer, pianist and renowned conductor of the Leipzig Gewandhaus concerts. His music is solid, in the Mendelssohnian tradition.

Fritz Reiner (1888–1963). Eminent Hungarian-born conductor who taught at the Curtis Institute. Leonard Bernstein studied with him. He was famous for his tiny beat. Some of his finest work was done as the leader of the Chicago Symphony Orchestra.

Ludwig Rellstab (1799–1860). German musician, novelist and influential Berlin music critic.

Sviatoslav Richter (b. 1914). One of the most important of Soviet pianists. His repertoire is all-encompassing, and his recordings are available everywhere. He made his New York debut to rapturous acclaim in 1960 in a series of six Carnegie Hall recitals.

Edouard Risler (1873–1929). Born in Baden-Baden, a student of Louis Diémer's at the Paris Conservatory. He played the thirty-two sonatas of Beethoven in London in 1906. Risler premiered the Dukas Sonata in 1901.

Artur Rodzinski (1892–1958). Polish-born conductor, music director of the New York Philharmonic from 1943 to 1947.

Moriz Rosenthal (1862–1946). Polish master of the piano, a pupil of Liszt. By all accounts, one of the titanic pianistic talents of all time. He didn't record until after the age of sixty, but some of his 78s of the late 1920s, including his own *Carnival de Vienne,* are breathtaking.

Mstislav Rostropovich (b. 1927). Born in Russia, he has had a major career as a cellist and conductor. He plays the piano with skill.

Albert Roussel (1869–1937). French composer. His piano music deserves exploration. The American pianist Joseph Bloch played the Roussel Concerto's U.S. premiere in 1949 in Indianapolis.

Anton Rubinstein (1829–1894). Russian pianist and composer. One of the greatest pianists of all time, he founded the St. Petersburg Conservatory, while his brother Nicholas (1835–1881) was the head of the Moscow Conservatory. As late as 1919 the critic James Huneker could write, "With the death of Rubinstein no artist of his emotional caliber has appeared upon the scene. . . . He was as torrid as midday in the tropics. His touch melted the heart in a Chopin nocturne."

Arthur Rubinstein (1887–1982). Polish-born pianist of universal fame, a student of Heinrich Barth's in Berlin. His two volumes of autobiography, *My Young Years* (1973) and *My Many Years* (1980), tell only a fraction of the story of a career that touched the whole musical world of the twentieth century.

DAVID SAPERTON (1889–1970). American pianist and teacher. Shura Cherkassky, Abbey Simon and Julius Katchen studied with him. His recordings of Godowsky's works are masterly displays of craftsmanship.

ERIK SATIE (1866–1925). French composer admired by Debussy and Ravel. His piano music is highly original.

EMIL VON SAUER (1862–1942). Pianist and teacher of distinction. He studied with Nicholas Rubinstein and Liszt. In 1938 he recorded both Liszt concerti with great style. Reissued on Turnabout THS65098 with Felix Weingartner (1863–1942) conducting.

PRINCESS CAROLYNE SAYN-WITTGENSTEIN (1819–1887). Polish writer. Lived with Liszt at Weimar for many years.

DOMENICO SCARLATTI (1685–1757). Italian-born master who wrote 600 sonatas for harpsichord in binary form, most of them in the last fifteen years of his life.

ARNOLD SCHOENBERG (1874–1951). Austrian-born composer, inventor of the "twelve-tone method." His Piano Concerto has had the advocacy of Brendel, Ax, Glenn Gould, Peter Serkin and Maurizio Pollini.

HAROLD SCHONBERG (b. 1915). Pulitzer Prize–winning music critic. His best-known book is *The Great Pianists*, published by Gollancz in 1964.

FRANZ SCHMIDT (1874–1939). Austrian composer. Wrote some excellent organ works and late-Romantic symphonies.

ARTUR SCHNABEL (1882–1951). Polish-born master pianist. Schnabel's Beethoven and Schubert discs have never been out of print and are essential listening. Schnabel also composed severe atonal music.

KARL ULRICH SCHNABEL (b. 1909). Pianist and author, son of Artur.

FRANZ SCHUBERT (1797–1828). Immortal Austrian composer. His piano sonatas are now at the heart of the Classical repertoire. Schubert never played the piano publicly. Upon playing his *Wanderer Fantasy* he declared to a listener that perhaps the devil could play it, but he could not.

ROBERT SCHUMANN (1810–1856). The great German master's piano music has been a source of unending joy to pianists of each generation. Schumann's first twenty-three opus numbers are for the piano. He has been called the most romantic of the Romantic composers. Schumann's critical writings are masterly.

CLARA SCHUMANN (neé Wieck, 1819–1896). German pianist and composer. The most honored woman pianist of the nineteenth century. She made her debut in 1832 with the Moscheles G minor Concerto. All who heard her admired her fine technique and impeccable musicianship. Her readings of the music of Robert Schumann, her husband, became gospel. Her conservative nature was in evidence in her revulsion to Wagner's

Tristan and Isolde, and in her pronouncement that "Liszt has the decline of piano playing on his conscience."

EDUARD SCHÜTT (1856–1933). Russian-born pianist and composer of salon music. Student of Leschetizky.

RUDOLF SERKIN (b. 1903). Austrian-born pianist. His Beethoven, Schubert, Brahms and Mozart are revered.

TIBOR SERLY (1900–1981). Hungarian composer and conductor.

DÉODAT DE SÉVERAC (1872–1921). French composer. His piano music is colorful and improvisatory.

GIOVANNI SGAMBATI (1841–1914). Famed Italian pianist-composer. Student of Liszt.

DIMITRI SHOSTAKOVICH (1906–1975). Russian composer. As a pianist he can be heard in several of his preludes and fugues, Seraphim 60024, and in his two delightful concerti, Seraphim 60161. His memoirs, *Testimony,* were published in 1979 by Harper & Row.

LEONARD SHURE (b. 1910). American pianist; best known in Beethoven and Schubert.

ALEXANDER SILOTI (1863–1945). Russian pianist, teacher and editor. Student of Nikolai Zverev and Nicholas Rubinstein, later of Liszt. Arranged works of Bach for piano solo.

JOSEPH SILVERSTEIN (b. 1932). American violinist-conductor.

BEDŘICH SMETANA (1824–1884). Czech composer of genius. His piano music has a nationalistic flavor.

RONALD SMITH (b. 1922). English pianist, best known for his powerful playing of the music of Charles Valentin Alkan (1813–1888). Smith also wrote the little volume *The Alkan Enigma,* published in London in 1976.

VLADIMIR SOFRONITSKY (1901–1961). A magical pianist. All who undertake the study of Scriabin should know Sofronitsky's many recordings of this music. He became a cult figure in musical circles in Moscow.

ANTONIO SOLER (1729–1783). Spanish composer. Wrote over 175 harpsichord sonatas, which show the influence of Domenico Scarlatti and popular Spanish rhythms. De Larrocha has often opened recitals with a group of them.

SIR GEORG SOLTI (b. 1912). Born in Budapest, he is one of the most honored of all conductors. He was the first to record the entire *Ring* of Wagner.

ROBERT STARER (b. 1924). Composer; born in Vienna. Lived in Israel and in the U.S. His "*Evanescents*" (1975) are recorded by Alan Mandel on Grenadilla 1020.

DANIEL STEIBELT (1765–1823). German pianist-composer. He had a stormy life, while his "*Storm Rondo,*" from his Third Concerto, had an enormous vogue. He was especially famous for the use of tremolo in his playing.

EDWARD STEUERMANN (1892–1964). Born in Poland, he studied piano with Busoni. He championed contemporary music, and gave the premiere in 1944 of the Schoenberg Concerto.

FREDERIC STOCK (1872–1942). German-born conductor and composer.

LEOPOLD STOKOWSKI (1882–1977). Amazing conductor, born in London. For years the maestro of the Philadelphia Orchestra. His career was the most glamorous of any conductor of the century.

IGOR STRAVINSKY (1882–1971). The Russian-born master was the most famous and influential composer of the twentieth century. He made several recordings of his own works. Especially good is the "*Serenade in A*," Seraphim 60183. He once said, "Composing begins for me as the feeling of intervals in my fingers."

RICHARD STRAUSS (1864–1949). Great German composer. His most important piano work is the *Burlesque* for Piano and Orchestra. Glenn Gould's last recording was of Strauss's early piano music.

JOSEF SUK (1874–1935). Czech composer. His piano music is overlooked, but it has considerable value.

GEORGE SZELL (1897–1970). Born in Budapest, Szell was a conductor of the first rank who made the Cleveland Orchestra into an ensemble of unprecedented quality.

JOSEPH SZIGETI (1892–1973). Notable Hungarian violinist.

KAROL SZYMANOWSKI (1883–1937). One of the most important Polish composers. He composed a quantity of difficult piano music, much of it neglected. Rubinstein, Horszowski, Jan Smeterlin and Jakob Gimpel often presented his music. The American pianist Donn-Alexander Feder plays all-Szymanowski recitals.

CARL TAUSIG (1843–1873). Polish pianist. One of Liszt's greatest students. He was one of the first to play uncompromising programs. He made many transcriptions and his daily exercises are still used.

ART TATUM (1909–1956). Fabulous jazz pianist who was blind for most of his life.

PETER ILYICH TCHAIKOVSKY (1840–1893). Great Russian composer who left over one hundred solo piano pieces, while the Concerto No. 1 in B-flat minor is the most played of all concerti. Tchaikovsky, in general, is the most performed of all Russian composers.

JACQUES THIBAUD (1880–1953). Venerable French violinist.

VIRGIL THOMSON (b. 1896). Brilliant American composer and writer on music. His chief contribution to the piano is found in his many "*Por-*

traits" of people he has known. He composes the work while the subject sits for him.

Arturo Toscanini (1867–1957). Born in Parma, the Italian maestro was the most idolized conductor in history. He gave the world premieres of *I Pagliacci* and *La Bohème,* as well as the Italian premieres of *Euryanthe, Die Götterdämmerung, Siegfried, Eugene Onegin* and *Pelléas et Mélisande.*

Sir Donald Francis Tovey (1875–1940). Composer, pianist and writer on music. His *Essays in Musical Analysis* are classics.

Isabelle Vengerova (1877–1956). One of the foremost teachers of her time. Leonard Bernstein, Leo Smit, Jacob Lateiner, Leonard Pennario and a host of others worked with her.

José Vianna da Motta (1868–1948). Portuguese pianist of stature. The International Piano Archive issued an LP of his discs.

Pauline Viardot-Garcia (1821–1910). French-born mezzo-soprano, teacher and composer. Her voice had an extraordinary compass.

Pantcho Vladigerov (b. 1899). Distinguished Bulgarian composer whose music is rooted in the folk music of his country.

Richard Wagner (1813–1883). Wagner is the most important of all German opera composers, though his piano works are of little value.

Bruno Walter (1876–1962). Distinguished German-born conductor. He was also a fine pianist, a composer and a foremost champion of Mahler's works. He wrote an autobiography, *Theme and Variations,* published in 1947.

Carl Maria von Weber (1786–1826). Great German composer who wrote some of the most distinctive piano music of his time. His four sonatas are occasionally played. His waltz, *Invitation to the Dance* (1819) launched the most popular dance craze of the nineteenth century.

Anton Webern (1883–1945). Austrian composer of far-reaching influence. His most important piano work is the Variations Op. 27 (1936) dedicated to Edward Steuermann. Pollini and Beveridge Webster play it with insight.

Paul Wittgenstein (1887–1961). Austrian pianist, student of Leschetizky.

Stefan Wolpe (1902–1945). Composer and composition teacher, born in Berlin, later settled in the U.S.

Maria Yudina (1899–1970). A student of Nikolayev, she was a fascinating and eccentric personality. Because of her religious fervor she was called a saint. Her concerts were always packed. She can be heard in the Hindemith Third Sonata and Shostakovich's Second Sonata on Melodiya D 07063.

Jakov Zak (1913–1976). Zak won the third Chopin International Competition in 1937.

SELECTED DISCOGRAPHY

The recordings chosen for this discography are among the most characteristic of the pianists' performances. In many cases, they represent the artists' own choices.

CLAUDIO ARRAU

BEETHOVEN Complete Piano Sonatas (thirty-two)
Thirteen-Record Set
Philips 6747035

LISZT Three *Études de Concert*
LISZT Twelve *Transcendental Etudes*
Two-Record Set
Philips 6747412

BRAHMS Four Ballades, Op. 10
BRAHMS Variations and Fugue on a Theme by Handel, Op. 24
Philips 9500446

DEBUSSY Twenty-four Preludes, Books I and II
Two-Record Set
Philips 9500676

SCHUMANN *Davidsbündlertänze,* Op. 6
SCHUMANN *Nachtstücke,* Op. 23
Philips 6500178

VLADIMIR ASHKENAZY

BEETHOVEN The Five Piano Concerti
Sir Georg Solti conducting the Chicago Symphony Orchestra
Four-Record Set
London 2404

SCRIABIN Sonata No. 2 in G-sharp minor, Op. 19 (Sonata-Fantasy)
SCRIABIN Sonata No. 7, Op. 64
SCRIABIN Sonata No. 10, Op. 70
SCRIABIN Quatre Morceaux, Op. 56
SCRIABIN Deux Poèmes, Op. 32
SCRIABIN Two Dances: *Guirlandes* and *Flammes Sombres,* Op. 73
London 7087

CHOPIN Scherzo No. 4 in E major, Op. 54
CHOPIN Nocturne in B major, Op. 62 No. 1
DEBUSSY *L'Ile Joyeuse*
RAVEL *Gaspard de la Nuit*
London 6472

PROKOFIEV Sonata No. 7, Op. 83 (1939–1942)
PROKOFIEV Sonata No. 8, Op. 84 (1939–1942)
PROKOFIEV Two Pieces from *Romeo and Juliet*
London 6573

SCHUBERT Sonata in G major, Op. 78 D. 894
London 6820

EMANUEL AX

SCHUMANN *Humoreske,* Op. 20
SCHUMANN *Fantasiestücke,* Op. 12
RCA ARC1-4275

CHOPIN *Andante Spianato* and *Grande Polonaise Brillante,* Op. 22
CHOPIN Nocturne in B major, Op. 62 No. 1
CHOPIN Scherzo No. 4 in E major, Op. 54
CHOPIN *Polonaise-Fantaisie* in A-flat major, Op. 61
RCA ARL1-1569

BEETHOVEN Sonata No. 23 in F minor, Op. 57 *(Appassionata)*
BEETHOVEN Sonata No. 26 in E-flat major, Op. 81a *(Les Adieux)*
BEETHOVEN Polonaise Op. 89
RCA ARL1-2752

BRAHMS Piano Concerto No. 1 in D minor, Op. 15
James Levine conducting the Chicago Symphony Orchestra
RCA ARC1-4962

CHOPIN Piano Concerto No. 1 in E minor, Op. 11
Eugene Ormandy conducting the Philadelphia Orchestra
RCA ATC1-4097

PAUL BADURA-SKODA

FRANK MARTIN Piano Concerto No. 2, 1968–1969
Frank Martin conducting the Orchestra of Radio Luxembourg
Candide CE 31055

Mozart Two-Record Set
MOZART Sonata in A minor K. 310
MOZART Sonata in C major K. 330
MOZART Sonata in A major K. 331
MOZART Sonata in F major K. 332
MOZART Sonata in B-flat major K. 333
Eurodisc 300342-420

MOZART Piano Concerto No. 21 in C major K. 467
MOZART Piano Concerto No. 24 in C minor K. 491
Paul Badura-Skoda conducting the Prague Chamber Orchestra
Quintessence PMC-7123

SCHUBERT Sonata in A minor D. 784
SCHUBERT Sonata in A major D. 959
RCA AGL1-2707

HINDEMITH Sonata No. 1 (1936)
HINDEMITH Sonata No. 3 (1936)
Westminster W-9309

DAVID BAR-ILLAN

BEETHOVEN Piano Sonata No. 3 in C major, Op. 2 No. 3
BEETHOVEN Piano Sonata No. 21 in C major, Op. 53 *(Waldstein)*
Audiofon 2009

BEETHOVEN Variations in E-flat major, Op. 35 *(Eroica)*
RAMEAU Gavotte and Six Doubles
SOLER Sonata No. 1 in D minor
SOLER Sonata No. 4 in D minor
MOZART Rondo in A minor K. 511
Audiofon 2013

MOSZKOWSKI Piano Concerto in E major, Op. 59
Alfredo Antonini conducts the Bavarian Radio Orchestra
Audiofon 2006

WEBER Piano Sonata No. 2 in A-flat major, Op. 39
LISZT Ballade No. 2 in B minor
LISZT *En Rêve.*
LISZT *Mephisto Waltz* No. 1
Audiofon 2002

STEPHEN BISHOP-KOVACEVICH

BRAHMS Sixteen Waltzes, Op. 39
BRAHMS Rhapsody in B minor, Op. 79 No. 1
BRAHMS Rhapsody in G minor, Op. 79 No. 2
BRAHMS Six Klavierstücke, Op. 118
Philips 6514229

BARTÓK Piano Concerto No. 2 (1931)
STRAVINSKY Concerto for Piano and Wind Instruments (1924)
Colin Davis conducts the BBC Symphony Orchestra
Philips 839761

BEETHOVEN Piano Sonata No. 28 in A major, Op. 101
BEETHOVEN Piano Sonata No. 30 in E major, Op. 109
Philips 9500569

MOZART Piano Concerto No. 20 in D minor K. 466
MOZART Piano Concerto No. 23 in A major K. 488
Colin Davis conducting the London Symphony Orchestra
Philips 9500570

CHOPIN *Polonaise-Fantaisie* in A-flat major, Op. 61
CHOPIN Impromptu No. 3 in G-flat major, Op. 51
CHOPIN Mazurka in B major, Op. 63 No. 1
CHOPIN Mazurka No. 40 in F minor, Op. 63 No. 2
CHOPIN Mazurka No. 41 in C-sharp minor, Op. 63 No. 3
CHOPIN Barcarolle in F-sharp major, Op. 60
CHOPIN Nocturne in B major, Op. 62 No. 1
CHOPIN Nocturne in E major, Op. 62 No. 2
Philips 6500393

JORGE BOLET

Bolet at Carnegie Hall Recorded Live February 25, 1974
Two-Record Set
BACH-BUSONI Chaconne in D minor
CHOPIN Twenty-four Preludes, Op. 28
STRAUSS-TAUSIG *One Lives but Once*
STRAUSS-TAUSIG *Nachtfalter* ("The Moth")
STRAUSS-SCHULZ-EVLER Arabesques on *The Beautiful Blue Danube*
WAGNER-LISZT *Tannhäuser* Overture
MOSZKOWSKI *La Jongleuse*, Op. 52 No. 4

RUBINSTEIN Etude in C major, Op. 23 No. 2 ("Staccato")
RCA ARL2-0512

BRAHMS Variations and Fugue on a Theme by Handel, Op. 24
REGER Variations and Fugue on a Theme by Telemann, Op. 134
London CS 7197

RACHMANINOFF "Polka de V.R."
RACHMANINOFF Prelude in G-flat major, Op. 23 No. 10
RACHMANINOFF Prelude in G-sharp minor, Op. 32 No. 12
RACHMANINOFF–RIMSKY-KORSAKOV *The Flight of the Bumblebee*
RACHMANINOFF-MUSSORGSKY *Hopak*
RACHMANINOFF-MENDELSSOHN Scherzo from *A Midsummer Night's Dream*
RACHMANINOFF-KREISLER *Liebesfreud*
RACHMANINOFF-KREISLER *Liebesleid*
RACHMANINOFF-BACH Preludio from Violin Partita No. 3 in E major
RACHMANINOFF-BIZET Minuet from *L'Arlésienne,* Suite No. 1
RACHMANINOFF-TCHAIKOVSKY *Lullaby*
RCA ARL1-0357

LISZT Two *Études de Concert* (*Waldesrauschen, Gnomenreigen*)
LISZT Three *Études de Concert* (*Il Lamento, La Leggierezza, Un Sospiro)*
MOZART-LISZT *Réminiscences de Don Juan (Don Juan Fantasy)*
L'Oiseau-Lyre DSLO-41

CHOPIN-GODOWSKY Arrangements of Eight Etudes and Six Waltzes
L'Oiseau-Lyre DSLO-26

ALFRED BRENDEL

LISZT Variations on Bach's Cantata *Weinen, Klagen, Sorgen, Zagen*
LISZT *Pensées des morts* (No. 4 from *Harmonies Poétiques et Religieuses)*
LISZT Fantasy and Fugue on the Theme B-A-C-H
LISZT *Bénédiction de Dieu dans la solitude*, No. 3 from *Harmonies Poétiques et Religieuses*
Philips 9500286

SCHUMANN Piano Concerto in A minor, Op. 54
WEBER Konzertstück in F minor for piano and orchestra, Op. 79
Claudio Abbado conducting the London Symphony Orchestra
Philips 9500677

Beethoven The Complete Piano Sonatas (thirty-two)
Thirteen Records
Philips 6768004

Schubert Sonata in D major, Op. 53 D. 850
Schubert Sixteen German Dances
Philips 6500763

Mozart Piano Concerto No. 15 in B-flat major K. 450
Mozart Piano Concerto No. 21 in C major K. 467
Neville Marriner conducting the Academy of St. Martin–in–the–Fields Orchestra
Philips 6514148

JOHN BROWNING

Barber Piano Concerto (1962)
George Szell conducting the Cleveland Orchestra
Columbia MS-6638

Barber Sonata, Op. 26 (1949)
Richard Cumming Twenty-four Preludes (1969)
Desto 7120

Prokofiev Piano Concerto No. 3 in C major (1921)
Ravel Piano Concerto in D for the Left Hand (1931)
Erich Leinsdorf conducting the Philharmonic Orchestra
Seraphim S-60224

Ravel Sonatine (1905)
Ravel *Gaspard de la Nuit* (1908)
Ravel *Le Tombeau de Couperin* (1917)
RCA LSC-3028

John Browning Recital
Bach *Chromatic Fantasy and Fugue* in D minor BWV. 903
Chopin Nocturne in D-flat major, Op. 27 No. 2
Chopin *Grande Valse Brillante,* Op. 18
Debussy *Reflets dans l'Eau*
Liszt *Mephisto Waltz*
Schubert Impromptu in B-flat major, Op. 142 No. 3
Seraphim S-60099

BELLA DAVIDOVICH

CHOPIN Twenty-four Preludes
Philips 9500666

SCHUMANN *Carnaval,* Op. 9
SCHUMANN *Humoreske,* Op. 20
Philips 9500667

CHOPIN Piano Concerto No. 1 in E minor, Op. 11
CHOPIN *Andante Spianato* and *Grande Polonaise Brillante,* for piano and orchestra, Op. 22
Neville Marriner conducting the London Symphony Orchestra
Philips 9500889

BEETHOVEN Sonata No. 14 in C-sharp minor, Op. 27 No. 2 *(Moonlight)*
BEETHOVEN *Für Elise*
BEETHOVEN Sonata No. 18 in E-flat major, Op. 31 No. 3
Philips 9500665

SAINT-SAËNS Piano Concerto No. 2 in G minor, Op. 22
RACHMANINOFF Rhapsody on a Theme of Paganini, Op. 43
Neeme Järvi conducting the Concertgebouw Orchestra of Amsterdam
Philips 6514164

ALICIA DE LARROCHA

GRANADOS Goyescas (complete)
London 7009

ALBENIZ *Iberia* (complete)
ALBENIZ *Cantos de España,* Op. 232 (five pieces)
ALBENIZ *Navarra*
Two-Record Set
London 2235

GRIEG Sonata in E minor, Op. 7
GRIEG Nocturne, Op. 54 No. 4
MENDELSSOHN *Variations Sérieuses,* Op. 54
MENDELSSOHN Capriccio in A minor, Op. 33 No. 1
London 6676

Xavier Montsalvatge *Concerto Breve* for piano and orchestra
Carlos Surinach Piano Concerto
Rafael Frühbeck de Burgos conducting the Royal Philharmonic Orchestra
London 6990

Schubert Sonata in A major, Op. 120 D. 664
Schumann *Carnaval*, Op. 9
London 7134

MISHA DICHTER

Brahms Piano Concerto No. 1 in D minor, Op. 15
Kurt Masur conducting the Leipzig Gewandhaus Orchestra
Philips 9500410

Beethoven Sonata No. 8 in C minor, Op. 13 *(Pathétique)*
Beethoven Sonata No. 14 in C-sharp minor, Op. 27 No. 2 *(Moonlight)*
Beethoven Sonata No. 28 in A major, Op. 101
Philips 9500319

Mussorgsky *Pictures at an Exhibition*
Stravinsky Three Movements from *Petrouchka*
Philips 6514323

Liszt Hungarian Rhapsody No. 6 in D-flat major
Liszt Hungarian Rhapsody No. 13 in A minor
Liszt *Vallée d'Obermann* (No. 6 from *Années de Pélerinage, Première Année: Suisse*)
Liszt *Eglogue* (No. 7 from *Années de Pélerinage, Première Année: Suisse*)
Liszt *Valse Oubliée* No. 1 in F-sharp major
Liszt *Valse Oubliée* No. 2 in A-flat major
Schumann-Liszt *Widmung*
Gounod-Liszt *Faust Waltz*
Philips 6514072

Liszt Piano Concerto No. 1 in E-flat major
Liszt Piano Concerto No. 2 in A major
André Previn conducting the Pittsburgh Symphony Orchestra
Philips 6514200

PHILIPPE ENTREMONT

RAVEL Piano Concerto in G major
FALLA *Nights in the Gardens of Spain* for piano and orchestra
Eugene Ormandy conducting the Philadelphia Orchestra
CBS MS 6629

SAINT-SAËNS Piano Concerto No. 1 in D major, Op. 17
SAINT-SAËNS Piano Concerto No. 5 in F major, Op. 103
Michael Plasson conducting the Orchestre du Capitole de Toulouse
CBS M 34512

KUHLAU Sonatina, Op. 20 No. 3
KUHLAU Sonatinas, Op. 55 Nos. 1–3
CLEMENTI Sonatinas, Op. 36 Nos. 1–6
DUSSEK Sonatina, Op. 20 No. 1
HAYDN Sonata in C major
MOZART Sonata in C major K. 545
BEETHOVEN Two Sonatas, Op. 49 Nos. 1 and 2
Two Records
CBS MG33202

BERNSTEIN *Age of Anxiety* (Symphony No. 2) for piano and orchestra
Leonard Bernstein conducting the New York Philharmonic
CBS MS 6885

DEBUSSY *Pour le piano* (1901)
DEBUSSY *Children's Corner Suite* (1908)
DEBUSSY *Images,* Book 1 (1905–1907)
DEBUSSY *Images,* Book 2 (1907)
CBS MS 6567

RUDOLF FIRKUŠNÝ

LEOŠ JANÁČEK Capriccio for Piano (left hand) and Wind Instruments
LEOŠ JANÁČEK Concertino for Piano and Chamber Ensemble
Rafael Kubelik conducting members of the Bavarian Radio Symphony Orchestra
LEOŠ JANÁČEK Tema con Variazioni
LEOŠ JANÁČEK Piano Sonata I.X. 1905 *(From the Street)*
LEOŠ JANÁČEK *On the Overgrown Path* (Fifteen Little Pieces)
LEOŠ JANÁČEK *In the Mists* (Four pieces)
Two-Record Set
Deutsche Grammophon DG 2721251

DUSSEK Sonata in F minor, Op. 70 *(L'Invocation)*
GEORG BENDA Sonata No. 9 in A minor
TOMÁŠEK Eglogue No. 2 in F major, Op. 35
VOŘISEK Impromptu No. 4 in A major, Op. 7
Candide 31086

DVOŘÁK Piano Concerto in G minor, Op. 33
Walter Susskind conducting the St. Louis Symphony Orchestra
Turnabout 34691

BEETHOVEN Sonata No. 8 in C minor, Op. 13 *(Pathétique)*
BEETHOVEN Sonata No. 14 in C-sharp minor, Op. 27 No. 2 *(Moonlight)*
BEETHOVEN Sonata No. 21 in C major, Op. 53 *(Waldstein)*
London 21080

SMETANA Czech Dances (ten)
Turnabout 34673

LEON FLEISHER

BEETHOVEN Five Piano Concerti (complete)
George Szell conducting the Cleveland Orchestra
Three-Record Set
Odyssey 35489

BRAHMS Variations and Fugue on a Theme of Handel, Op. 24
BRAHMS The Waltzes, Op. 39
Odyssey Y35920

BRITTEN *Diversions on a Theme for Left Hand and Orchestra,* Op. 21
Sergiu Comissiona conducting the Baltimore Symphony Orchestra
Desto DC-7168

COPLAND Piano Sonata (1940)
ROREM Three Barcarolles (1949)
KIRCHNER Piano Sonata (1948)
SESSIONS *From My Diary (1937–1940)*
Epic LC3862

GRIEG Piano Concerto in A minor, Op. 16
SCHUMANN Piano Concerto in A minor, Op. 54
George Szell conducting the Cleveland Orchestra
Odyssey Y-30668

GLENN GOULD

BACH *Goldberg Variations* BWV. 988
CBS 1M-37779

BACH *The Well-Tempered Clavier* BWV. 846/93
Book I—Three-Record Set
CBS D3S-733
Book II—Three-Record Set
CBS D3M-31526

BEETHOVEN Five Piano Concerti, Complete
BEETHOVEN Piano Concerto No. 1 in C major, Op. 15
Vladimir Golschmann conducting the Columbia Symphony Orchestra
BEETHOVEN Piano Concerto No. 2 in B-flat major, Op. 19
Leonard Bernstein conducting the Columbia Symphony Orchestra
BEETHOVEN Piano Concerto No. 3 in C minor, Op. 37
Leonard Bernstein conducting the Columbia Symphony Orchestra
BEETHOVEN Piano concerto No. 4 in G major, Op. 58
Leonard Bernstein conducting the New York Philharmonic
BEETHOVEN Piano Concerto No. 5 in E-flat major *(Emperor)* Op. 73
Leopold Stokowski conducting the American Symphony Orchestra
Four-Record Set
Odyssey Y4-34640

BYRD First Pavan and Galliard
BYRD *Hughe Ashton's Ground*
BYRD Sixth Pavan and Galliard
BYRD A Voluntary
BYRD *Sellinger's Round*
GIBBONS Fantasy in C
GIBBONS Allemande, or Italian Ground
GIBBONS *Lord of Salisbury Pavan and Galliard*
CBS M30825

SIBELIUS Three Sonatines, Op. 67
SIBELIUS *Kyllikki,* Three Lyric Pieces for Piano, Op. 41
CBS M34555

GARY GRAFFMAN

BEETHOVEN Piano Sonata No. 31 in A-flat major, Op. 110
BEETHOVEN Piano Sonata No. 32 in C minor, Op. 111
CBS M-33890

Bartók Suite, Op. 14
Benjamin Lees Sonata No. 4 (1964)
Prokofiev Sonata No. 2 in D minor, Op. 14
Odyssey Y-35203

Prokofiev Piano Concerto No. 1 in D-flat major, Op. 10
Prokofiev Piano Concerto No. 3 in C major, Op. 26
Prokofiev Piano Sonata No. 3 in A minor, Op. 28
George Szell conducting the Cleveland Orchestra
CBS MS 6925

Tchaikovsky Piano Concerto No. 1 in B-flat minor, Op. 23
George Szell conducting the Cleveland Symphony Orchestra
Tchaikovsky Piano concerto No. 2 in G major, Op. 44
Tchaikovsky Piano Concerto No. 3 in E-flat major, Op. 75
Eugene Ormandy conducting the Philadelphia Orchestra
Two-Record Set
CBS MG 30838

Brahms Variations on a Theme of Paganini, Op. 35
Brahms Variations and Fugue on a Theme of Handel, Op. 24
CBS MS 7276

VLADIMIR HOROWITZ

An Historic Return—Horowitz at Carnegie Hall
Bach-Busoni Organ Toccata in C major
Schumann Fantasia in C major, Op. 17
Scriabin Sonata No. 9, Op. 68
Scriabin Poem in F-sharp major, Op. 32 No. 1
Chopin Mazurka in C-sharp minor, Op. 30 No. 4
Chopin Etude in F major, Op. 10 No. 8
Chopin Ballade in G minor, Op. 23
Debussy *Serenade for the Doll* (from *Children's Corner*)
Scriabin Etude in C-sharp minor, Op. 2 No. 1
Moszkowski Etude in A-flat major, Op. 72 No. 11
Schumann *Träumerei* (from *Kinderszenen*, Op. 15)
Two-Record Set
CBS M2S728

Scarlatti Twelve Sonatas
CBS MS-6658

Clementi Sonata in G minor, Op. 34 No. 2
Clementi Sonata in F minor, Op. 14 No. 3

CLEMENTI Sonata in F-sharp minor, Op. 26 No. 2
RCA ARM1-3689

Horowitz in Concert—from 1966 Carnegie Hall Recitals
HAYDN Sonata in F major
SCHUMANN *Blumenstück*, Op. 19
SCRIABIN Sonata No. 10, Op. 70
DEBUSSY *L'Ile Joyeuse*
MOZART Sonata in A major K. 331
CHOPIN Nocturne in E minor, Op. 72 No. 1
CHOPIN Mazurka in B minor, Op. 33 No. 4
LISZT *Vallée d'Obermann* (from *Années de Pélerinage Première Année: Suisse*)
Two-Record Set
CBS M2S757

SCHUMANN *Kreisleriana*, Op. 16
SCHUMANN Variations on a Theme by Clara Wieck (from the Sonata in F minor, Op. 14)
CBS 7264

EUGENE ISTOMIN

SCHUMANN Piano Concerto in A minor, Op. 54
Bruno Walter conducting the Columbia Symphony Orchestra
CHOPIN Piano Concerto No. 2 in F minor, Op. 21
Eugene Ormandy conducting the Philadelphia Orchestra
Odyssey Y34618

TCHAIKOVSKY Piano Concerto No. 1 in B-flat minor, Op. 23
Eugene Ormandy conducting the Philadelphia Orchestra
Odyssey Y34606

BRAHMS Piano Concerto No. 2 in B-flat major, Op. 83
Eugene Ormandy conducting the Philadelphia Orchestra
CBS MS6715

SCHUBERT Piano Sonata in D major D. 850
CBS MS 7443

BEETHOVEN Piano Concerto No. 4 in G major, Op. 58
Eugene Ormandy conducting the Philadelphia Orchestra
CBS MS7199

BYRON JANIS

LISZT Piano Concerto No. 1 in E-flat major
Kyril Kondrashin conducting the Moscow Philharmonic
LISZT Piano Concerto No. 2 in A major
Gennady Rozhdestvensky conducting the Moscow Radio Symphony
Mercury SR90329

LISZT *Totentanz* for piano and orchestra
SCHUMANN Concerto in A minor, Op. 54
Fritz Reiner conducting the Chicago Symphony Orchestra
RCA ARP1-4668

CHOPIN Etude in F major, Op. 25
CHOPIN Waltz in A minor, Op. 34 No. 2
FALLA *The Miller's Dance* from *The Three-Cornered Hat*
GUION *The Harmonica Player*
LISZT Hungarian Rhapsody No. 6 in D-flat major
LISZT *Valse Oubliée* No. 1
LISZT *Sonetto 104 del Petrarca*
MENDELSSOHN Song Without Words *("May Breezes")*, Op. 62 No. 1
PINTO Three Pieces from *Scenes from Childhood*
PROKOFIEV Toccata
SCHUMANN Romance in F-sharp major
SCHUMANN Novellette in F major
Mercury SR90305

RACHMANINOFF Piano Concerto No. 3 in D minor, Op. 30 (1909)
Antal Dorati conducting the London Symphony Orchestra
Mercury SR90283

RACHMANINOFF Concerto No. 1 in F-sharp minor, Op. 1
STRAUSS *Burleske* for piano and orchestra
Fritz Reiner conducting the Chicago Symphony Orchestra
RCA VICS-1101

GRANT JOHANNESEN

FAURÉ The Complete Piano Works
Six-Record Set
Golden Crest CR 40348

FRANCK *Prelude, Chorale and Fugue*
DUKAS *Variations, Interlude and Finale on a Theme by Rameau*
FAURÉ Nocturne No. 7, Op. 74
FAURÉ Impromptu No. 3, Op. 34
FAURÉ Impromptu No. 5, Op. 102
CHAUSSON *Quelques Danses*
SAINT-SAËNS Bourrée (Etude for the Left Hand)
CHABRIER *Bourrée Fantasque*
CHABRIER *Ballabile*
CHABRIER Impromptu
SÉVERAC *Sous les Lauriers Rosés*
SÉVERAC *Pipperment-Get (Valse Brillante de Concert)*
ROUSSEL Bourrée (from Suite for Piano, Op. 14)
ROUSSEL Three Pieces for Piano, Op. 49
D'INDY *Chant des Bruyères*
DEBUSSY *Children's Corner Suite*
RAVEL *Sérénade Grotesque*
MILHAUD Four Romances
MILHAUD *Hymne de Glorification*
SATIE *Préludes Flasques pour un Chien*
SATIE *Croquis et Agaceries d'un Gros Bonhomme en Bois*
SATIE *Poudre d'Or* (Waltz)
Three-Record Set
Vox SVBX 5483

STRAVINSKY "Ragtime" (1918)
STRAVINSKY "Tango" (1940)
STRAVINSKY "Piano Rag-Music" (1919)
MILHAUD *Caramel-Mou* (1920)
MILHAUD Three Rag-Caprices
MILHAUD *Tango des Fratellini* (1919)
CASTRO Tango (Suite in G)
BARBER Hesitation Tango (from *Souvenirs*)
THOMSON Parallel Chords (Tango)
THOMSON Ragtime Bass
Golden Crest GC-S 4132

CASADESUS Sonata No. 2, Op. 31 (1941–1942)
MILHAUD *Album de Mme. Bovary* (seventeen short pieces)
Golden Crest GC-S 4060

BEETHOVEN-LISZT Six Goethe-Lieder, from Opp. 75, 83, 84
BEETHOVEN-LISZT *Adelaide,* Op. 46
BEETHOVEN-LISZT Six Lieder by Gellert, Op. 48
BEETHOVEN-LISZT *An die Ferne Geliebte,* Op. 98 (six songs)
Pantheon FSM 53903

GUNNAR JOHANSEN

BACH The Complete Keyboard Works
Forty-three albums

BUSONI The Complete Piano Works
Seven albums

LISZT
Fifty-one albums

Gunnar Johansen's records were done for his own label:
Artist-Direct
Blue Mounds, Wisconsin

RUTH LAREDO

The Complete Solo Piano Music of Rachmaninoff
Seven-Record Set
CBS Masterworks 79700

The Complete Sonatas of Alexander Scriabin
Eight Etudes Op. 42, *Vers la Flamme* Op. 72
Three records
Connoisseur Society CS2032, CS2034, CS2035

RAVEL *La Valse*
RAVEL Sonatine
RAVEL *Miroirs*
RAVEL *Menuet sur le nom d'Haydn*
CBS Masterworks M36734

SAMUEL BARBER Piano Sonata, Op. 26
SAMUEL BARBER *Souvenirs*
SAMUEL BARBER Nocturne (Homage to John Field)
Nonesuch D79032

SCRIABIN Twenty-four Preludes, Op. 11
SCRIABIN Poem, Op. 32 No. 1
SCRIABIN Five Preludes, Op. 74
Desto DC 7145

GARRICK OHLSSON

CHOPIN Polonaises (complete)
Two-Record Set
Angel S-3794

CHOPIN Nocturnes (complete) (twenty-one)
Two-Record Set
Angel SZ 3889

LISZT *Bénédiction de Dieu dans la Solitude*
LISZT *Funérailles*
LISZT Three *Liebesträume*
LISZT *Mephisto Waltz* No. 1
Angel S-37125

BRAHMS Piano Concerto No. 1 in D minor, Op. 15
Klaus Tennstedt conducting the London Philharmonic Orchestra
Angel SZ-37568

RACHMANINOFF Various transcriptions
Angel S-37219

MURRAY PERAHIA

CHOPIN Sonata No. 2 in B-flat minor, Op. 35 *(Funeral March Sonata)*
CHOPIN Sonata No. 3 in B minor, Op. 58
CBS M-32780

MOZART Piano Concerto No. 14 in E-flat major, K. 449
MOZART Piano Concerto No. 24 in C minor K. 491
Murray Perahia conducting the English Chamber Orchestra
CBS M-34219

SCHUBERT Eight Impromptus
Four Op. 90, D. 899
Four Op. 142, D. 935
CBS 1M-37291

SCHUMANN *Symphonic Etudes,* Op. 13 (including the five posthumous etudes)
SCHUMANN *Papillons,* Op. 2
CBS M-34539

MOZART Piano Concerto No. 9 in E-flat major K. 271
MOZART Piano Concerto No. 21 in C major K. 467
Murray Perahia conducting the English Chamber Orchestra
CBS M-34562

IVO POGORELICH

CHOPIN Piano Sonata No. 2 in B-flat minor, Op. 35
CHOPIN Prelude in C-sharp minor, Op. 45
CHOPIN Scherzo in C-sharp minor, Op. 39
CHOPIN Nocturne in E-flat major, Op. 55 No. 2
CHOPIN Etude in F major, Op. 10 No. 8
CHOPIN Etude in A-flat major, Op. 10 No. 10
CHOPIN Etude in G-sharp minor, Op. 25 No. 6
Deutsche Grammophon DG 2531346

PROKOFIEV Sonata No. 6 Op. 82
DEBUSSY *Bruyères* (Prelude No. 5, Book II)
KELEMEN Theme with Variations in C-sharp minor (1949)
Vox Cum Laude VCL9049

CHOPIN Piano Concerto No. 2 in F minor, Op. 21
Claudio Abbado conducting the Chicago Symphony Orchestra
CHOPIN Polonaise in F-sharp minor, Op. 44
Deutsche Grammophon DG 410507-1

BEETHOVEN Sonata No. 32 in C minor, Op.111
SCHUMANN *Symphonic Etudes,* Op. 13
SCHUMANN Toccatta, Op. 7
Deutsche Grammophon DG 2532036

RAVEL *Gaspard de la Nuit*
PROKOFIEV Piano Sonata No. 6, Op. 82
Deutsche Grammophon DG 2532093

CHARLES ROSEN

BACH *The Art of the Fugue*
BACH *Goldberg Variations*
BACH *Musical Offering*
Three-Record Set
Odyssey 32360020

BEETHOVEN Sonata No. 16 in G major, Op. 31 No. 1
BEETHOVEN Sonata No. 17 in D minor, Op. 31 No. 2 *(Tempest)*
BEETHOVEN Sonata No. 18 in E-flat major, Op. 31 No. 3
BEETHOVEN Sonata No. 21 in C major, Op. 53 *(Waldstein)*
BEETHOVEN Sonata No. 23 in F minor, Op. 57 *(Appassionata)*
BEETHOVEN Sonata No. 24 in F-sharp major, Op. 78
BEETHOVEN Sonata No. 26 in E-flat major, Op. 81[a] *(Les Adieux)*
Three-Record Set
Nonesuch 78010

BEETHOVEN *Diabelli Variations*
Peters PLE-042

CARTER *Night Fantasies* (1980)
CARTER Sonata for Piano (1946)
Etcetera ETC 1008

LISZT Piano Concerto No. 1 in E-flat major
CHOPIN Piano Concerto No. 2 in F minor, Op. 21
John Pritchard conducting the New Philharmonia
Odyssey Y-31529

GYORGY SANDOR

BRAHMS Piano Concerto No. 2 in B-flat major, Op. 83
Rølf Reinhardt conducting the Southwest German Radio Symphony
Vox 510990

PROKOFIEV The Complete Solo Piano Music
Volumes I and II
Six records
Vox SVBX 5408-5409

BARTÓK The Complete Solo Piano Music
Volumes I, II and III
Nine records
Vox SVBX 5425-5426-5427

KODÁLY Works for Piano
Candide CE 31077

BARTÓK Piano Concerto No. 3
Michael Gielen conducting the Vienna Pro Musica
Turnabout 34483

ANDRAS SCHIFF

BACH *Goldberg Variations* BWV. 988
BACH *Chromatic Fantasy and Fugue* BWV. 903
BACH Four Duets BWV. 802–805
Two-Record Set
London LDR 7201

MOZART Sonata in A major K. 331
MOZART Sonata in A minor K. 310
MOZART Sonata in D major K. 576
London CS 7246

MOZART Sonata in B-flat major K. 333
MOZART Sonata in C minor K. 457
MOZART Fantasy in C minor K. 475
MOZART Sonata in C major K. 545
London CS 7240

BARTÓK Dance Suite
BARTÓK Roumanian Folk Dances
BARTÓK Three Rondos on Hungarian Folk Tunes
BARTÓK Fifteen Hungarian Peasant Songs
Denon OX 7215 ND

MENDELSSOHN Concerto No. 1 in G minor, Op. 25
MENDELSSOHN Concerto No. 2 in D minor, Op. 40
Charles Dutoit conducting the Bavarian Radio Orchestra
London LDR 71123

PETER SERKIN

SCHUBERT Sonata in E-flat major, Op. 122, D. 568
SCHUMANN *Waldszenen*, Op. 82
RCA LSC-2955

MESSIAEN *Vingt Regards sur l'Enfant Jésus*
Three-Record Set
RCA CRL3-0759

MOZART Piano Concerti Nos. 14–19
No. 14 in E-flat major K. 449

No. 15 in B-flat major K. 450
No. 16 in D major K. 451
No. 17 in G major K. 453
No. 18 in B-flat major K. 456
No. 19 in F major K. 459
Alexander Schneider conducting the English Chamber Orchestra
Three records
RCA ARL3-0732

Bartók Piano Concerti Nos. 1 and 3
Seiji Ozawa conducting the Chicago Symphony Orchestra
RCA LSC 2929

Beethoven Piano Concerto in D major (Beethoven's own arrangement of the Violin Concerto)
Riccardo Muti conducting the New Philharmonia Orchestra
RCA LSC-3152

ROSALYN TURECK

Bach *Italian Concerto* BWV. 971
Bach *Chromatic Fantasia and Fugue* BWV. 903
Bach Four Duets BWV. 802–805
CBS M35822

Bach Aria and Ten Variations in the Italian Style
Bach Suite in A major
Bach Suite in E minor
Bach Prelude and Fugue in A minor BWV. 989
Bach Fantasia in G minor
Bach Invention in C major (two versions)
Bach Selections from *Anna Magdalena Büchlein*
CBS 37275

Bach *Goldberg Variations* BWV. 988
Everest 3397

Bach *Goldberg Variations* (on the harpsichord)
CBS M2 35900

Bach *The Well-Tempered Clavier,* Book I, Nos. 1–8
Decca DL 710120

TAMÁS VÁSÁRY

CHOPIN The Four Scherzi
No. 1 in B minor, Op. 20
No. 2 in B-flat minor, Op. 31
No. 3 in C-sharp minor, Op. 39
No. 4 in E major, Op. 54
Deutsche Grammophon DG 2535285

MOZART Piano Concerto No. 14 in E-flat major K. 449
MOZART Piano Concerto No. 26 in D major K. 537 *(Coronation)*
Tamás Vásáry conducting the Berlin Philharmonic
Deutsche Grammophon DG 2531207

LISZT Piano Concerto No. 1 in E-flat major
LISZT Piano Concerto No. 2 in A major
Felix Prohaska conducting the Bamberg Symphony Orchestra
LISZT Legend No. 2 *(St. Francis of Paolo Walking on the Water)*
LISZT *Paganini Etude* No. 2 in E-flat major
Deutsche Grammophon DG 2535131

DEBUSSY *Suite Bergamasque*
DEBUSSY Danse
DEBUSSY Deux Arabesques
DEBUSSY *Pour le Piano*
DEBUSSY *La plus que lente*
DEBUSSY *L'Ile Joyeuse*
DEBUSSY *Masques*
Deutsche Grammophon DG 139458

CHOPIN The Four Ballades
No. 1 in G minor, Op. 23
No. 2 in F major, Op. 38
No. 3 in A-flat major, Op. 47
No. 4 in F minor, Op. 52
CHOPIN The Four Impromptus
No. 1 in A-flat major, Op. 29
No. 2 in F-sharp major, Op. 36
No. 3 in G-flat major, Op. 51
No. 4, *Fantaisie-Impromptu,* Op. 66
Deutsche Grammophon DG 136455

ANDRÉ WATTS

SCHUBERT Waltzes, Op. 18
SCHUBERT Sonata in A minor, Op. 143, D. 784
SCHUBERT Fantasy in C major *(The Wanderer)* D. 760
Columbia M33073

André Watts *Live in Tokyo*
SCARLATTI Sonata in F minor L. 187
SCARLATTI Sonata in A major L. 391
HAYDN Sonata No. 48 in C major
BRAHMS Intermezzo, Op. 119 No. 2
BRAHMS Intermezzo, Op. 119 No. 3
RAVEL *Oiseaux Tristes* from *Miroirs* (1906)
DEBUSSY *The Children's Corner Suite* (1908)
CBS 37792

FRANCK *Symphonic Variations for piano and orchestra*
LISZT *Totentanz* for piano and orchestra
Erich Leinsdorf conducting the London Symphony Orchestra
Columbia M-33072

BRAHMS Concerto No. 2 in B-flat major, Op. 83
Leonard Bernstein conducting the New York Philharmonic
Columbia MS-7134

GERSHWIN Three Preludes for Piano
GERSHWIN *Rhapsody in Blue* (solo version)
GERSWHIN Thirteen Songs, arranged by Gershwin
Columbia M 34221

ALEXIS WEISSENBERG

BACH *Goldberg Variations* BWV. 988
Two-Record Set
Angel DS-3926

RACHMANINOFF Piano Concerto No. 3 in D minor, Op. 30
George Prètre conducting the Chicago Symphony Orchestra
RCA AGlI-3366

SCHUMANN *Humoreske* in B-flat major, Op. 20
SCHUMANN *Davidsbündlertänze,* Op. 6

SCHUMANN *Träumerei* (from *Kinderszenen,* Op. 15)
SCHUMANN *"The Prophet Bird"* (from *Waldszenen,* Op. 82)
Pathé Marconi EMI C069-16210

BARTÓK Piano concerto No. 2
Eugene Ormandy Conducting the Philadelphia Orchestra
RCA AGL1-4090

CHOPIN Nocturnes (complete)
Two-Record Set
Angel S-3747

EARL WILD

The Art of the Transcription—Live from Carnegie Hall, Two-Record Set
GLUCK-SGAMBATI Mélodie
RAMEAU-GODOWSKY Rigaudon, Elegie, Tambourin
BACH-TAUSIG Toccata and Fugue in D minor
WAGNER-MOSZKOWSKI *Isoldes Tod*
RIMSKY-KORSAKOV–RACHMANINOFF *The Flight of the Bumblebee*
KREISLER-RACHMANINOFF *Liebesleid*
MENDELSSOHN-RACHMANINOFF Scherzo from *A Midsummer Night's Dream*
ROSSINI-THALBERG *Grand Fantaisie sur l'Opéra Sémiramide*
CHOPIN-LISZT "Mes joies"
TCHAIKOVSKY-WILD Pas de Quatre sur *Lac des Cygnes*
STRAUSS-SCHULZ-EVLER Concert Arabesques on *The Beautiful Blue Danube*
Two-Record Set
Audiofon 2008-2

RACHMANINOFF Twelve Songs, transcribed for Piano by Earl Wild
Del' Arte DBS-7001

RACHMANINOFF The Complete Piano Concerti (four) and the Rhapsody on a theme of Paganini
Jasha Horenstein conducting the Royal Philharmonic Orchestra
Quintessence 3PC-3700

FAURÉ Ballade for Piano and Orchestra, Op. 19
Charles Gerhardt conducting the Metropolitan Symphony Orchestra
CHOPIN Concerto No. 1 in E minor, Op. 11

Sir Malcolm Sargent conducting the Royal Philharmonic Orchestra
Quintessence PMC-7141

MEYERBEER-LISZT *Réminiscences de Robert le Diable—Valse Infernale*
MOZART-LISZT *Réminiscences de Don Juan*
GOUNOD-LISZT *Faust Waltz*
LISZT *Gnomenreigen—Etude de concert*
LISZT *Mephisto Polka*
LISZT *Mephisto Waltz* No. 1
Vanguard VCS-10041

INDEX